Skye Stories

Volume 1 the Linicro Years

By Raymond Moore

First published in 2021 by Redshank Books

Redshank Books is an imprint of Libri Publishing.

Copyright © Libri Publishing.

The right of Raymond Moore to be identified as the author of this work has been asserted in accordance with the Copyright, Designs and Patents Act, 1988.

ISBN 978-1-912969-18-0

A CIP catalogue record for this book is available from The British Library

Cover and book design by Carnegie Publishing

Libri Publishing
Brunel House
Volunteer Way
Faringdon
Oxfordshire
SN7 7YR

Tel: +44 (0)845 873 3837

www.libripublishing.co.uk

Dedication
For My Dad, Big Gerry.
Love ya Big Man.

Big Gerry

Contents

céud míle fáilte

('a hundred thousand welcomes')

Five years for an adult passes in about five minutes, it seems.
Five years for me, a Glasgow child passed a whole lot slower.
Each year really was a year, not these ephemeral things we have
today. My mother's mother, my Granny Cuisack was from the
Misty Isle, so the hills and heather were not strangers to me.
From perambulating baby to a young teenager Skye was the
destination for many holidays.

I arrived on the Isle of Skye for what would be my school
summer holiday of 1977 that I would spend with my Great
Granny and My Great Auntie Margaret.

This holiday was not a problem, it was a joyful escape. My
problem would be when I returned to school in Glasgow.

Prior to this school vacation, a bike stealing attempt in
Springburn Park had left me exposed to the possibility of going
into second year at All Saints and being bullied by one of the
bike thieves and his big brother. I needed a plan. I didn't have a
plan.

What if I asked my Aunt Margaret if I could stay in Linicro and
go to school in Portree? No chance! She would never go for it.
Or would she? It took me around a month to build up the
courage to ask her, which I eventually blurted out red faced and
sweaty. She calmly said ok. Wow!

Over the next five years, my life would be altered in ways that
still influence me today. Skye changed my life forever and by
that, I mean changed my life in a positive sense. What follows
is, to the best of my memory, what happened to me in the first
of those five years. Told as wee stories or as I like to call them
'memory moments' and also in poetry; some rhyme – some
don't.

Foreword

The Isle of Skye is justly famed for its timeless seascapes, mountains, and moorland, but the real character of a place is determined by its people. Skye homes are centres of legendary Highland hospitality, where visitors are welcome, but family are taken to the bosom.

Skye natives, meeting for the first time in the diaspora, will have two questions for each other in the ancient language; 'Cò as a tha thu?' ('Where do you come from?' meaning, which part of Skye) 'Agus cò leis thu?' ('And to whom do you belong?' meaning, which is your family). This phenomenon is called 'clannishness' and is a last remnant of the Clan (family) system which once dominated the Scottish Highlands and Islands. It promotes a warm feeling of belonging, a love of place and people. This, in our island, has led to a strong sense of community and neighbourliness.

The 1970s was a transition period for rural Skye. The post-war decades had seen continued population decline due to absence of work and housing for local families. The traditional industries of crofting and fishing were no longer yielding a living wage. Migration to the towns and cities, or even abroad, had been the options for lots of young people. The island's long association with Inverness-shire County Council was being called into question. We were no longer happy to be ignored, on the edge of an east-coast-centred local authority.

Reform of local government in 1974 (sadly short-lived), whereby the Skye and Lochalsh District Council now had responsibility for local affairs, produced a much-needed boost for the island. To take charge of one's own important matters instils vibrancy in a community.

Portree High School was also 'on the up'. James Rodger, a former professional footballer, was now at the helm and a progression of young teachers was recruited, several of them former pupils, keen to allow their own children to grow up in a safe and stable environment.

There was the tentative beginning of revival of the Gaelic language and its associated musical culture. Truly comprehensive education was brought in and all Skye teenagers attended the same secondary school, thus abolishing the perceived inferiority felt between country and town. Among the older generation however, there was fear at the encroachment of rampant materialism and dilution of traditional values.

It was onto this stage, and this changing scene in 1977 that another young teenager was to join the rural inhabitants of the island.

How would he be perceived and how would he view his new domain?

I. G. Macdonald.

Former Deputy Headmaster,

Portree High School.

Introduction

Don't they say that everyone has at least one book in them to write? I guess I believe that to be true. For the longest time I wanted to document the experience I had of moving from Glasgow to Linicro on the Isle of Skye in the summer of 1977. I thought, written the right way, at the very least it would bring a wee smile to the most jaded of hearts. There was only one problem. That problem was my incredible laziness. I have suffered this affliction for most of my adult life and have spent many man hours on perfecting the art of lazy. I can give you an example of how lazy I can be, when I lived and worked in Al Ain, Abu Dhabi. One of my close friends Vince lived up the stairs from me and both our apartments had brand spanking new microwave ovens delivered. Mine lay on my kitchen floor boxed and I would hop on the elevator up to Vince's flat to heat something up in his microwave! I was too lazy to lift mine out of the box and set it up!

Luckily, a few years ago I joined a Facebook group called 'Skye and Lochalsh Memories'. This group was set up so that people from far and wide who had a connection to the Isle of Skye could share photos and memories. Thankfully, they accepted me as a member. As I live in the Kingdom of Saudi Arabia, I have no access to my Skye photos, most of which live in a biscuit tin and several albums in my mother's living room closet. Wanting to contribute something to the group, I began writing about my time in Linicro, Uig and Portree. These wee stories seemed to go down quite well, and I was encouraged to keep on writing. Later I joined 'Something Skye' Facebook group and continued to write and submit stories and poems.

Many members of both groups suggested I collect all my stories and poems and put them in a book. They promised they would love to buy it! I live and work in the Kingdom of Saudi Arabia as a Nurse Manager. My family had left me on March 2020 to spend their annual three months in our house in Thailand (my wife is Thai). A week later everything shut down due to the COVID-19 pandemic. It soon became obvious to me that they would not be able to return and that Thailand was far safer than coming back to the Kingdom. This meant that I would now have a lot of time on my regularly washed hands. Now there was no excuse. I got down and got writing ... not one book, but two!

The books deal with my years on Skye. Both are loosely chronological and although I might have used a wee bit of poetic licence (here and there), everything I have written is pretty much true and how I remember it. I'm no J. D. Salinger or Harper Lee, I'm just an RN in the desert hoping to entertain people.

My love affair with the Isle of Skye started as a baby in a pram in 1965 and although I have not set foot on my cherished island since 1997, my love affair is endless. The years between 1977 and 1982 changed the trajectory of my life. Skye made me the person I am today and whatever I do, wherever I go, and wherever I live, a piece of Skye is always with me.

I named these books 'Skye Stories' and I realise now that all my stories, even the ones after 1982 when I left the island are and continue to be Skye Stories because without Skye I would not be who I am and where I am today. If I can bring a smile to one reader's face, then my job is done.

Glossary

I was advised that it would be a good idea to include an explanation of some of the words that your eyes will feast on as you make your way through my book. Having spent 12 years in Glasgow, 5 years on Skye, 14 years in Edinburgh and over 20 years in the Middle East my accent and dialect are a wee bit mixed up (to say the very least). In my hopeful attempt at being funny and entertaining I use Gaelic, Glaswegian and Scottish words to describe my Highland adventures. I also use, what Steve, my editor calls 'Mooreisms' or 'made up words' e.g. chesticles! Should any word confuse you please refer to this glossary for a relatively poor explanation of what it means. For aficionados of the beautiful Gaelic language accept my apology in advance of any spelling mistakes. Saudi Arabia is a veritable desert for finding a fluent Gaelic speaker! Sometimes words that I thought were Gaelic are Arabic and vice versa. My Arabic is about as good as my Gaelic!

With regards to my poems, I defend my use of certain words (including Mooreisms) using the shield of 'poetic licence'. My aim is to entertain and to engage people like myself who do not read much poetry in their daily life. Forget about iambic pentameter or heroic couplets and read them like you would a lyric sheet that accompanies your favourite album. I find that the rhyming poems work better if you read them fast in a faux Glasgow accent! If it seems I'm obsessed with passing place signs, tractors, hills and heather, mountains in the distance and the salty sea then I plead guilty as charged. I also appear to use the word God frequently in a number of my poems. When you read 'God' think 'love' because that's what I mean.

For those who have never experienced the beauty of Eilean a' Cheo (see glossary) my fervent hope is that my writings will spark a wee flame of desire and that you will one day get over the sea to Skye. If you pass by Linicro have a look and see if you can find my old bike in a ditch somewhere. A handsome reward may be available depending on the status of my depressingly empty wallet.

An Buth Bheag – Gaelic for the small shop. An Buth Bheag was a candy shop on Wentworth Street, Portree.

Athens of the North – A name for the city of Edinburgh. Given when the city's 'New Town' was built between 1757 and 1850 for the rich folks. Thus, separating them from the smelly poor folk of the 'Old Town'.

Auld Reekie – A name by which the city of Edinburgh is known. A few hundred years ago Edinburgh's 'Old Town' was over-populated and had very poor sanitation. The tendency for people to empty their chamber pots onto the streets gave the place its individual aroma (reek) – hence Auld or Old Reekie.

Bahoochy – Bum or backside. A much-used term in this part of the world.

Baldy – Someone with male pattern baldness. Frequently accompanied with a comb-over.

Battered – Meaning beaten up or assaulted. Used a lot in Glasgow as a threat. 'I'm gonna batter ye'.

Bealach – Gaelic for small mountain pass. Used to describe the back road to Staffin by locals. Also, a shortcut down the hill from the top of Uig.

Bi samhach – Gaelic for 'be quiet' as in shut your mouth! Or as we say in Glasgow 'shut yer geggie'.

Braw – A Scottish word for great, beautiful, brilliant, wonderful.

The blaes – The name by which our school's 'red ash' sports pitch was known. Why? I don't know!

Braces – Elasticated over shoulder belt for holding up your troosers!

Brass neck – Not shy, over-confident, used a lot in Glasgow particularly when one is 'trying it on'. As in 'he had the brass neck to ask me out when he knew I had a boyfriend'.

Breeks – Trousers as in troosers.

The bog – Toilet or an area of muddy land. As in 'Where's your bog I need to pee'.

Bodach – Gaelic for old man. The Bodach is the head of the house. The guy in charge. Numero Uno. The big cheese. The guy you don't mess with. His word is the law! The way it was said though was in an affectionate way.

Bogging black – Very dirty. As in lifting the peats made my hands bogging black! Frequently used to describe dirt-covered kids.

Byre – A Scottish barn for wintering livestock. Also, a good place to hide to get out of chores. Unless the chores were to 'muck out the byre'.

Burn – A Scottish stream of water. The burn besides the wee hoose only ran when it was pouring down. No water flowed during a sunny summer (which wasn't that often).

But and Ben – Scottish for a wee house that lacks many creature comforts!

Caileach – Gaelic for old woman. Used as a term of endearment to describe your Skye Mum. Or my Great Aunt Margaret and Great Grannie Annie.

Caileag – Gaelic for girl or a young lassie. Common name for female dogs. Was the name of our Collie during my time in Linicro.

Camus Beag – Gaelic for small bay or harbour. An area by the sea in Earlish, Uig.

Camus Mor – Gaelic for big bay or harbour. An area by the sea in Kilmuir.

Chesticles – Meaning breasticles or ladies' upper frontal area.

Coil – A hay mound. Made by crofters when their hay was dry. Not made well by me. Precursor to individual coils being made into bigger haystacks.

Cludgie – Toilet. Rhymes with budgie as in my ex-Edinburgh flat mate's song 'Today I flushed my budgie doon the cludgie'.

Cracking – A beauty, the best. As in 'that's a cracking book you have just written Raymond'.

The dipper – A chemical bath for sheep generally for removing unwanted beasties. Found in a fank.

Dose gun – A gun for administering anti-worm medicine to sheep.

Doon – I think it's from Glasgow. It means down as in 'I'm going doon to the pub'. Which is something I have never said in Saudi Arabia!

Dram – A measure of alcohol mostly used along with whisky. Non-specific on how big or small the drink might be.

Deoch – Gaelic for drink. Can be used endearingly like 'he is on the deoch' as in an alcohol binge!

Eilean a' Cheo – Gaelic for Islands of the mist. Or to the lay person it's always effin pouring it doon!

Effin – I swear a lot so rather than have the F word…

Electric meter – Specifically the coin-operated electric meter in My Aunt's big house that swallowed 50 pence coins like candies.

Fank – An enclosed area for sheep shearing and other sheep-related activities.

Feart – Scottish word for afraid as in 'Am no feart of anybody except my wife'!

Gaff – A place of residence. As in 'my gaff is a total mess because my wife is in Thailand'.

Grealuin – A beautiful crofting community now in ruins besides Linicro fank.

Gaeilovore – Islands that I think about all the time that can be seen from Linicro when you look across the Minch to Stornoway.

Govan launch – A ship launch from Govan, Glasgow's famous shipbuilding district.

Inversneckie – A nickname for Inverness only used by really cool people.

Ithe ur biadh – Gaelic for 'eat your food'. As in 'shut your mouth and eat your food'.

Keek – I think it's Scottish for having a quick look as in 'I had a keek through the keyhole'.

Keks – Trousers or troosers or breeks.

Kerry Oot – Glaswegian for 'Carry Out' as in buying beer and spirits from the bar after last call for alcohol.

Knocked back – Something I got quite a lot of during my adult life. Meaning the answer 'no' as it pertains to asking a lassie out. 'She gave me a knock back'. 'I was the King of knock backs' (me?).

Laldy – Loud as in he was singing loud. Gien it laldy!

Maddies – As in more than one madman or a collection of madmen.

The Minch – Part of the Atlantic that separates the Outer Hebrides and the Inner Hebrides. Not suitable for swimming if you are sensitive to the cold.

Monkstadt – An area and house across from Linicro made famous by Bonnie Prince Charlie and Flora Macdonald.

MV Hebrides – The passenger ferry that sailed people to and from Uig and the Outer Hebrides from the 1960s till the 1980s. Survived by the Hebridean Princess that tours the western waters.

Old Smiddy – Blacksmith's workshop that once stood in Linicro.

Poly bags – Ubiquitous disposable plastic shopping bags.

Puirt à Beul style – Mouth music. Traditional Scottish music taught verbally through generations.

Quid – Great British Pounds.

Quirang road – The bealach road or the road to Staffin via Quirang.

Racket – Making a lot of loud noise. I made many.

Skelp – Slap as in 'slap your arse'.

Sweeties – Candy. As in 'I want candy'.

Strupag – Gaelic for cup of tea as in 'come in for a wee strupag'. Skye was full of strupag addicts, probably still is!

Steaming – Scottish colloquialism for being very drunk.

Stocious – See above and add another 'very'. Note abundance of terms for intoxicated – similar to the number of words Inuits have for 'snow'.

Tatties – Potatoes. My favourite veg!

Taps aff – Meaning tops off, used in Glasgow when the weather is nice and people, mostly guys (unfortunately), would go shirtless.

Tobar – Gaelic for well or freshwater spring.

Tobar an Dualchais – Meaning 'Kist o Riches' which is a project that aims to preserve and digitize material gathered in Scottish Gaelic, Scots and English by the School of Scottish Studies (of the University of Edinburgh).

Troosers – Trousers or breeks or keks!

Tootsies – The medical term for toes (isn't it?).

Tumster – Rhymes with Yumster.

Wallys or Wallies – False teeth. Prone to slippage.

Wee – As in short in stature, or a small amount of time, or a little drop as in 'a wee dram of whisky'!

Weegie – Someone from Glasgow short for Glaswegian. Me.

Yumster – Made up word that only I use.

Z-Bed – A foldable bed popular post war. Usually used when room space is in short supply.

A Raleigh Jeep
Changed My Life

My Skye story, inevitably, has to begin in Glasgow. For many people, the bond between Glasgow and Skye is as strong as the strongest glue. The island and the city are interlinked. So it's there, in Springburn, where this book begins.

Your life can change in a split second and it's true that for every action there is a reaction! Case in point, me in Galloway Street in 1976. All I could dream about was getting my own bike, and that's all it was, a dream! I was determined though, so with the money I was earning from my brief stint as an 'Evening Times' seller, of which I was giving half to my Mum to save, my plan was to make my bike dream come true. I vividly remember when I reached the princely sum of ten pounds. Wow! What an amount of money, honey, I was rich!

Luckily at about the same time one of the Peebles boys who lived opposite us was selling their Raleigh Jeep bicycle for that exact amount. Their Father was a real bike nut who had a fancy racer, and he had modded this Jeep to have dropped 'racing' handlebars. I really loved that bike and now I did not have to rely on borrowing someone's sister's bike for our regular 'bike runs' or ask for a 'shot' of someone's bike on the street.

When I look back on this purchase, it's hard to believe the ramifications of what would seem a relatively small life thing to do? I will get to that in a wee minute, but I just wanted to reminisce about having my own transport for a while! One of the regular runs a group of us 'biker boys' from Galloway Street would go on was to the Campsies. This involved us leaving the city boundaries and heading to the local hill area via Bishopbriggs. It would take some time, but it was always worth it as we would end up at a well-known spot by the river. This was us city boys getting some countryside action, and it was always fantastic fun if tiring on the young legs!

Galloway Street
Early-1970s

That bike changed my life, and it also saved my life? As the school summer holidays fast approached in 1977, I was about to finish first year at All Saints Secondary School in Barmulloch. I will be honest and say that other than the long walk to and from the school, it was an OK school. I was lucky mostly in that I experienced no bullying, and in one year I had only one fight (which I won). It was school, and you just accepted it!

One sunny summer evening Tariq Benison, who lived in the Tenements opposite me and myself, took our bikes out to Springburn Park. It was bright and warm, and we had nothing better to do. Close to the swings, the ones near the boating pond, we were accosted by three guys who I recognized but did not know personally as they were not from our area. They were maybe a year younger than us and they had designs on my Jeep! I was in total fear that they would 'knock it' and as I didn't know where they stayed there would be little hope of me ever seeing my golden chariot again! One of the guys named Eddie had an older brother at my school so if I were to get into a fight and hurt him my second year of school life would have been a living hell. Drastic action was called for! He was on the bike circling us when I made a grab for the handlebars, he spun round and fell off, and with a shove I was on the bike and pedalling like a madman to get back to Galloway Street.

In the meantime, I had lost my pal Tariq. Sweaty and relieved, I made it safely to my house, my bike secured on our landing. I remember that because it was hot, my Mum had been sunbathing on our 'veranda' and she had left the pillows there. I went out and plopped myself down, thinking I had had a lucky escape! Before too long our doorbell rang and it was Tariq at my door with this guy Eddie who had tried to nab my bike! WTF? It turns out in the middle of my bike recovery he had lost his school bag and books and he wanted to see if I had them? No was the answer, and he left very unhappy! I returned to my seat on the veranda and played out all that happened in my mind. One thing that occurred to me was that this guy would come into first year after the school summer holidays and, with his older brother, he might try to make my life a total nightmare! What a downer!

Eventually the school holidays began, and I was transported to Linicro via a Wallace Arnold bus. I tried my best to forget about the bike incident and enjoy my time on the Isle of Skye. As the days turned to weeks, and the end of my holiday was slowly approaching, the thought of returning to All Saints was not a pleasant one. My two Totescore pals Archie and Duncan Macinnes knew of my plight and they suggested that I ask my Great Aunt Margaret if I could stay and go to Portree High School. Whilst this was very attractive, I was too scared to even bring up the subject with Margaret. She could be very intimidating and asking her to live in Linicro just seemed so impossible. My stomach turned every time I thought about it. Archie and Duncan kept at me though, saying how brilliant it would be to have me there full time. I loved Skye and Linicro for as long as I could remember, and the thought of living there was just beyond my wildest dreams!

How many times did I play out the scene where I asked my Aunt if I could stay? Every time I felt physically sick at the thought of her saying no. It was getting closer and closer to August now and the fear of going back to All Saints pushed my anxiety up a

Margaret and
My Granny at
Linicro

level causing me a lot of stress! With all these thoughts going on in my head, I concluded, 'What's the worst thing that can happen?' Margaret could only say no, and there seemed a slight chance that she could say yes! Still, I had to build up the courage to ask her. Ultimately, it was a rather anti-climactic affair and the weeks of worry were for nothing! She said YES! Yippee!! Our relationship over the years might have been fractious, but I love her for agreeing to let me live in Linicro. She probably regretted it though!

So, the action of me saving up for a bike and then it nearly getting stolen had the reaction that now would change my life forever, and for the better!

There is a postscript to this wee story in around 2001 when I was working as an Agency Nurse at Stobhill Hospital, which is near to my old Galloway Street home. I was on a night shift in the A&E when I took a call from a guy asking advice if he should come in or wait to see his GP in the morning. This of itself was a rare thing as he did not want to waste the A&E staff's time. His symptoms sounded too severe to be left till morning, so I told him to 'come on down'.

I was not assigned to look after him, but I just went to say hello as it was a slow night. We got to talking, and it turned out that

4

he was a year younger than me and that he went to All Saints Secondary. I felt compelled to ask him if he knew this guy, 'Eddie', (the one trying to pilfer my bike way back at the beginning of this story).

This is the God's honest truth, when I tell you he not only knew the guy, he was one of his best friends! Cryptically I asked him if he could say thank you to 'Eddie' for trying to 'borrow' my bike all those years ago? He looked at me kind of strange, but he said that he would. Thanks 'Eddie' – you and your pals changed my life that summer evening a long time ago.

Wallace Arnold

Summer holidays, 1977. Up near the top of Sauchiehall Street early morning. This is where the bus was that would take me away from Glasgow and deposit me in Portree to be picked up by my cousin Bobby. I was travelling alone, and my old man asked the Wallace Arnold bus driver to keep an eye on me just in case I got lost. He promised he would and kept that promise.

I remember the driver was a tall baldy guy who wore a kilt! Throughout the journey he would tell wee stories and make the passengers laugh. As we wound around the tight roads of Loch Lomond, he said that if the bus drove off the road and into the chilly loch waters, he would be the only one that would survive because his kilt would help him float!

To a 13-year-old the journey seemed to take days and although the seats on the WA bus were far more comfy than the Highland Scottish bus, it was a hard journey. My stomach was not great at travelling long distances, and it took me a good few years before I could eat anything on the way to Skye. Eventually we reached Kyle and as we crossed on the Cal Mac ferry, my excitement really kicked in. Once on the island I felt immediately happy. It's hard to explain but when you have a deep

Linicro Sign Wee Hoose

connection to Skye there is just something that feels 'right' when you are there. The journey from Kyleakin to Portree continued to be vomit inducing, but at least the end was near.

As we came out of the trees past the filling station and in towards Somerled Square, I could barely sit down! When at last we stopped and parked, I was told by the big baldy driver to wait until someone came to pick me up. The other passengers said their goodbyes to me, the lone kid and weegie and I waited for Bobby.

The funniest thing, it still makes me laugh today, bearing in mind this was a Wallace Arnold bus with large WA's on either side my cousin stepped onto the bus. He then asked (and this I remember as if it was this morning), he asked the driver 'is this the Alice Warnold bus'? The driver laughed and confirmed that this indeed was the WALLACE ARNOLD bus!

Bobby collected me and my suitcase and we boarded the local MacLeod bus, dumped my stuff and went for a wander around Portree until it was time for 'John the bus' to take us to Linicro. Little did I know then that I would become intimately familiar with that bus and the road as we shoogled all the way to Kilmuir! A summer of adventures awaited me, and I was ready. It would be an unforgettable summer and one that changed everything for me.

Totescore

The chiming clock on the wee hoose dresser smugly sits, knowing that it controls time.
That tik tok ticking clock also controls me and my lifeline.
My day is one of waiting for three hours of joy in the Totescore evening, this I'm estimating.
It's time for dinner tik tok.
The chiming clock is laughing.
Two hours to go until seven.
Ticking, tocking my feet want walking but here I am just sitting.
For my pals in Totescore and for the carrying on I'm anticipating.
With one hour to go, my mind is racing.
For courage is needed to voice the words that my mouth is accumulating.
Tik tok goes that naughty clock.
My hands sweating, my nerves jangling, I know fun is waiting.
Will my Auntie set me free at seven o'clock?
Tik tok growing louder in my two ears.
With five minutes to go, why does time run so slow my courage is on the wane?
That mocking, tik toking, says if I don't ask, I will never know, then I've only myself to blame.
Seven chimes ring through the air and out the wee hoose door.
The tik tok drowning, as my voice gathers volume, and the words are on my tongues tip.
My Aunt is frowning and my heartbeat begins to skip.
This anticipation I can't hold anymore.
I blurt out 'can I go to Totescore'?
Tik tok that clock is waiting for an answer along with me.

Seconds like hours are agony, I stand in animation, suspended.
Tocking tiking my Aunt is still thinking.
What will her answer be?
Yes, brings joy like a newly bought toy.
No, the slow death of me.
The chiming clock has stopped time until a yes appears in my ears.
Tok tik lightening quick, I leave the wee hoose far behind.
With a song in my soul the Minch by my side I know all is dandy a
fine.
For soon I will be far from that ticking tok, embracing my
Totescore time.

The Wee Hoose and the Big Hoose

As far back as my Linicro memories will take me, there has always been a 'wee hoose' and a 'big hoose'. Known to me as hooses and not houses. This was the Glaswegian in me and even though I no longer stayed in Glasgow, I still called them hooses. Still do!

The wee hoose is a stone-gabled corrugated iron covered cottage. Today, from the outside, it does not look much different from how it did way back in the dim distant past. Inside, I know it has changed quite a bit. This hoose was a former shop which dates back to the 1940s. It had two rooms downstairs and two rooms upstairs. On the ground floor there was a kitchen/living room and a bedroom with two double beds. When my sister Angela and I would go to Linicro during the summer we would sleep in one of the double beds and my Great Granny and Great Aunt would sleep in the other. We loved it. It may not have been fancy, but it was cosy. In 1977, when I lived there, I slept in the bedroom above the living room. My cousin Bobby slept in the other room. We accessed these bedrooms from a rather steep stair just inside the front door. It was more like a ladder to be honest with you! My bedroom was where they kept all the junk. My bed just behind the door was an ancient 'Z-Bed' which had three different thin mattresses on it. This meant that the bed was not totally flat. It had a slight incline on it, and more than once I turned over in my sleep and rolled onto the floor. They had placed most of the other objects in my room as there was no other space for them in the hoose. There was an old spinning wheel which probably was used by my Granny. A few butter churns, one of which was a wooden barrel type that had a handle you turned to rotate the barrel. Various vases and wee tables. A couple of old oil lamps and a faded white wooden shelving unit that contained some dusty old books and a selection of old Portree High School magazines from the 1960s. There was no electric in this room, so I used a torch and when I had no batteries, I used a candle. I liked it. I read my comics by candlelight and when the comics ran out, I would read some old books from the shelves, including the PHS magazines.

Big Hoose 1970s

Bobby's room was more luxurious. It had a proper metal framed bed in the far corner. A rug on the floor and far less stuff in storage. There was also a wee stone fireplace in the middle of his wall. In the corner opposite his bed there was a storage area where we found an old record player and some 45 singles. The only one I remember was Andy Stewart's 'Donald Where's Yer Troosers' and the reason I remember this so well is that after the main song is finished Andy does a really funny impression of Elvis singing the song. The B side was 'A Scottish Soldier'. When Bobby was away, I would sleep in that room. Both rooms had one window which had an iron bar with holes so we could open it a little or a lot, depending on which hole you used.

Downstairs in the living room there was a big table in the far corner that was used as a work surface for preparing food. It backed on to the wall that separated the room from the bedroom. There was no running water in the house and no toilet! On the big table always sat two big blue plastic buckets filled with water. For years we had to collect the water from the 'tobar' (water well) at the side of the neighbouring shepherd's house. This spring water was fresh, cold and clean. My Granny would say it had healing properties and was very good for you. When thirsty we would use a metal measuring jug to scoop out the H2O and glug it down. As young kids, we thought it magical that you drank water that poured out of the ground. As a young teen it was not so magical dragging two full buckets of water sloshing all over the croft! Latterly my Aunt had a tap and massive porcelain sink installed outside the main door of the byre and that's where we would collect the wee hoose water. I would still go to the 'tobar' if my Granny requested it.

In the other corner was a smaller table with three wooden chairs. This is where we sat and ate and also socialised. In the far corner near the front window was my Granny's chair and beside her was one of those old brown sofas that could be made into a bed. They almost looked like leather with wooden arms. The sofa was a two-seater and was not that comfy. Years later when I lived in my flat in Bruntsfield, Edinburgh, we would have the exact same sofa. It still was not comfy but surprisingly made into a pretty decent bed! Next to the sofa, past the window was my Aunt's Baby Belling cooker. Most of the cooking was done on a gas camping stove near the big worktable. In the middle of the back wall there was a big brown dresser. Was it Welsh? I don't know, but it was that pre-war utilitarian type; functional, but not particularly pretty. The top half housed stuff like a chiming clock and dishes. The double cupboard at the bottom is where the freshly squeezed Murdy milk was stored (Murdy was my Aunt's milking cow). The wee hoose did not have a fridge, so this dark cupboard had to do. On one side there was one of those big white, blue-rimmed enamel basins. This is where the fresh milk was stored. On the other side was another enamel basin, and this is where my Aunt would store the cream that would be put into a churn and made into butter. When there was a layer of cream on the fresh milk Margaret would scoop it with a scallop shell into the neighbouring basin. I was not a big fan of the home-made butter. It took me a few years to learn to like it. I was an Echo margarine boy or, if I was lucky, a Blue Band margarine boy!

The wee hoose had two doors. The main outside door and an inside wooden door that led to the living room. One summer Bobby decided to saw that door in half which was a brilliant idea as it meant the top half was always open, allowing more light in, and the bottom half remained shut to keep the dogs in. I have very fond memories of that hoose and enjoyed living in it for several summers.

My Aunt also had the big hoose up behind the wee one. This is a more traditional Skye croft house, which has been updated and added to by my Aunt Annie, who now lives there. For as long as I can remember, this house was rented out to tourists during the summer. Most came and stayed for two weeks at a time. From my recollection, most of the tourists were English. Margaret used to advertise in *Daltons Weekly*. This house had three top floor bedrooms – two double bedrooms, on either side of a small middle single room. Downstairs there was a living room and a back-kitchen extension. Opposite the living room was another room that was always kept locked from the tourists. As young kids, it was a treat for us to go into that room in between renters! We were not allowed in unsupervised, though. In there were a lot of personal items belonging to my Aunt and Granny and stuff belonging to our deceased Great-great Uncles.

During the summer months, the only time we could use a proper bathroom and toilet was during the changeover when Margaret was cleaning the place for her next guests. It was then that Bobby and I took the opportunity to have a nice warm bath and sit on a proper flushing toilet! Pure luxury!

By summer's end, usually around mid-September, we would decant from the wee hoose to the big hoose and spend the winters there. My bedroom was the double room above the locked room. Bobby slept in the wee single room. Margaret and Granny were in the other double room. The big hoose back then was not what one would call luxurious, more Skye functional.

There was no central heating back in the 1970s, only the living room's coal fire. There was an uncomfortable three-seater sofa and two wooden cushioned chairs either side of the fireplace. My usual seat was one of them below the budgie cage that was home to Margaret's annoying bird named Lemon. Margaret usually sat on the sofa and my Granny in the chair opposite me. The kitchen is where we ate, and it was not what one would call nice and warm – especially in the middle of a dark Skye winter. There was a Spartan dining table with metal chairs. A Belling cooker (not Baby) and an Aga-type stove. This stove was very rarely used because there was some issue with the chimney in that it kept blowing the smoke back down the lum and into the kitchen. Which is a shame because had it functioned properly, like the Macinnes family's range in Totescore, and was always on, the kitchen would have been nice and toasty! There was a double Shanks China sink, one of which was deep. A wringer, which was used to wring clothes before we had an automatic spinner, separated these. I don't recall if we had a twin tub back then, but we might have had. There was a pulley above the sinks for our clothes to hang. The kitchen door was really the main door as we very rarely opened the front.

My bedroom was always fridge like in the winter – my single bed pushed up against the tongue-and-groove wood on the walls. I had one utilitarian chest of drawers for my meagre supply of clothes. I hated waking up in the cold winter mornings, it was freezing as I got dressed for school. Ultimately Margaret bought me this wee white convector heater that had one hair-like strand as an element and a small fan. It had an orange bulb inside so when it was on it kind of looked like it was putting out heat, but it was all a deception. It was effin freezing most mornings. I would jump out of bed and turn that heater on, lay my shirt and jumper over it, stay in bed for maybe ten minutes and eventually get up – and at least the chill was taken from my top clothes. At night I would take a scalding rubber hot-water bottle to chase away the cold from my feet. I have a memory that Margaret also bought me an electric blanket, but I'm not sure if that was just wishful thinking. Outside at the top of the creaking wooden stairs there was a coin-operated electricity meter that swallowed 50-pence pieces. Those coins would not last long, especially when you had the water heater on for your Sunday night bath!

Wee Hoose Dresser

Holding court in the room's middle, dark brown hardwood, strong and utilitarian.
My Aunt Margaret's dresser was multi-tasking and where she stored her milk.

Opening the bottom cupboards, wooden doors revealed two large enamelled bowls.
One on your right was for freshly squeezed Murdy milk, the other stored cream whole.

Innocent eyes watched in awe as Margaret skimmed the cream with a white scallop shell.
Transporting the creamy goodness, scooped into the cream wishing well.

In the dark and lonely coolness, the collected cream awaited its croft fate.
Ending life in a wooden barrel churn, slightly salted butter on scones we ate.

Above on the dresser's top sat my Aunt's ticking, chiming clock.
The one that made me wait for my Totescore trip till it chimed 7 o'clock.

On other shelves hidden were Post Office bought Pan Drops and Oddfellows.

Sometimes, for us kids, Highland toffee if we behaved and my
*   Aunt was feeling mellow.*

Seven Seas cod liver oil and effervescent aspirin hidden behind
*   electricity bills.*
Glass doors shielded other pieces of paper, a crofting filing
*   cabinet with no frills.*

Where are you now my wooden pal, are you still in use or has
*   your life come to an end?*
No worries, you're here in my mind keeping other Linicro
*   memories company my friend.*

Who Took the Dogs Out (Not Me)

There were always dogs in Linicro. Usually a Terrier and a Collie. During my time we had Caileag the Collie and Corrie who was some sort of Terrier. Caileag was a big softy who always liked to be petted. Corrie, to my mind, was this gruesome, smelly black thing. Margaret loved that wee dog. He was not particularly friendly to anyone except her and was known to snap at people. He could only be let outside on a leash whilst Caileag was free to roam leashless.

Corrie's only one saving grace was that he liked to howl – if you started first, he would soon join in with you. This I thought was funny. Apart from that, I did not like him one wee bit. There was one time in the big hoose when my Granny had thrown a bit of a scone on the floor for him to eat. He was a fussy eater and rather than eat it, he just guarded it. Caileag was the opposite. She would eat anything, and she tried to steal it from under his nose. He growled and the next thing he snapped at my Granny's stocking-covered leg. He was biting it and she was screaming. Margaret was in the kitchen. The only thing I

Margaret,
Granny and
the Dogs

thought to do was to kick the wee smelly bugger into touch. So I booted him with my sock-covered foot. This was just as Margaret came running in. Corrie let go and yelped. The first thing Margaret did was come over to me and kick me! All my Granny could think about was the dog. Her leg was bleeding, but that she ignored. I got really upset and stormed out crying. That's how much Margaret loved that dog. She said sorry afterwards. The dog was unharmed and my Granny's leg was bandaged.

After my Granny passed, Margaret would take Corrie up to sleep in her room. I think she liked the company. Both dogs lived to a real good age. I had heard that when Corrie died, Margaret kept him in her bedroom for one last night before they buried him the next day. She was very upset for a long time.

At the 11th Hour

Wooden staircase groans underfoot as I slink my way to bed.
Candlelight flickering, I forage to find a book I haven't already
read.

Slanted and enchanted shadows follow my every floor creaking
move.
My Z-bed grimacing under my body, squirming to find a
comfortable reading groove.

Starved for stories I found a book lying at the bottom of the white
wooden shelves.
Dusty and lonely, behind the butter churn, where only a
desperate boy would delve.

The triple mattress left me on an incline, when at last I could
open my newly found book.
Into the French Alps evading Nazis, the pages transplanted me
to where I was labelled a crook

Every page of this foosty old book, I turned with trepidation.
A solitary Corncrake sings in a lonely field, a midnight
declaration.

The wee hoose silent now as I carry on reading, underneath I hear
my Granny's snore.
Page after yellowed page I turn, imagining Nazis at my front
wooden door.

It's after two and the book I'm still reading, I'm on my second
candle now.
Through the window I hear something coughing, I'm hoping it
was our cow.

I'm nearing the end of this 1950s novel. The suspense is killing
me.
Finally, the last page with the heroine escaping, she makes it
back to her French family.

I'm fighting sleep with every blink, eventually it manages to
overpower.
The book's story continues as I dream, I'm back in France at the
eleventh hour.

Love Island

Merriam Webster's defines love as:

Love noun

(1): strong affection for another arising out of kinship or personal ties

maternal love for a child

(2): attraction based on sexual desire: affection and tenderness felt by lovers

After all these years, they are still very much in love.

(3): affection based on admiration, benevolence, or common interests

love for his old schoolmates

A: an assurance of affection

Give her my love

B: warm attachment, enthusiasm, or devotion

love of the sea

In the (slightly more than) half century I have graced this globe I have been extremely lucky. I was born into a loving Glasgow family and as I grew into (im)maturity I found and lost love (more than a few times). It has been my pleasure to have met, loved and lost friends, but love for them remains in the pulsating mass of muscle that lives in my chest. I attended a High School that I loved which led to a career that I love (though sometimes don't) which has enabled my skinny frame to travel the world and discover the true meaning of being lucky in life. It might have taken a good while, but I was fortunate enough to find the love of a wife who's gifted me three children. Their eyes project onto me the accurate definition of unconditional love and for me proof of a loving

Haiku

A Japanese poem of seventeen syllables, in three lines of five, seven, and five, traditionally evoking images of the natural world.

A poem in English written in the form of a haiku.

This is the Oxford Dictionary definition that I took from Google.

What I have created is Skye Haiku, which I have called a Skyeku. Now I'm not saying I followed the formula for Haiku diligently. I have used some "poetic licence". They all try to convey a thought or feeling I had way back in the days of my youth. Hopefully, for you dear reader they will stir something in your soul's memory.

Skyeku 1

Morning mist sweet cold

Corncrake hidden songs swing low

Crofter boots well worn.

creator. From my first visit as a perambulating child till this moment as I type, I have a love for the Isle of Skye that is organic, pure and as real as the air that I breathe. As an expat I can freely admit to having an overly sentimental heart that wears rose-coloured bifocals when it comes to my lifelong love of Linicro. Though it has been nearly a century's quarter since my Samba wearing feet have walked there, in my mind I visit at least once (if not more times) a day. I remember every single blade of croft green grass that surrounds my Aunt's Linicro home. They are my friends and are forever in my soul. As is the sun and the rain that crowned my head as it shone or poured down feeding the Linicro land.

Not a day goes by that I don't recall the Macinnes family of Totescore. The mischief and the kindness that was part of my daily life with them. My love for my Granny and Aunt Margaret, for it was them that said yes to my living in Linicro request. My cousin Bobby, who unbeknownst to him (or me) proved to be a role model and who I'm lucky to still be in touch with, courtesy of Facebook Messenger. The long-gone Kilmuir neighbours are alive and well and remain fondly in my memory. Making hay and feeding the hens!

Big Margaret

Margaret Arnott was my Great Aunt on my Mother's side and known in the family as Big Margaret. Margaret Lucas is my Aunt known in the family as Wee Margaret. Wee Margaret was actually bigger than Big Margaret! Clear now?

Over the years in my mind I may have been a bit harsh in my feelings towards Margaret, she could be pretty tough, and the honest truth was that for the first few years in Linicro I feared her. I suppose scared of the power she wielded over me in that she could send me back to Glasgow if I misbehaved too much. She almost did a few times!

Nowadays I have nothing but love for the old girl and I understand that it could not have been easy looking after a teenage boy!

It had been a bit of a tradition for our extended family to live in Skye. My Aunt Margaret's sister Katie who was my Mum's Mum and lived in Glasgow sent my Mum's two sisters to live in Linicro. Big Margaret and my Aunt Annie, Bobby's Mum. During the late 1960s when my Mum was in hospital with TB they sent my sister Angela to live in Linicro and to go to school in Kilmuir. She was very curly and cute then, and I know that both my Great Granny Annie and Big Margaret had a real soft spot for her because of the time she spent with them.

Angela and I would spend school summer holidays together in Linicro until 1977 when I went alone. It is thanks to Big Margaret as she was the one who allowed me to stay there after I had built up the courage to ask! Luckily my Granny supported it! Margaret was not a big woman, was pretty skinny and short but she was strong and Skye hardy. Margaret did not have it easy and I know she gave up a lot of her personal life to look after my Granny. Margaret should have been married years before. I know she had a guy who was intent on marrying her in Glasgow. This didn't happen and Margaret spent her life as a crofter in Linicro looking after her Mum. Smoking Players No 6 and sporting the same enormous nose as her brother Willie, Margaret was well known and well liked in Kilmuir. She looked after her Mother right up till my Granny's death in 1978.

Margaret was strict with me in that I was not as free as my besties the Macinnes boys. She would only ever allow me to go to Totescore between the hours of seven and ten and if I was late, I not only got a verbal punishment she would also stop me from going for a couple of nights! She didn't want me to go to local dances but usually capitulated on the insistence of Bobby or the Macinnes. She knew we were underage drinking and did not want us to get into trouble!

Those years I lived in Linicro had their ups and downs. I was growing into a full teen and testing Margaret's patience to the limits. Something would eventually give.

Over the years when I returned to Skye, I always did my best to see Margaret and would call her every so often to check in. This became more frequent after her cancer diagnosis. She lived for over five years with the illness and I consider myself lucky in that I saw her a few months before she passed and we talked a wee bit about my time in Linicro and I felt that I finally made my peace with her.

Margaret passed away in the summer of 1997 and we buried her beside her mother in Uig cemetery. I miss the old girl and I realise now that it really is her I have to thank because she could easily have said no to me living in Linicro and going to school in Portree and if that had happened my life would have taken a different trajectory. Thank you, Margaret and lots of love from me.

My Cousin Bobby

Without my cousin Bobby, my first years in Linicro would have been a lot more difficult to handle. He, like me, was a Glasgow refugee. Unlike me, Bobby was born on Skye and his first years were spent up the road at Stonegate cottage, Totescore. Now in ruins, it was once was a traditional thatched cottage. My Uncle Peter and Auntie Annie lived there with my two cousins until one day the roof caught fire. Thank God nobody was hurt! They went to live in Glasgow, but in 1977 Bobby was in Linicro. He lived in the 'nice' wee hoose bedroom as opposed to my room, which really was a storeroom and not even glorified! Bobby eventually moved out to his folks' caravan at the side of wee hoose and I moved into his old room. Yass! During the winter he stayed in the big hoose's wee middle bedroom. It's thanks to him I discovered Pink Floyd and Boston as these were in his small tape collection when I arrived and till this day Animals and Wish You Were Here are still two of my favourite albums.

Like a big brother, Bobby financed me throughout the first couple of years in Linicro. He got a job via the council's 'Job Creation' scheme and he and Donnie Glen worked opposite us in Totescore digging drains! If I remember rightly, he also worked on a fishing boat out of Uig. Luckily for me he was not scared of my Auntie Margaret and he would always take the blame if anything happened so made my life easier. Bobby also owned a portable black and white television that we could watch a very snowy Top of the Pops on. In the wee hoose we would put it on the old sofa beside the window and twist the aerial to receive a picture. In wintertime he had the TV in his room and we would watch the likes of Dr Who on dark winter Saturdays, with me trying to squeeze to sit on his compact single bed!

Luckily, he had a great sense of humour and was full of devilment and we got up to some serious mischief when he was there! At the end of 1978, he left for a while. He went to Glasgow, or was it Shetland? He had to come back up to look after the house and me when Margaret was admitted to Raigmore

Skyeku 2

Headlights dip cat's eye

Night owls gaze hill rolling dark

Silence sounds abound.

Hospital in Inverness following a sheep butting incident, more on this later. He was a decent cook too! After she returned, he then went to Shetland. It was there he met Sheila and got married; I was the best man and had a superb time during my first and only visit to those Shetland islands. Both he and I wore kilts, and we were the only ones at the wedding in that attire! Margaret came from Linicro and we all enjoyed the warmth and hospitality of Sheila's friends and family. There is a video of the proceedings I have not seen, but one of these days I will get a watch of it.

The last time I saw Bobby would have been at my Aunt Margaret's funeral in 1997. We loosely kept in touch but now thanks to the wonders of modern technology we regularly video call each other and send wee messages on Messenger. For this I'm glad, because I missed him throughout the years!

Dam

Another lazy Sunday afternoon lies ahead, and we scratch our heads.
What to do to pass the afternoon hours?
My cousin germinates a plan.

Quarry, let's go to the quarry, said Bobby, I have a great idea?
Great I said as I stopped scratching my head, and as ordered I put on my welly boots.

We headed out this winter afternoon, our destination was only five minutes away.
The Totescore quarry, all lonely and forlorn, welcomed us in to play.

Beneath the mossy mini waterfall is where we made our base.
The sky above showed kindness and let the winter sun our
*   bodies embrace.*

We're going to build a dam, boy. My cousin let the words fall from
*   his smiling face.*
We need boulders boy, lots of boulders, like the ones scattered all
*   around this place.*

In the quarry's mouth he found two planks of wood, abandoned
*   to their rotten fate.*
Placed in the icy stream, with the boulders in-between, the
*   genesis of our water gate.*

Dirt boy, we need lots of dirt, and like mad miners, by hand we
*   would excavate.*
A fast and furious muddy hour saw our construction take dirty
*   shape.*

And all at once the stream's flow was stemmed, our cold bath
*   water began to accumulate.*
Inch by dirty foamy inch, the stream showed no sign of abate.

What a sight to behold as the water rose, post dam no cold liquid
*   flowed.*
And in that perfect winter afternoon, God's eye upon our
*   workload.*

The flowing force of nature, time and tide could not hold back for
*   long.*
As the frothy brown gallons gathered, the dam's strength would
*   soon be gone.*

I ran to the road, hanging like washing over the wooden rail.
And I waited for the water rush as it ran under the tarred road.
All at once I could hear an oncoming whoosh of white water
*   ready to explode.*

What a day. We slapped each other's backs, mud stained we
*   headed for home.*
For a minute we were water gods, all powerful in the Totescore
*   gloom.*

Duncan and Archie the Boys from Totescore

What can I say about my Totescore pals? If I did not have these two brothers in my life indeed the whole Macinnes family, my Linicro life would have been a lot lonelier.

As I try and cast my mind back to first meeting them it feels that I have always known them! Duncan is the same age as my sister Angela so two years older than me with Archie was just a wee bit older than me. My primary memory of my two mates was them walking to church on a Sunday. We would chat with them for a wee while on their way there and then again on their way home! It being a Sunday meant that they could not spend much time with us. Both wore their Sunday best. At this time I remember their height not being so different. It would have been the summer of 1975 when we next saw them. Sunday again. Wearing their Sunday best. The only difference was that Duncan seemed to have doubled in height! It was amazing to us who had grown very little in the last year or two! That summer I have wonderful memories of playing with them and having a lot of fun and being very unhappy when I had to return to Glasgow!

The summer of 1977 we were inseparable, and I did my best to spend as much time in Totescore as my Aunt Margaret would allow. I had to be back by 10pm and if I returned too late, she would complain and then not let me go again for a few evenings!

Both of the brothers were incredibly generous to me and their kindness was unconditional, the complete opposite of what I had experienced with friends in Glasgow. I suppose for them it was a novelty having a city boy as a pal!

It was with them I discussed the idea of going to school in Portree and living permanently in Linicro. They really encouraged me and eventually with their help I built up the

Duncan, Archie and Parents

courage to ask Margaret and the rest, as they say, is history.

We did loads of stuff together and got up to lots of 'carrying on' over the years. It was not all exciting stuff to write about but for me it was the best time of my life. I loved them like brothers (still do). I know that some people might think I have a tendency to look back on that period with rose-tinted spectacles, and that it could not have been 'that good'. I'm not saying every day was totally brilliant and it's not like I did not have bad moments but even during the worst times not once did I ever say to myself 'that's it I have had enough I want to go back to Glasgow'! I never, ever thought that. To be brutally frank, I did not miss my family that much at all. I suppose at that age you are selfish – it just was not something that I thought much about.

The three of us grew up together and even after they both left school we still hung around. The summer of 1980, when I got a job at Uig Hotel, Archie and I shared a room that whole summer. We saw

Skyeku 3

Winter wet face blue

Sea shanty sung softly floats

Waves boulder smooth.

Duncan regularly at the weekends, especially when we went to local dances. Even during the last two years that I was living in Uig Hotel we still got together, albeit less often as they had to work.

After I left Skye in 1982, I always tried to get to see them during my infrequent visits back over the years. With the likes of Facebook I'm loosely in touch with them and although it has been many years since I have seen them they will always be like brothers to me. I have to thank them for everything that they did for me during those years, and I'm lucky to have all these brilliant memories that I'm now sharing with you.

Top of Totescore Looking out to Harris

Wilks

*We needed money, so we put our heads together, and the picking
of wilks was the answer.*
*With our plastic buckets, sacks in our hand, to Scudaburgh on
the word of an advisor.*

*The Macinnes boys and I made our way to the shore, black shelled
gold on our mind.*
*Across green field and fence, on soggy ground, we treaded in
excitement at what we might find.*

*Our fortune was in as the tide was out, what we discovered was a
wilk wonderland.*
*With a song in our heart and buckets ready, we got busy
bending with our hands.*

*An overcast day did not dampen our enthusiasm as bucket after
bucket we filled.*
*Spurred on by the thought of filthy lucre, hour after hour, at
wilk picking us three became skilled.*

*Frozen hand turning blue, our eyesight affected, we picked, and
we picked some more.*
*Until sacks became full and our legs got cramp, all of us had
heads that were sore.*

*Two solid days we battled the waves, and the elements began to
take its toll.*
*That's it, said the boys, I've had enough of this, and the full
sacks meant we'd reached our goal.*

*All we had to do now was arrange getting our booty from shore to
single track road.*
*One thing we forgot was that it was Communion week, which
meant no tractors left their abode.*

*The wilks would be useless if not lifted soon, but there was
absolutely nothing we could do.*
*With disgruntled acceptance and our pockets empty, we had to
bid our wilks adieu.*

Summer Sounds of 77

Unbeknownst to me, 1977 would be the last school summer holiday that I would have from Glasgow to Skye. Subsequent school holidays would be from Skye to Glasgow. My memories of that 1977 Linicro summer might be clouded by Isle affection but didn't the sun shine all summer long? It was not the heat wave of the previous year, but my memory tells me it was 'taps aff' weather? The evenings produced warm clear blue fading skies and it never quite got dark. The Minch's salty water replaced with glass by God's glazier hand, producing a still blackness all the way to the Outer Hebrides. Ok, so it might have rained now and again, but I don't remember the sky's tears at all.

One of the major influences on my young teen life was my cousin Bobby, who was living in Linicro that summer. He might not have been the perfect role model, but beggars can't be choosers (only kidding Bobby)! That summer was the first time that I saw the old static caravan that his parents had procured and positioned to the side of the Wee Hoose where an old black house had once stood many years before. Unlike the caravan that lives there now, this one was basic! It was large with two double beds and a kitchen area, but it truly had seen better days.

They tasked Bobby with giving it a makeover, which would not be easy! It was purchased from somewhere near Uig's pier and looked like it had seen some Hippie action. Judging by the paint on the wooden walls, man! Needless to say we spent many hours in that curious caravan ostensibly 'doing it up' but most times just mucking around (Bob did all the hard graft).

We had music though, by way of Bobby's green Sharp cassette deck. The problem for me was that I was 13 and raised on the pop of TOTP and my musical ears had yet to mature. Unfortunately (as I saw it) Bobby only had a handful of tapes with weird bands! I only recognised the obvious Ringo Starr and Boston's 'More than a Feeling' had some Scottish airplay the year before, but it did not float my (Skye) boat! The other cassettes were from Pink Floyd, who I knew nothing about.

One of the wonderful things about music is that if you are constantly exposed to songs repeatedly, it's torture to your uninitiated ear drums – then, without a word of warning, you start to like what you are hearing. 'Blast from Your Past' was easy listening. Mr Starr may not have had the best vocal cords but songs like 'Photograph', 'You're Sixteen' and 'Back off Boogaloo' have made this album a minor 70s classic! Boston's 'Boston' rapidly became my favourite album with some cracking AOR tunes like 'Hitch a Ride', 'Something about You' and the aforementioned 'More Than a Feeling'.

The Floyd albums took longer to make sense to my ears and brain! Slowly, Dark-Side of the Moon became singalongable with classics like 'Us and Them', 'Brain Damage' and 'Money'. Then came Animals, which at first was far too weird for me, but it soon stirred something deep in the nether regions of my soul, with tracks like 'Dogs' and 'Sheep'. It's not that I understood what the hell Roger Waters was writing about, but on a spiritual level that album did (and still does) something to my heart and mind!

The most difficult of Bobby's meagre tape collection to get into (and to understand) was 'Wish You Were Here', with its long instrumental pieces and occasional songs. It was just too difficult for me to get ma wee weegie heid round! I really had no clue about how to listen to it! That all changed when I heard the title track and from that moment my love affair with Pink Floyd (Dark Side till Final Cut era) was set in stone and never could we divorce!

Summer of 77 not only saw me leave Glasgow and become a Linicro resident, it was the beginning of my musical life. I would learn the power a tune has to change your emotions, and that this life of song would colour the rest of my teen years and have a major impact on my metamorphosis into an (immature) adult.

Skyeku 4

Sheep red cloud sky

Booted smiles on the moor

Collie tongues flap.

Today I still listen to these albums other than 'Blast from Your Past' (sorry Ringo), and on these occasions I'm transported back to those summer days when anything was possible, life was easy and the blue Skye sky covered my head and told me everything would be all right (and mostly it was)!

Big Norman

Norman Macinnes, what a guy and an enormous influence on my young Linicro life. The eldest of the Macinnes brothers, Norman was a hard-working, decent guy who was built like the proverbial brick poop house! One of my first memories of Skye was being lifted into the tractor trailer in Totescore by the big man! Again, as everyone knows, Norman had a blue Austin 1100 (maybe 1300) and was the primary driver of the Macinnes David Brown tractor. He was beloved by my Aunt Margaret and my Great Granny. He was a handsome devil, albeit shy with the ladies! Big, hairy with muscles and a fine head of short back and sides Highland hair. A weather-worn ruddy complexion perhaps made him seem older than he was, and he was definitely one of my heroes as a kid. He had the patience of a saint and was generous to a fault. I used to love hanging around with him. Duncan, Archie and I would often make his life hell and annoy him, but back then he used to just take it all in his stride! On a summer's evening I would hope that he would pass by in his car and stop in for a cup of tea. He liked to stand on the outside of the wee hoose half door, and he could be there an hour or two talking!

Norman would cut my Aunt Margaret's hay in his David Brown, and there was no better fun than walking behind the mower and unclogging it when the blades were stuffed with thistles and grass. When on the road he would let me steer the tractor, only taking control when there was oncoming traffic. He used to do handyman stuff at our neighbour Miss Morton's house

'Big' Norman
Macinnes

and me and Bobby would go over and hang out and hopefully get a shot of her petrol-driven Flymo!

Attending my first ever Portree High School Christmas dance in 1977 was made possible by him coming to pick me up after it had finished.

I went out many times to the hill with him to help gather sheep, and at Linicro fank (the place where they shear sheep). Norman was probably the fastest sheep shearer there was!

How many dances he took us all to? He never drank except once when I saw him take a swig of whisky. Unlike us younger idiots who got steaming, he was the sensible one. We used to make fun of his taste in music, which was pretty much Gaelic signing, accordion music and some American country music.

Norman would take us on runs to Staffin, if we were lucky, sometimes to Portree. There he would always buy Archie and me chips or sweeties. He was an all-round, superb guy. My abiding memories of him are that he was very hard-working whether on the Totescore croft or doing other work for locals, including my Aunt. Many a time he would take me on one of his jobs and I would do my best to help. More than once he gave me pocket money when I was totally broke!

It has been many years since I last saw him, but he is never far from my mind and I hope he knows how important and influential he was to me growing up in Linicro.

Austin

*The road was narrow in the summer heat, tourists passed from
    countries near and far.*
*My well-scrubbed summer face waved to all, but my eye only
    wanted to see one car.*

*From its corrugated home in Totescore, the four wheeled object of
    my desire would wake.*
*The familiar silhouette of its driver, wavy-haired, weather worn,
    booted foot on the blue car's brake.*

*On these lucky days, the driver's brothers and I would pile into the
    back.*
*All arms and legs with smelly feet as the rubber burned on the
    Linicro tarmac.*

*Big Norman, our lumberjack shirt wearing chauffeur, smelling of
    Brut 45 and diesel.*
*One big callused hand gripping the steering wheel, the other
    searching for a tape that would meet our approval.*

*We drove to the top of Uig, en route to the bealach, with the
    MacDonald sisters blasting loudly in the back.*
*Us three in the rear, screaming and shouting for him to change
    the tune to something resembling rock.*

The hill road quiet in the summer still, we rolled down both the back windows.
I stuck my head out to grab some relief from the heat, my hair flapping in the bealach air flow.

We travelled all the way to Staffin, turning off on the road, racing past Digg.
Past the Flod and our sleeping school bus, heading to Score is what we did.

I loved that wee blue car and the fun we had, carrying on like triple loons.
The ever patient elder Macinnes boy laughed in the rear mirror at us Kilmuir goons.

We zoomed past the Kilmuir Post Office, wishing for a chocolate snack.
All at once we arrived outside the wee hoose half door. They set me free from the back.

The three boys took off in that blue Austin waving and shouting till they disappeared.
And I would wait impatiently, for the next time that the car and the boys would reappear.

My (Great) Granny Annie Arnott

Annie was the mother of Katie Mackenzie who was my Mum's Mum. She was my Great Granny. We just called her Granny. She was a real character. Well-known and respected on Skye. Well known in Glasgow too. Here is what Wikipedia have to say about her:

Great Granny Linicro

'Anna 'Annie' Arnott (née Mackenzie) (1887–1978) was a Scottish singer who sang in Scottish Gaelic in the puirt à beul style.

Annie Arnott was born and raised in Linicro, near Uig on the Isle of Skye in Scotland. She learned many songs from her mother who was descended from the MacDonald bards.

She was regarded as one of the foremost exponents of traditional Gaelic song. Her singing was recorded in 1950 by Derick Thomson and later by Calum Maclean and by others from the School of Scottish Studies at the University of Edinburgh. Many of her recordings are archived on Tobar and Dualchais. The song Seallaibh Curaigh Eoghainn (Look at Ewen's Coracle) was included on a compilation of music from the Western Isles.'

She was a housewife, crofter and also had a shop in Linicro. She lived in Glasgow for many years, eventually returning to Skye.'

To all of us kids she always seemed ancient and small, but inside was a personality big enough to take on the world. She could be a strict task master in her younger days, but all my memories are just of her as my Granny. Easy to coax into song and although her voice had seen better days, she had a memory like an elephant. Her brain stored 100s of old Gaelic songs and she could sing them all lyrically flawless.

Her memory continues to live online where you can find many recording of her made by the Edinburgh School of Scottish Studies. In the 1950s and 60s they recorded her singing and chatting about her early life. It's fascinating to hear her voice as if she was still here with us. I recommend that anyone with an interest in Gaelic history, Scottish Music and Skye in general just 'Google' her and you will find links to her singing.

For me she is and always will be that we wrinkly woman in the big cardies and thick socks – singing in the corner of the wee hoose.

By the time I arrived to stay in Linicro she was in her 90s and seemingly indestructible. I consider myself to be very lucky to have been part of her last few years of Linicro life. Love you Granny.

GG and Me

Sunday Afternoon

*All is quiet in the big hoose living room and you can hear a hat
    pin drop.*
*I'm on the sofa staring at the clock which barely moves past 12
    o'clock.*

*On the corner chair, my Granny is dozing, dreaming about tea
    and oatcake.*
*Whilst my Auntie is walking her favourite dog, I'm staring
    through windows, opaque.*

*Less than four hours of daylight left for me to get outside and try
    to amuse myself.*
*If I don't get moving and start my grooving I'm going to end up
    on the shelf.*

*Big jacket on and welly boots, I make a beeline for the kitchen's
    back door.*
*On the path to the wee hoose, I pass my Aunt who orders my
    return by four.*

*From the shed, I grab my trusty steed in the shape of my old
    woman's bike.*
*And I'm on the road pushing like mad with no particular place to
    go.*
All around me, surrounded by silence, this Sunday in Linicro.

What to do, I wonder?
Where to go I ponder?
When the sky lets loose its rain.
*From my moist blue eye I spy my shelter at the end of the old
    Stonegate road.*
*The terrain is a strain on my bum and spokes as I make it to the
    old garage abode.*

*I park my bike, and I park my rear on top of an old cardboard
    box.*
*The rain bouncing off the corrugated roof severely limits my
    options to play.*
No Macinnes boys to carry on with, on this the Sabbath day.

*It's too wet and too far to go to Uig's pier, and the mud-soaked
    quarry is a no go.*

When at last an idea formulates, above my head a light bulb glow.

I squish my way down the stream, to the tunnel beneath the Totescore road.
And I bend my neck, straddle the flow, and use the cement circle as a commode.

For once nature is on my side, a sunbeam appears from Waternish.
Soon it spreads its love, and the sky above reveals a faint hint of blue.

I get on my bike and make it to the top of Totescore, gaze all across the land.
My love of this view will never cease, God's love and I'm in his hands.

Bat out of hell like, I pedal two feet to the metal; I head back to the hoose.
At least a few hours wasted. My tummy empty, I wait for my Sunday riposte.

Time on this day moves snail like, I wait for the clock to strike seven.
When I'm allowed to watch the Saint and enjoy three hours of black-and-white TV heaven.

W.C. Fields

Some toilet humour or make that some humour about toilets (or lack of them)! Previously I have alluded to the fact that the 1970s wee hoose in Linicro had no running water. This also meant an absence of a 'comfort room' as my Filipino colleagues like to call the bog! To some this would seem like an inconvenience, but to us kids not only was it fun it was a challenge.

A quick backtrack first.

You may recall that the big hoose was rented out during the summer months and we lived in the wee hoose during this time! Toilet activities were covered during the winter because the big hoose had

A. Running water and

B. A bathroom!

So, no complications in the bodily functions department!

Back to the wee hoose toilet challenge. Number ones were easy as a child. Just go outside and let the water flow freely! Just remember to switch peeing places as we would not want any unpleasant odours wafting into the wee hoose living room via the wee hoose window. For number twos this entailed a trip to the byre where you would find secreted in a corner stall, a chemical cludgie.

Whereas most people might look upon this arrangement with some disdain, I loved it. Toilet time was an adventure, and nothing seemed more natural than sitting in that dark corner doing your thing. Rain or shine, when Mother Nature called, a trip to the byre was in order. This could be tricky (and scary), if you had the call late at night, and if this happened you would need the company of a toilet chum and a torch!

In the bedroom of the wee hoose, there in one corner, was this homemade commode for my Granny. It was just a wooden-legged chair that had been boxed. The seat would lift to reveal a none too comfortable toilet seat and a metal bucket below. Nightly Margaret would take the pee-filled container to the burn besides us and throw the contents over. That burn did not run all the time though. Only in heavy rains. In pleasant weather there was a pungent smell wafting across the road.

My Aunt Margaret ensured that the chemical cludgie was regularly cleaned and topped up with the blue poo-eating chemical. Not once did she ever ask me to perform this chore, and for that I'm forever grateful! She also ensured that the supply of soft bog roll was never in shortage! So thank you

Margaret for doing that unenviable task!

The two top wee hoose bedrooms housed my cousin Bobby and I and, being incredibly lazy teenagers, if we woke in the middle of the

Skyeku 5

Griddle fresh taste treats

Hot hands grab cheese munched

Freshly baked mouth full.

night, with that familiar bladder stabbing pain we would inevitably choose the porcelain chanty under the bed, rather than getting dressed and going outside. Taking laziness to new heights, we would choose not to do the right thing the next day, by disposing of the chanty contents responsibly. Rather, we chose to open the bedroom window and pour said contents into the guttering! We assumed that the rain would come to dilute and flush the contents away. All appeared well but fine summer weather prohibited the rain and my Aunt noticed a familiar toilet type aroma. She quizzed us about the smell, but we assured her that we were nothing but dutiful when it came to emptying our chamber pots. Later, with some water from the nearby 'tobar' we hurriedly washed away any traces of our wrongdoing! During the times between big hoose guests leaving and the next arriving, we had the luxury of a flushable throne and we made good use of our short time on it.

Today no such worries as the wee hoose has been totally renovated and toilet type dilemmas are consigned to the history books or Facebook group pages.

Chemical Loo

In middle of the wee hoose night, in 70s Linicro when Mother Nature called.
From my creaking Z-bed, barely dressed, down the wooden steps I crawled.

Wellies over bare feet, wee red and white torch on, desperately in need of a number two.
Dodging nettles and fresh footpath cow pats, I stumbled to the byre's chemical loo.

*The dark and hay dusty stalls held nothing but ghosts, except for
the one in the corner.*
*A metal bucket and toilet seat sat alone. Beauty truly was in the
eye of the beholder.*

*With my breeks at my ankles, the silence of the byre was great for
contemplation.*
*And the blue liquid beneath your bum so adept at
decontamination.*

*In the half light of a summer night, sounds struck you with doom
and fear.*
*What was that heavy breathing and those weird footsteps and
are they coming near?*

*Loo roll, tied with blue bailing twine, hung from the wooden hen
house wall.*
*Running water from the tap outside froze your fingers after
finishing in the stall.*

*Not a thought did I give to my poor Aunt, whose chore was
emptying that poop bucket.*
*Hosing and cleaning and filling with blue the gruesomeness, I
can now appreciate.*

*My aunt, long past and many summers since that byre, held its
portable potty chum.*
*More than forty years have there been since two moonlights, one
in the shape of my bare bum.*

A (Dog's) Life Less Ordinary

To date, my Glasgow family owned two dogs. The first being a
Dalmatian called 'Jackson', my memories of him are from
warmly saturated 70s Kodak colour snaps that live in a biscuit
tin in my mother's living room cupboard. We only had him a

short while as the confines of a Galloway Street maisonette proved too challenging for us and him. A friend of my father who lived in a less built-up area and had their own garden adopted him.

As the 1970s neared their end, I was transported from Springburn and living in Linicro with my Great Aunt and Great Granny. Around the summer of 77 my mother was in Linicro with her sister and my cousin Flora. We all took a trip to the Uig Bakery, after which the adults went to 'Boyd's' (The Ferry Inn) for an afternoon refreshment. Being around 13 at the time, they parked me outside the door of the public bar.

This was not the Ferry Inn of today. This was when the public bar was a Spartan affair, save for a few locals propping up the bar. My seat was directly in front of the men's toilet, looking out to the road and the grassy area in front of the pub. The weather must have been fine, as I seemed to have spent a good hour sitting on the concrete. After a while a local (who my mind's eye can still see but can't name), appeared at the bar with two or three pups. Black and fawn coloured, as I recall. Cute, like all

Caileag and Me,
Linicro

puppies, I got my boredom relieved by playing with them whilst their owner went for a pint. He eventually took the pups inside the bar and to cut a long story short, my mother took the light-coloured one and my cousin took the black one.

I didn't get much chance to play with the pup as my Mum returned to Glasgow soon after. They named the four-legged bundle of cuteness Skye! He was a mongrel, part Labrador mixed with Groucho Marx and Albert Einstein! I did not see him again till the following year when I spent some weeks of my summer holiday in Springburn. By this time, he had grown as big as he ever would be. He was not huge at all but had a cute Lab-like face, a wiry body and curled tail. He was very smart and constantly hungry.

Over the years I grew to love him like the rest of my family did and although he would not see me for long periods, when I returned home he would always recognize me with a whipping of that curled tail and a smile. Yep, you read right. A smile! Someone had taught him how to (kind of) smile where he would raise his top lip (do dogs have lips?) and show his front gnashers. Funny and cute. He was also very protective of my mother so that if you went to close to her and pretended to kiss her, he would growl, snarl and bark until you backed off.

Skye was intelligent and when it was time for his walk my siblings and I would argue whose turn it was to take him 'oot' and when he heard either 'oot' or 'out' he would go totally bonkers until his lead was on and he was rushing out the door. It got so that when we argued about whose turn it was we had to spell 'o. o. t' or 'o. u. t' to stop him going mad, he soon learned how to spell!

Taking him out was a total nightmare. He might have been slim built, but he was strong and he would drag you up and down Galloway Street wheezing like a hanged man. With him pulling so tight on his lead he was in a constant state of semi-asphyxiation!

Skyeku 6

Rhubarb green growing red

Corner garden dirt goodness

Sugar poke sweetly sour.

42

Skye liked to try and sneak out too and often waited for a chance to bolt out the front door between your unsuspecting legs! He could be gone for days. Then, you would hear a gentle rap of the letterbox and you would find him in the corridor totally bogging black and looking apologetic! He hated to have a baff (bath) and we had to surreptitiously run the water and spell b.a.f.f. He would desperately need a wash post escape as he usually smelled to high heaven. We would trap him in the bathroom and do our best to soap away the smell. Why he hated the water so much I don't know.

That wee dog was always hungry, he would eat absolutely anything, including blocks of Whitecap lard that he would purloin from the fridge! Whenever he would make his great escape, his first port of call was zooming up the stairs outside the tenements opposite us and could be seen springing up to the first-floor window to get a peek at his Jack Russell pal 'Nipper'. Skye was not an aggressive dog, but he had the dog's equivalent of 'short man's syndrome'. With dogs his own size or smaller he liked to play but if you were out walking with him on the lead and you passed a big dog e.g. an Alsatian he would go wild and jump for their neck!

With acute hearing he could hear a pin drop on cotton wool and would bark his louder than you would think (for his size) bark. Funnily though, and unfortunately for my mother, during the numerous burglaries at our place he never barked once! In fact, one of the robbers used his bed (an old sleeping bag) to load up their booty. We used to joke that he would show them where the stealing stuff was as long as they did not hurt him!

In the late 80s, my mother moved from Galloway Street to the far nicer Park Road in the West End. Skye got confused by this move and during one of his escapes he disappeared for days and was seen in Springburn by my brother! Eventually he made it back to the West End! As the 80s gave way to the 90s, he began to slow down but rallied when the promise of a walk in Kelvingrove Park was made. My mother's flat was on the top floor and latterly he struggled with his hind legs so we would lift them and wheel-barrow him to the top!

His ultimate adventure was the funniest of all. I think he suffered a wee bit of dementia, but true to form this old dog managed one last escape! This time he did not reappear and was taken for dead. Weeks passed when my brother, Gary, walking along Great Western Road, spotted Skye on a leash with a strange female? He immediately confronted her and claimed that the dog belonged to my mother. She denied this and said the dog was hers! I think she was feeding Skye well as he played dumb, but it was obvious he recognized Gary. The woman was not keen to relinquish ownership of our dog, but after meeting with my Mum and Sister she had no choice but to say bye-bye to Skye! By this time, he was around 17 years old and spent the rest of his time sleeping, although when I went home, his cataract eyes still recognized me and his tail still wagged. He would eventually succumb to illness, but what a 17 years he had! How many doggy years is that? A lot I know! Gone, but I will never forget his wee smile.

Dyke

On the croft behind the big hoose, stretched across the green land is a dyke.
Formed by Mother Nature yawning and leaving a seat for man and boy alike.

A sofa of mud, stone, and grazed grass, housing holes for Linicro rabbits.
On sunny Skye days you will find me there, close to where the ruined bothy sits.

I'm cooled by the wind behind me as it rolls down from the heathered hill.
On its way to the rocky salt shore, skimming across the Minch, glass still.

From where I sit I see a kaleidoscope of colours, an artist's dream, waiting to be captured.
And on the water, dotted here and there, are sun silver fishing boats all bound homeward.

*In the evening still you can hear disembodied voices creep all
across the land.*
*Neighbour secrets, secret no longer, as radar ears gather gossip
in hand.*

*I'm surrounded by four-legged animals, chomping away on my
Aunt's green grass.*
*And she goes about her croft chores, I hide out of her sight,
underneath this land mass.*

*All at once day turns to evening, and evening turns to summer
night.*
*A calm settles all across our township, the neighbours turn on
their outside big lights.*

*My tummy tells me it's time to go and get a cheese-filled treacle
scone.*
*And if I'm lucky, a piece of sponge might be handed to my wee
Glasgow hand.*

*When at last my life light begins to dim, and I answer God's
calling home.*
*Post fire, take what's left in an urn to the dyke, let me scatter in
the gloam.*

$$\backsim$$

King of the Castle

Every time I stroll past freshly mown grass, my nasal passages
trigger memories of Skye summers long ago. This time the
memory smell was triggered by the small patch of recently
mown Saudi green, outside my apartment building's front door!
As I walked past in the morning desert heat, this small oasis
and its earthy green odour transported me, Tardis-like back to
1977 Linicro. Just along from the wee hoose, heading to Uig,
where my Aunt Annie's neighbours, the Mackenzies live now.
Between the road and the croft fence there was grassed hillock

45

with a number of lumpy green levels all the way down to the ditch at the side of the road. This small patch of natural fun would prove ideal land for us kiddies to play King of the Castle. Where brave Linicro Knights would fight for dominion and stand alone, proud at the top of this green grassy bump!

The 1977 Knights in question were my two Glasgow cousins Andrew and Jason who were on holiday in Linicro with their Dad, my Uncle James. In the warmth of the Skye summer sun we would battle it out, throwing each other down the hill towards the ditch. Andrew was two years younger than me and Jason was a very cute bit younger than us both. He fought well, though! Rolling around on the grass with no fear of injury, we would play there for hours (weather permitting). Green grass stained we would run back to the wee hoose for a jug-scooped drink of cool water from the nearby 'tobar'. Then we would make our way back to the battleground.

How we never broke a bone is a medical mystery. Our rubber limbs would make any professional stuntman turn a dark shade of envious green. Late into the evening we would wrestle and roll, pick ourselves up, climb the hill and go at it again! Whenever I was crowned King, I would sing at my voice's top, the Ringo Starr song chorus from 'I'm the Greatest' ad-libbing

Gaeilovore Island with Harris Hills

and adding 'I'm the Greatest King of the Castle'. My words carrying along the crofter's fields, down to the shore, bouncing from salt rock to rock pool and across the Minch so that the inhabitants of the Outer Isles and beyond would know that I truly was the King!

The Hill

The hill knows me, my feet it recognizes, whether welly booted or not.
Its slopes of heather and grass green, as familiar to me as breath is to my lungs.
The hill has always been there, through iced rain and sun, not hot.

Its common, my play field as far as the eye can see.
Surrounded by rock and stream, its sounds no stranger, its peaks no danger.
The hill has always been by my side on lonely walks and in company.
Its Sunday silence, my friend.
The supplier of sustenance for beast and boy.
The hill an endless journey, until grass meets gravel, then grass again.

Waterlogged and tinder dry, peppered with rocks rolled down from high.
The hill my shelter from heaven's tears.
It exposes my fragility with crevice and cliff.

The purveyor of bird's-eye views, in its mud tracked beauty, my body basks.
The hill unchanged since baby eyes first blinked.

Its cold coat worn in winter's depth.
Replaced in spring with lighter things, summer is on its way.
My hill, it knows me, knows me well until my dying day.

Fishing and Loving the Limpet

That same King of the Castle summer saw my cousins, Uncle and I walk to Uig Pier – fishing lines in our wee excited hands. As we neared the top of Uig, Andrew, Jason and I could not wait to get to the end of the pier and get some saltwater fishing action! From the top of Uig the pier looks deceptively close, but as you try to get closer the further it moves away from you! It took only minutes to bolt down the Bealach, landing at the start of Idrigal's long and winding road down to the shore's edge.

This was the old pier that belonged to my long-time friend the MV Hebrides. The closer we got, the more excited we became, with visions of catching a trawler's haul with our puny fishing hooks!

Our chosen spot is before the pier's end. Our destination was to step carefully down the slimy stairs that fishing boats used to land and decant. The tide was low enough that we stood on the bottom landing. Leaning on the salt-rusted metal handrail, we looked over the shell-encrusted legs of Uig Pier. The old legs giving the appearance of terrible varicose veins as the sun glinted off the blue green sea. We did not have any bait. What could we use? My Uncle James pointed at some limpet shells sucked and stuck to the pier's slippery steps, and with a swift kick one came loose! What to do with this, we wondered? None of us kids had the foresight or the finances to bring a pen knife. No bother to James, as he showed us what to do. With his adult thumb he scooped into the poor wee gastropod (I Googled that)! The innards in his palm we thought were too big for our tiny hooks, so how to make it smaller without a sharp, Sheffield-steeled cutting accoutrement? Easy, he bit into the salty beastie and nipped off a sliver for us to hook on our lines! Wow! You can bite these limpets and not die?

Our tiny minds blown, it was our turn next! As if sensing our approach, the shelled animals flexed their foot muscles and hung on for dear life, as a rain down of small feet tried to kick them loose.

Skyeku 7

Candle lit page turn

Night eyes hungry for more read late

Bed springs groan approval.

Successful, we then had to squish our thumb into the shell's body and pop out the now dead sea creature. 'Do we have to bite into it?' But bite we did. The leathery salt taste was not unpleasant as we nipped it into tiny bits of limpet! We then hooked the flesh and, with a small lead weight attached, threw the line over the stair rail. This metal rail was shaky and the only thing keeping us from a cold salty bath! Water visibility was right to the seabed and soon we attracted the attention of these small fish that seem to hang around piers. I don't know what they are called, but there was a school of them trying to nibble on our baited lines? The problem with our gear was that the hooks were a bit on the big side and these fish, maybe only 3 or 4 inches. Their petite fishy mouths far too small for our big barbed hooks. My Uncle though had the right kind of fisherman's moves and he caught several slippery wee reddish, greenish brown fishy things. His technique? He patiently waited till a sizeable swimmer nibbled above his hook. Then, with a strong jerk of the line, he could hook them long enough to pull to the surface and render them dead! It was an excellent technique that us kids tried to emulate, but I have no memories of catching anything that day!

We vicariously enjoyed my Uncle's success, albeit with some envy! Hours we spent trying our luck when eventually, tired and hungry, we made for the long walk back to Linicro. I think my Uncle James gutted his small haul, and we fried them for us to eat. My memory tells me that though bony, the flesh when fried, tasted yummy! That was the last time that I got to spend with Andrew and Jason as they would return to Glasgow, leaving me with fishing lessons learned. Occasionally, over the next couple of years, I would cycle to the pier's slimy steps once more and try my luck, with modest success and a salty after taste!

Pier Sunday

*Sunday sitting on the pier, a world of water beneath my dangling
feet.*
*Spring fresh, the sun cold and super bright, daffodil yellow in
the air so sweet.*

*Time and tide have washed the concrete legs, scrubbed schoolboy
clean.*
*The frothy saline soaks the boats, bobbing on a sea of grey, blue
and green.*

*Overhead some rogue seagulls are scrounging for lunch and leave
disappointed.*
*A slimy shiny seal, swimming to Cuil, turns to spy me, pupils
deep black and dilated.*

*The rivers Conon and the Rha rush race, white faced into the
briny bay.*
*Peat water, smoothing stones for aeons, runs from the hills so
far away.*

*No sign of human beings. The roads grey and deserted tell me I'm
on my own.*
*Whilst Sunday roasts get carved, Sunday papers get read in
quiet Sunday homes.*

*A rain cloud, fast and angry, floats across from Earlish, ever
nearing.*
*And I jump my silver pedalling machine, to reach Linicro by
early evening.*

I Fought the Law and
the Law Won

I have always been a law-abiding citizen and have never been in trouble with the police, apart from a fine I got when we were stopped by a police van in Glasgow as we were coming home from my Dad's in a private taxi. The reason being that they spotted Isis, who was only a baby, not secured in the back with a seat belt. Guilty your honour. I duly paid the 60 quid fine! They did not take into account mitigating circumstances, which was that we had to rush down to my Dad's unexpectedly because of a trouser emergency. The following day was Isis's christening, and we had discovered that he did not have a decent pair of keks to wear! We had to rush into town, buy a few pairs and then rush to his wee flat in Govanhill to make sure they fitted. Luckily, they did! Also, luckily for us that the Police van pulled us over near Cessnock Underground, as we had to leave the taxi because there was no child's seat and walk!

Let's go all the way back to the summer holidays of 1977. This was not long after my Aunt Margaret had agreed that I could stay and go to school, so I was a lucky person. This Saturday evening there was a football match in Staffin between Kilmuir and Staffin, and me and my accomplices (who shall remain nameless) had decided to go and support our local team! We got dropped off by a certain person who then promised to come and pick us up after the game. I have no memory of the match itself, but to my embarrassment now, I remember absolutely everything that happened after!

Post-game we waited for our lift, which failed to appear. One of us had the idea to start walking along the road and hopefully we would be picked up by that certain person's car and be transported home. Big mistake! We were young and stupid and left to walk along the road towards Digg we got up to some mischief. There was a toilet sign that we bent and wrapped round its pole. Not smart, I know, but we laughed like maddies as we did it. The car had still to pick us up when we passed some Council road works, and there were some concrete pipes being used for drainage. We rolled a few of them down a hill and watched them smash at the bottom! I know, I know we really were stupid. Finally, we removed somebody's garden gate from its hinges and rolled it down a hill. To another round of laughing! Thankfully, by that time our transport had arrived, and we could get up to no more mischief!

Not long after this, I don't remember exactly, perhaps a few days. I got a visit from the Uig Policeman asking if I knew anything about what had occurred on the Saturday night previous. It had been reported to him that the four of us had been seen walking along the road and that some signs got bent and concrete pipes got busted! I remained cool under pressure, thinking I can lie my way out of it and declared my innocence. This did not last too long as he already had the story from my honest accomplices and at that point I cried like a big baby! And to be honest now, and I know that this is just between you and me, right? My tears were not for getting caught, although I felt scared. My waterfall was at the thought of being sent home to Glasgow by my Aunt Margaret!

I could not think of anything else! After all the goodness of her to let me live in Linicro, I now had ruined it by being a naughty boy. We all fessed up and surprisingly Margaret took it quite well. My Granny was a star as she just laughed and said 'boys will be boys'. Still, someone had to pay and as I was underage, it would not be me! A fine was issued after a brief appearance in Portree, and subsequently it was paid. The money was to pay for the broken pipes and to replace the sign and the garden gate. Fair enough!

Skyeku 8

Bike boy Totescore bound

Winded and puffing uphill

Soon speeding downhill.

One evening, the fine payer and I went back to the scene of the crime. Only to find that someone had just straightened out the sign (and that sign was still there years later), and the gate was back on its hinges. So why did it have to be paid for? Some words were said about that issue. The payer of the fine never got a discount. Hardly the crime of the century I know, but it was big north end news although I'm pretty sure that it did not make it into the West Highland Free Press (if it did, would someone send me a clipping)?

We had all learned our lesson about damaging other people's property, so we removed that from our mischief making and just got up to 'legal' naughty stuff (not quite legal when it came to the deoch, but that's another story)!

Passing Place

Standing guard, straight and true, I remember you.
Are you still standing there today?

Through nights as dark as the devil's soul.
My loneliness you offered a light reflection.

From the top of Totescore's road to the Post Office phone box, your
    company I kept.
Diamond black and white, a face friendly and kind, my hand
    held in the night rain.

The quarries creeps you kept at bay on starless winter evenings.
The ghosts of Stonegate kept their distance as I passed your
    luminous face.

In the evening summer light stretched south to north, east to west,
    always on call.
No complaints you filed when we changed A to I, and laughter
    replaced the corncrake.

We turned your head; we kicked you hard, but no sign of anger
    you showed.
And when again the dark came and sucked out the light, you
    never abandoned me.

A head of white on a moonlit night, a torch procession stood still
    and straight.
Passing place, I miss your face on single tracked Linicro you
    wait.

Stand tall my metal friends, please don't disappear, wait for my island return.
Until that time keep strong, upright, and don't let the water bite.
Let cars and buses pass each other, keeping islanders safe and guests alike.

$\backsim$

First day at Portree High School

After the stress of asking my Aunt Margaret if I could stay in Linicro and getting to go to school in Portree, I then gave myself more anxiety, as I thought the school would not allow me to attend. I don't know why but I thought because I went to All Saints for the first year I had to finish my schooling there. Anyway, that stress was all for nothing as Portree High School just required a phone call from my folks and that was it!

Come the Sunday before my first day, I was nervous but also excited. I did not have a school uniform, and the only clothes I had were the ones I had taken to Skye for my summer holiday. I think the reason my folks did not buy me a uniform (other than the exorbitant price of a school blazer) was that they thought that maybe I would not like it and that I would want to return to Glasgow toot sweet (they were dead wrong)!

But what to wear? I had a pair of black brogues (these were fashionable back in the 1970s). A pair of black 'made to measure' flairs from Glasgow's Burtons the Tailor. A white short-sleeved 'army shirt' from Dee of Trongate (these were also fashionable at the time). And I had a grey school-type jumper that was given to me by the Macinnes boys. Big Norman Macinnes gave me a tie but as I did not know how to tie a tie, I never wore it!

That Monday morning in the Wee Hoose I had butterflies on top of my butterflies. I nervously waited for 'John the Bus', in his bus, to come pick me up! Eventually he arrived and as I entered, the sea of maroon blazers all had eyes only looking at me. I sat in the first seat beside John. As we passed the top of Totescore, I could see the familiar shapes of my two best pals Duncan and Archie Macinnes. That made me feel much better. Both of them boarded and tried to persuade me to sit down to the back of the bus, but I refused. I sat alone all the way to Portree. Once we decanted, Duncan showed me the door to the administration where I had to announce myself. I think the first person I spoke to was the secretary who was a good friend of Miss Herdman, the Home Economics teacher. I remember her name: Anne.

After waiting a while, a wee guy came to show me to my form room. I don't remember if he told me his name but as he had a fine moustache under his nose. I assumed that he was older than me. I was to be in G2 and the guy who showed me to class was none other than Donnie 'Noddy' Nicholson, who was in the same year as me! The rest of the day was just trying to fit in and find my feet. At lunchtime I met up with the Macinnes boys and we went into the town centre for something to eat. Later, I was to find out that as I stayed with my Great Granny and my Great Auntie, who did not work, I was eligible for free school dinners.

I remember the dinner tickets as they were red and looked like big bus tickets. You tore one off each lunchtime. The difference between the paid and free tickets was that the free ones had a line drawn by an ink marker down the middle.

I was not impressed by the food in the cafeteria. The portions were minuscule and unlike the school dinners at All Saints you could not line up for 'seconds'!

Those first couple of weeks at PHS were a bit of a blur as you not only had to get used to your surroundings but you had to make new friends and explain why you were there instead of being in Glasgow. Throughout the long day, I could only think about being back in Linicro. I had some model tanks and at the side of the burn behind the big hoose I had made a tank base diorama for them with some toy soldiers. This was all I could think about, and four o'clock could not come fast enough for my young self.

Kids are resilient and I quickly found my brogued feet and made friends with guys like Gudge and Lorenzo who were in my form class. People often asked me if I missed my family in Galloway Street. If I'm being honest the truth is, I did not miss them or Springburn! I called home every Sunday night to let them know how things were going, but I never once laid on my bed thinking 'I wish I was back in Glasgow attending All Saints'!

It only took a couple of months at Portree High until I stopped thinking about being back in Linicro all the time and began to look forward to going to school every day. Not for the academic part but for the social part and the fact that being in Portree and looking at the nice girls in my year was infinitely better than being stuck in the wee hoose/big hoose staring at my Aunt's two dogs!

Drowning Not Waving

My Granny decided this sunny summer afternoon that she wanted to go for a walk. Me being a teenager did not take much notice, and my Aunt Margaret was not around. I sat in the wee hoose and would occasionally get up to see where Granny had got to. She was heading towards Morton's house. Another check by me after a period of time I saw that she had passed Morton's gate and appeared to be sitting on the grass dyke enjoying the weather. She waved. I waved back and went inside.

Ten or so minutes later I went outside to have a look, and she seemed fine there at the side of the road. She waved. I waved back and once again returned inside. It would be a further 20 minutes before I would check on her again and when I did, she waved, and I waved back, but this time I noticed she was using her walking stick to wave! Strange, I thought, but she seemed ok. I sat back in and thought no more about it until I decided I would walk her back. As I came outside the wee hoose door she was waving furiously with her stick. I quickened my steps towards her. As I got close it soon dawned on me that she was stuck on the dyke and could not get up. She was not just waving; she was looking for help and I ignored her! Thankfully she had not hurt herself and was ok other than that she needed the loo. My outstretched arm pulled from the grass verge and we walked back to the wee hoose arm in arm.

Great Granny and Tourist
Early-1970s

Funky Moped (Our Fast but Not Furious Suzuki 125)

That first summer of 1977 I discovered that Bobby had got himself a motorbike. It was a gold-coloured Suzuki road bike with a white storage box on the back and L signs on front and rear. He stored it in one of the stalls in the byre and I constantly begged him to take me on it for a spin. Being a learner he could not take any pillion passengers but hey this was the 70s with very few passing policemen! He used it regularly when he got a Job Creation 'job'. Luckily for him, this was near to old Hojan's house opposite us. There he worked with the late Donnie 'Glen' digging a drain or something. I'm not even sure they did any work. Most of the time they sat in the portable shed that was placed there for them by the council.

On Sundays I would pester him to get the bike out so we could have some biking fun. It didn't take much persuasion! The only problem (for me) was that he had only one helmet. Which he wore! Apart from that, we did not worry about the Police. Sundays were quiet days for the Uig Officer! Most days would see us go to the Camus Mor. Occasionally we would ride up to the top of Uig and go along the bealach road. There we found some relatively flat off-road surfaces and we would ride the bike over the grass. Whilst on the grass I was brave enough to try my hand at some stunts! Usually I would get up on the seat and stand straight whilst holding on to Bobby's shoulder. I nearly fell off a few times as we went over some bumps in the grass, but I figured if I fell off I would not hurt myself landing in the soft green. Of course, a more mature person might think I could easily fall off head first and land on a covert rock! I didn't. I was brave and stupid!

One time Bobby, Norman Macinnes and I were standing chatting outside of the wee hoose when Norman asked for a shot of the bike. He straddled it, making it look like a toy with his height. Stupidly, I was hanging on to the back storage box when he took off. Scraping along the road I got scared and let go, but the balance of the bike had been changed, which meant Norman lost control of the swerving Suzuki! Luckily, he was not going fast, but that bike was heavy, man. He came off it but managed to stay upright but could not save the bike from half spinning to the ground. The back brake light got smashed on one side and the petrol tank received a dent because of my idiocy!

Skyeku 9

A scone in the hand

Oven hot and tinned treacle

Butter cheese delight.

There was also one bitter day we headed down to Kilmuir and as I had no gloves, I put my hands in Bobby's motorbike jacket pockets for warmth. These pockets had zips. Not far from Kilmuir Post Office a couple of cars passed so Bobby moved close to the road's edge which everyone knows has a lot of gravel. The bike slipped sideways, and we both ended up in the road. Luckily, he was not travelling at speed so we did not get hurt too bad. My only injuries came from those pockets' zips. I ripped both my hands, and it left a zip tattoo on my skin. Both wounds were superficial and healed quickly.

The last of the Suzuki tales was not so funny, though. Bobby was out on the bike one evening. I remember vividly sitting in the wee hoose when I heard the bike go past the window and stop at the side of the house. Bobby walked in and looked as pale as me (and a sheet). His trousers were ripped at the leg and he had dirt over him. Scared, I asked what had happened, but he could only keep asking me to go and look at the bike to see if it was damaged. Then, out of nowhere, he started crying. By now I was really scared. That was the first and last time I saw him cry. To appease him, I went outside to look at the bike. It had some damage and scuffs to the paint work but nothing too bad. I went back into tell him when I saw the blood on his trousers near the knee. The fear took over me, especially when it looked like he had really done some serious damage to his knee. There was a rather deep and bloody wound. It transpired that he came off the bike near the Idrigal road in Uig. He was hurting. Eventually he was taken to hospital in Portree and ended up in Broadford as he needed knee surgery. The big boy must have been an in-patient for two weeks. He was a patient when Prince Charles visited. He came into the ward that Bobby was in and everyone stood to attention except my cousin! We laughed about that for ages. He eventually sold the Suzuki after that accident. By then he had started driving his father's old Hillman Avenger. It was slightly safer for both of us!

∽

Carry On (in the) Caravan

That 1977 summer saw the arrival of an old caravan which was parked at the side of the wee hoose. It stood where an old thatched cottage 'black house' had once been. The caravan was my Aunt Annie and Uncle Peter's, my cousin Bobby's folks. They had purchased it in Uig, where it had been static somewhere near the pier. It was rumoured (not spread by me) that it was once a caravan of ill repute, but I don't know if there is any truth in it. It certainly was not new and needed a fair amount of work on it to make it habitable. Bobby would do most of this. Sometimes I would help (or hinder). Uncle Peter would work on it when he was home from Glasgow.

Inside, it was spacious. It had two double beds, a wee kitchen with a toilet area in the corner. If my memory serves me right the décor of the place when it arrived was a bit on the hippie side. Bobby had to do a lot of wood sanding and laying on a fair few coats of paint to make the place look OK. In the middle of the living area there was space for a Calor gas heater. The sofa area near the far windows could be pulled out for one double bed. Opposite, in a cupboard, was another pull down bed. Bobby did a good job, and it ended up being reasonably nice and comfortable. He eventually moved into it full time. This was all right with me as I got into his bedroom in the wee hoose.

That caravan stood there for years and was used by various members of the family for holidays. I stayed in it myself a few times in the 1980s. They eventually replaced it with a more modern static affair, which, although more comfortable, did not have the same character as the original.

Camping

One cold winter night in Score, we decided it would be fun to camp in a two-man tent.

The sky above us was black hole dark, no star light could escape its chasm.

Undaunted, torch in hand, we made it to a grass plateau, below waves lonely crashed.

Across the way, the castle stood, night-time creepy and foreboding.

We wrestled with our tent and the chilly sea breeze, singing AC/ DC songs as we pitched.

From Pete's house we purloined some wood for a campfire cosy time.

In a moment of midnight madness, we headed to the shore for fire flotsam.

The heat comforted our hands, and ears and the yellow flames licked the dark.

Until a blowing breeze from the bay threatened to burn down our house.

God's eye was kind, and the wind subsided. Into the wee hours, we talked and laughed.

As the embers glowed their last, we dined on scones, thanks to my Auntie's baking hand.

Sleepy eyed sausages. Wrapped in our sleeping bags, we eventually succumbed to dreamland.

The morning rain subsided, and the sun made a guest appearance, albeit all too brief.

We rolled up the tent, stashing for later, awaiting the sight of John coming towards us.

Our Portree plans made, our arrival soon, we dozed in the warmth of the bus.

If Sport is the Question (What's the Answer?)

It was probably the first week of school when I was in the games hall changing room getting ready for P.E. Donnie Nicholson (Noddy), who had befriended me, asked if I was any good at football. I said, 'pretty good'. I lied. I was pretty hopeless, but what I lacked in skill I made up with enthusiasm and I enjoyed many sports at PHS. Even shinty. I enjoyed running around the blaise (known as 'red ash' in Glasgow) chasing a ball that I rarely caught whilst others like Ali Aitken and Donnie were excellent players.

Over my years at PHS, I made it into a couple of sports teams. Believe it, baby! Even though I did not enjoy it that much I always tried to do my best when we had to run 'cross country' during P.E. That run up the hill behind the school could be soul destroying, but I was determined to at least not be last. Donnie was always first. Usually followed by John 'Piggy' Robinson. I was usually around sixth or seventh, occasionally fourth. One injury I would receive on these runs was caused by the material of my Admiral Leeds United football top. It was terrible for chafing your nipples! Especially in the wet and cold.

I got picked for the school cross-country team and we were to go to Inverness to compete against other Highland schools. That night I remember I stayed with Alan Stewart, whose father was a banker. What I remember most was that they had a Parker-Knoll recliner, which to me was the height of luxury. I opted to sleep on it. To be honest, it was probably great for watching TV, but not that comfortable to sleep on. We awoke the next day to find Portree covered in a thick blanket of snow, and they cancelled the sports meet.

I also enjoyed playing rugby. Again, I was not that good, and my skinny frame did not do me any favours, but I relished the chance at trying my best to bring people to the ground. One P.E. day we were playing on the sports field at the side of the

Technical Block and I was on the opposing team of big (massive) Donald (from Dunvegan, I think). This guy in the fourth year was built like Juggernaut from the Deadpool 2 movie!

He had the ball and was running down the wing when I made a dive at him. This dive might have been a wee bit too high as I wrapped my arms around his neck. He ran on and I was trying to bring him to the grass with little success. It looked like he was wearing a meat scarf as my pale white frame flapped in the wind!

I also played rugby during Friday activities, and this was with the big guys! This was good because it was the only time you could legally try to hurt some of the annoying older boys with no consequences. Throughout the winter of fourth year I would be on that muddy field out past the blaise (It has a name which I have forgotten). We would return to the dressing room by the Gym caked in mud but as I was too shy to have a shower with these big Highland lads, I would just put my clothes on over the dirt and wait till I got back home to clean myself up! I got a concussion one Friday as I remember running low to pick up a loose ball when Robert Nelmes (who was a good player) sped into me. His knee caught me full on in the temple region. The pain was excruciating, and I wandered about like the walking dead for the rest of the afternoon. I don't think I sustained any lasting damage!

Mr Philip, our science teacher and rugby coach, surprisingly added me to the team that would go to Inversneckie to play Inverness Royal Academy and then Millburn. I don't remember what position I played, but I do remember having a good laugh. The bus was a mixed bus as we went with our ladies' hockey team. The Royal Academy game stands out more because they treated us very nicely. The facilities were excellent and although we were beaten, I scored a try! Purely by accident! I grabbed a loose ball and immediately was pounced upon by various big guys from Portree and Inverness. I kept my grip on that ball and somehow the momentum of the bodies took us over the line. When everyone was peeled off, I still held the ball! Robert Nelmes converted easily. I did not do much else of note for the rest of the game!

The Millburn game was less exciting. The facilities were not that good, and we got beat! What was funny though was that during throws a few of their team members tried to psyche people out with threats of violence! I remember them saying stuff like 'I'm gonna effin get you' and 'you're dead'. Not particularly scary in a Highland accent. They hurt nobody during the game, and I did not score a try! Jokingly in the changing room I tried to sell my PHS rugby top. Nobody was interested! I remember on the long and laborious bus journey home a few of us at the back, girls and boys were singing along to the likes of REO Speedwagon 'Keep on Loving You' and Kim Wilde's 'View from a Bridge'!

I also played some Skye league football for Dunvegan and Uig. Not because I was any good, but because they needed me to make up the numbers! I played one of the first games on the then new Uig football pitch, which I remember being anything but flat or smooth. I don't think I once got a touch of the ball! I also recall a humiliating defeat against Sleat when I got subbed on to the field for Dunvegan. It was a wet and miserable day and although I don't remember the score; it was rather top heavy. I managed to get myself in a photo for the West Highland Free Press. I had quickly changed back into my clothes to warm up when the photographer gathered the bodies for a team shot. I decided not to be in it but someone shouted for me to move in so I sheepishly moved closer to the posing group. If you saw that photo it looks like I had nothing to do with the game and just tried to photo bomb the team! Sad and funny at the same time!

Blaes

Winter wet sheets of water, icy cold and bone shivery, engulfed the
*   two Friday teams.*
The colour red, on those who fell a badge of honour, worn on
*   the bus all the way home.*

For some, knee and palms skinned, Blaise infiltrated their
*   superficial wounds.*
A good bath left the water brown and red, with particulates
*   clinging to the Shanks Vitreous.*

No luxury of green grass afforded us unfortunates on an activities
*   afternoon.*
Big guys knocked us about like a bowling pins, white and
*   shaking, ready to fall.*

Goals scored to no applause as pupils skirted the red border, on
*   their way to warmth.*
PE torture in the frost field of red did not stop us from enjoying
*   our hour of class freedom.*

Many lunchtime breaks we spent at one goalpost, as a few of us
*   tried to score.*
Some fell, some tripped, the sandpaper surface ripped the
*   trousers red, bloodless.*

Sweating and laughing, we played on until the call of the
*   afternoon bell.*
The years did not soften that gritty pitch and many battle scars
*   grace elbows and knees.*

Much fun was to be had when the sun shone kindly and you
*   remained upright.*
But as the years rolled on, many, including me, abandoned the
*   red field for others to play.*

Still, we walked across it from hut to school criss-crossing, bloody
*   shoe prints aplenty.*
Long gone the red roughness might be, but the pain memory for
*   many fallen remains.*

Pudding Lover

Who doesn't love pudding? I do! The difference between my years in Galloway Street and my time in Linicro was that pudding in Glasgow was a rare treat. Pudding on Skye was nearly every day! The Linicro pudding selection was done on an informal rota basis, to include custard, farola, semolina and tapioca. My absolute favourite was custard (still is).

These sweet delights would be accompanied by a crumble. Sometimes apple but mostly rhubarb. To mix it up I would add a slice of a sponge cake if my Aunt Margaret had recently made one for strupag guests. Margaret made tasty crumble although the rhubarb was not sweet enough for my sweet tooth! Usually I would eat all the crumble and custard and leave the rhubarb. With the apple I scoffed the lot. For the semolina, tapioca and farola these would be topped with whatever homemade jam was available. Mostly raspberry and gooseberry and – if they had grown without all being scavenged by the local rabbits – strawberry!

I totally loved my Aunt's strawberry jam on anything! There was one time though she made a very large pot of and got the thickener ingredients wrong. We ended up with over twenty jars of liquid strawberry jam that poured like water! This didn't stop me from eating it all. Many of the locals would drop off a jar or two of their recently made sweet spread. No metal lid just a grease-paper circle kept in place by an elastic band. All these deliveries gratefully accepted by an always hungry me.

There was a problem, however. Most of these yummy products were usually served cold! Most Skye kitchens prepared their sweets long before dinner. These would be poured hot into a clear oval dish and left to 'set'. This meant that by the time you ate your dinner the pudding would be viscous in its consistency and worse of all (for me at least) would develop a 'skin' on top! I don't know about you, but I like my puddings hot and runny – with the exception of trifle. Cold tapioca and semolina were not too tasty. Cold farola was just plain weird! That cold 'skin' layer on top was absolutely disgusting. I would do my best to scoop the pudding from under it and leave that leathery topping to someone else! Bobby ate the skin, but he was not as sensitive as me! I even hated the skin that formed on instant coffee made from milk. It's an alien consistency for food. No skin for me please.

This was long before microwave ovens made an appearance so there were no 'heating up' options. It was either cold pudding or nothing. Very occasionally Margaret made the pudding right before dinner so at least your custard had some heat! The crumbles were served cold too! It's just not right. These need to be hot. I ate them all anyway what else was a Linicro lad to do?

My Auntie's Scones

*Wish I could have a wee taste of one of my auntie's scones, made
    on her black iron griddle.*
*Feather flour dusted and slightly burnt, what a yummy wee
    hoose summer treat.*

My favourites were her treacle ones: brown, tasty, flat and chewy.
Stork margarine spread thickly, topped with Orkney cheese.
*Strawberry jam red and thick was definitely the mouth-
    watering bee's knees.*

*The smell of the baking rounds wafting all around made your
    tum tum rumble.*
Hot off the pan and melted butter, fresh from the wooden churn.
*What I'd give for one of these stuffed with cheese, all the money I
    have in my hand.*

*In winter, for a tongue tasting treat she would sometimes make in
    the big hoose oven.*
*And on a Sunday night before watching The Saint my taste buds
    were in scone heaven.*

*Long-time passed since I had the chance to fill my stomach to the
    brim.*
*My Aunt Margaret and her scones might be long gone, but I
    remember them still.*

Linicro Post Office

Sundays were phone home nights for Bobby and me, which meant a walk down the road to Linicro Post Office run by the Martin family. To the side of their house was a call box. If the weather was dry, then Bobby would take his Sharp radio cassette player and we would listen to Radio Luxembourg. This station had the best reception, in fact I think if you were on Mars you would get a decent Radio Luxembourg signal. Sometimes you would manage to tune into Radio 1, and it was not too crackly, but when you were on the move, the signal could be patchy. Usually I would call home first, and I stuck to the same script every Sunday. 'Hello, I would like to make a reverse charge call to Glasgow please.' I would then talk to my family for a wee while and fill them in with what had been happening over the previous week. Bobby would then call his folks.

Occasionally after the calls we might feel the need for some sweeties so we would ring the Martins' bell. In all the time that I remember, Calum and Ina would provide a service on any day at any time! Inside their vestibule we would stand, one of them would come out of their living room and open up the 'Post Office', which was like a remodelled box room which had a wooden fold down counter! They did not have a vast selection of sweets, but they had Pan Drops for my Aunt Margaret, Oddfellows for my Granny and McGowan's Highland Toffee for us! They always served you with a smile.

On other occasions we would use the phone box as a source of amusement. Sometimes we would make prank phone calls if we had any spare change. If you can remember, in these red boxes there were lists of various cities' telephone codes stuck up behind the phone. I would randomly choose a code and then try to make up a number! If it rang, I would try something funny (or at least funny to us). A standard prank call was, 'Hello, can I speak to Mr Wall?' they would say who, and that there was nobody of that name there. I would say, 'Is there a Mrs Wall there?' to which the answer was 'No'. Then I would say, 'Are there any Walls there?' 'No.' Then I would shout, 'Then how the eff to you hold up your roof?' Then hang up! OK not that funny but I laughed a lot! I seem to remember making an inordinate amount of these calls to a place called Chipping Sodbury as I thought it sounded funny!

You have to understand that Sunday nights were long and boring so going down to the Post office for an hour or so broke up the monotony and you could chew something sweet on the road back up to the wee or big hoose!

Post Box

Standing guard for so many years, looking spiffy in your coat of red.
A silent soul who never speaks on letters and postcards you're fed.

How many cars have passed you, never giving a second glance?
Enamel shiny and upright, you serve bereft of love and
*   romance.*

Through winter's winds blowing sharp and swift, not once did
*   you complain?*
Rain runs riot across the Minch up Totescore's fields into your
*   red veins.*

A 70s Renault 4 one day had an argument with your stance.
Its front smashed in and windscreen crumbled, it never stood a
*   chance.*

In summertime when heat appears your coat glows apple red.
As your neighbours pass on four legs and two, on their way to bed.

And when a young boy walks home on a dark lonely road,
*   glimpsing your silhouette at night.*
In his mind he conjures demons and ghosts, as he draws near
*   his face is in fright.*

How old are you now, my red metal friend, and when will you
*   retire?*
Have email and digital paper, left you lonely and ready to expire?

But still you stand on the Totescore's road, rude red for all eyes to
*   see.*
My friend, my hope is when I return, your enamelled mind will
*   remember me.*

Ali Aitken the Guy from Glendale

He mumbled something in what I thought was an English accent. I asked him to repeat himself and this time I understood what he said: 'You want a fight?' It was late 1977 or early 1978. The place was Portree High School.

I was in G2, and he was in B2 form class. He stood in front of me in his maroon blazer, and with an unusually thick head of hair. Kind of dishevelled, with his knotted tie hanging loose to one side, his shirt tails poking out from beneath an oversized jumper! Some might say an unusual way to start a friendship, but Mr Ali Aitken walked his own path and not too long after his offer of a fight (which I declined) we became firm friends.

We hung out most lunchtimes. Walking into Wentworth Street hoping to chat up a girl or two. Mostly we tried our charms on girls from the years above us. For some reason it was easier (certainly for me) to talk and flirt with the older girls than it was to chat (up) the ladies of our own year at school. There were several girls who we tried to impress, but I won't embarrass them (or me) by naming anyone. Suffice to say most 2nd, 3rd and 4th year boys had crushes on them.

What a pair we were. I had yet to purchase a school uniform (not until 4th year did I don those threads).

My school attire was limited to the aforementioned Glasgow bought togs. At one point I thought I looked cool, but by 3rd year's end the backside of my ageing breeks shined like a newly polished piece of ebony. The material was wafer thin and threatened to expose the whiteness of my rear at any given moment! The heels on my leather-soled shoes worn down to the quick, and no cobbler, no matter how skilled, could resuscitate them! In stark contrast, Ali was rather well turned out and adhered reasonably well to PHS's dress code. I believe he had brown, slightly flared cords and wore these wide toed leather shoes that seemed in vogue with the Portree High guys.

Most often we would visit the same places each day which included the Caley Cafe, An Buth Bheag and occasionally the chippy near the shore. We had a good routine going for getting people to part with their sweeties. We attended the school canteen as I got 'free' dinner tickets on account of me living with my Great Aunt and Great Granny, who partook of the social welfare system. Mr Aitken and I spent many a dinner time there.

As third year rolled into 4th year, we had outgrown going into the town centre and had taken to hanging out in one hut (Mr Nicholson's) which was the G form room. There Angus Gordon and Donnie Nicholson would join us. These lunch times mostly found us talking about girls. I can only tell you the truth and say that I (unlike Messrs Aitken, Nicholson and Gordon), did not have a girlfriend at school (sad me) unless you count a 2-week awkward holding of hands with the lovely Margaret Gunn, who along with the equally lovely Lorna Cormack, spent hours with Ali and me at the back of Mr Glennie's history class. There we giggled a lot and occasionally there was some learning of historical facts! If it was not girls, then we mostly talked about music and it was not unusual for us to be singing the latest TOTP hits and giving it 'laldy' in our prefabricated form room!

I have very fond memories of that time. Everything was fun, and our discussions appeared deep and important. I would call us the AlDonRayAng Gang nobody thought it was cool or amusing, just me!

Here's the funny thing, though. Ali and I were very close, but it took him till fourth year to admit that he was a talented singer/ songwriter! I remember it as if it was this afternoon. The surprise that my best pal could not only play the guitar and hold a tune. He also had the knack of stringing words together to make some beautifully moving songs. Some of them remain in my brain to this day (remember the foot stomper 'Baby I Don't Care'?). My attempt at a song, 'You're a Friend' sentimentally simple, was taken by him and fashioned into a decent teenage ballad. The highlight for me was when a group of us

Skyeku 10

Morning fresh eggs found.

Secreted in green den cosy

Fried on bread and butter.

including fine female singers Lorna and Margaret, doing backing vocals, Jimmy McKinnon on drums and Neil McLennan (possibly Duncan McDonald), Ali and myself belted out my heartfelt ditty in a room in the boys' hostel. The lovely ladies joining in with the chorus made it very special, and we recorded it! I have a cassette copy somewhere in Glasgow.

Later I would go on to manage Ali's first band DC Desouza and he would then form the rather splendid Rootlove. Time, as it does, marches on and although we drifted apart and lost contact, we have recently exchanged some messages on Facebook.

I thought it would be nice to include some of the lyrics from both songs I wrote, which Ali made sound innocently good. Allow me some leeway as it was over 40 years ago!

You're a Friend

It's been a long, long time
Gotta move on down the line
But I won't forget your face
And I can't forget this place
Or the first time we met
(Chorus)
You're a friend
You're a friend
And we'll hold till the end
Me and you
Just us two.
Coz you're a friend
Remember the days of trouble
Remember the fight we had

We were young and in love
But with the same girl
Now that's all over
That's all done
(Chorus)
We had so many good times
Hell forget about the bad times
Remember how we used to laugh and play
Now it's time for us to part
We must go our separate ways
But I won't forget this place
And the time we met
(Chorus)

Christine

I thought it would never end.
You said it would last.
I thought whatever we had was so strong.
And now you've left me without even saying goodbye.
I know it's silly but I just want to cry.
(Chorus)
And now you're gone
I wonder if you knew
Just how much
I loved you
Christine
My life feels so empty now
Without you being here.
Did you even love me?
Did you really care?
Now I must live my life
Without you being there
(Chorus)

I have never forgotten the laughs we had and the trials of being best pals. There is more to be written on that subject, but I would like to finish using a wee bit of poetic licence with a quote from the Stephen King story/movie 'Stand by Me'. 'I never had friends later on like the ones I had when I was a teenager at school. Jesus, does anyone?'

Rosebud's Gaelic Class

The first subject I knew I wanted to drop when I arrived at PHS in 1977 was French. I chose Gaelic instead. Not that I hated French, but I had come from a Glasgow school that had a French teacher who was not particularly nice, so it really put me off learning what is a beautiful language. This shows the importance of having excellent teachers at school, and today I wanted to celebrate two of my former tutors.

First, Miss 'Rosebud' MacLean, daughter of Sorley who was good friends with my Great Granny Annie Arnott. During my first week at Portree High they put me into her class and I duly sat up the back, besides Alasdair MacRaild. Truth is, her class was too advanced for me, but she welcomed me nevertheless. She knew my Great Aunt and Great Granny and this made my life a little easier in her class (but not by much). My memory of her is that she was a very dedicated (and quite strict) teacher whose love of the Gaelic language was obvious. We had to write screeds of Gaelic that she chalked on the blackboard.

Everyone had to read a passage and then translate, but when it came to me I was often only given a word or two to translate. Alasdair was very helpful and frequently let me copy his work! I spent one year with Rosebud and although it was difficult and the homework was painful, I enjoyed her class. Having changed Gaelic teachers in third year, she would often stop me and ask after my family and how I was getting on. I was particularly saddened when I heard that she passed at a very young age and I'm glad to have had the opportunity to have been one of her pupils.

After Miss Maclean, I ended up with one of my favourite PHS teachers, Mr John Norman MacDonald who lived in Broadford. He taught me English and Gaelic. JN was a good sport with a naughty sense of humour. He looked like a 1970s sitcom teacher and behaved like one too! I loved that he was easily distracted and us pupils (one of whom was Calum, his son) would do our level best to get him off the (teaching) subject and onto another that did not involve us doing much work!

Calum and I spent most of our time ignoring his father and talking about music and if I recall he was a big Police fan. When I posted this wee story on the Skye and Lochalsh Memories Facebook page, it garnered a lot of comments about both teachers. One in particular was from JN's daughter and I was happy to hear that the old man is still with us and that she would pass on many members' good wishes, including mine.

I feel very privileged to have attended Portree High School and lucky that I really enjoyed my years of mischief ... I mean learning!

So thank you Miss MacLean (Mrs DR Macdonald) and thank you Mr John Norman for being influential teachers and having a very positive impact on my teenage life.

You both are forever in my heart.

P.S. I failed Gaelic O level (twice) but managed a Higher in English!

Camus Beag Creep Out

As a child, I had a recurring dream in the mid-1970s. I was on a bike riding down the fields of Earlish on a hot summery day. Magically taking off over the rocky cliff and landing in the freshly tepid salty sea! Safe and happy!

Wow! What a pleasurable dream!

The reality would have been rain was pelting down and if I cycled down to the cliff's edge, there would have been no magic, only my body, eggshell broken on the jaggy rocks below! Ouch!

Although this happened before I moved to Skye permanently, I wanted to write it down as it's as fresh in my mind today as the day that it occurred. It must have been the summer of 1975 because my big sister Angela was on Skye with me. My cousin Bobby and his folks were at home, and we took a visit to the 'Fiddler' house in Earlish. Whilst the adults took their strupag, Bobby took us on an adventure. We made our way down the crofts to the Camus Beag, which is this cool wee cove opposite Idrigal Point. A set off location for rowing boated fishermen!

There we fannied about (as kids do). Throwing pebbles into the deep, blue grey brine. There is a stream's end that drains into Uig Bay. Bobby took us on an upstream jaunt. We gladly followed!

This stream is under a canopy of leafy green trees that made the adventure all the more exciting. The sun streaked through the branches as we made our way up on the stream's bank when suddenly, Bobby disappeared into the undergrowth! He reappeared telling us that there was a gang of gypsies and that they were after us! WTF? My childish heart pounded like a jack hammer on turbo as he told us to follow him and hide! My sister and I tried to hide our fear, but we did not make a wonderful job of that. It scared us poopless! This unseen enemy was (allegedly) following us, and we had to move fast. Bobby was the only one to see them, but I'm sure I heard them as they followed our trail. I remember asking him, 'How many were there?' He replied, 'Four or five'! Ever more fearful I said, 'What will we do if they catch us?' He said he thought he could fight them off! And we believed his every word! All I could think about was getting back to the comfort and safety of the house as quickly as my skinny white legs would take me!

Eventually, we made the clearing, and houses were in sight. This gave me some succour, but Bobby urged us on, ever quicker, just in case the invisible enemy sprung out of the trees and nabbed us! We got back to his grandparents' house unscathed but mentally scarred when he announced with a big annoying smile on his big annoying face that nobody was chasing us. He had made it all up!

What about noises I heard of people's feet following us? My overactive imagination was obviously in top gear as we ran through broken branches and dirty dirt!

That was our last visit to the Creepy Camus Beag!

Tobar

*Warm summer evenings saw us, blue buckets grasped in each
    hand.*
*And we laughed at our adventure across the croft onto the
    Shepherd's land.*

*We climbed the fence at the strainer, scraped thighs on the rust
    red barbed wire.*
*The water from the well fresher and colder than that from the
    tap outside the byre.*

*Past the old shepherd's house the gallons rush sang songs to our
    ears.*
*From earth's mouth came the life sustainer, drunk by Linicro
    locals over many years.*

A mini Fingal's Cave greeted our sand shoed and white stocking feet.
*With our hands we cleared spiders' webs, and the green
    overgrown we had to defeat.*

Our legs akimbo, balanced precariously on two wet, slimy rocks.
*Back bents low, we sunk the first bucket, the freezing wet soaked
    our socks.*

*Each bucket took us an age to fill, our technique left a lot of
    floaters.*
*Finally, both buckets, brim full, we moved away from the
    streaming nature's nectar.*

To the road, this time we staggered to ensure the least water lost.
*The creaky wooden gate groaned in pain as our bodies
    successfully crossed.*

*Wee hoose bound with our liquid treasure trove proudly hanging
    from each hand.*
*The kitchen table beside the stove, the buckets home, in our wee
    hoose wonderland.*

White plastic lids in place. Our evening's work is almost complete.
*As we scooped a glug in a metal jug, thirst quenching cold water
    our treat.*

First Crush (Is the Deepest)

This story I had not planned to tell because I felt embarrassed. I do it now because I think it's cute and funny. I mean to cause no embarrassment to the girl who was the object of my affection, and I have to name her as it's a crucial part of the tale. So apologies Alison, and if you ever read this, I hope it will make you laugh too.

Everyone at Portree High School had to choose an 'activity' to take part in on a Friday afternoon. Recently coming from Glasgow, I thought this was strange and great. There were loads of things you could do, from sports to arts and crafts. It was cool. I don't recall if it was every Friday it might have been twice a month. Anyway, I chose to be inside with table tennis. Not that I was any good at it, but I liked to play, so it was fine for me. They would set us up in the games hall. There would be a few green tables sharing the floor with badminton nets and players.

A few weeks into this 'activity' thing, I was bored. I then noticed that there were people climbing the wall using ropes and harnesses. It piqued my interest, so I meandered over. In charge was Mr 'Oddbod' Roberts. I watched as climbers made their way up to various ledges with a rope being held by someone on the ground. It was then I noticed this pretty girl who obviously knew what she was doing, so I chatted with her. She was very friendly and nice and asked if I wanted a shot at climbing. I jumped at the chance and was sprinting up that wall like a deer on acid. Feeling safe because someone was taking a lot of my weight on the ground.

I wanted more of this, so I swapped activity. Not only did we do climbing, we also did canoeing. We would take the canoes and set sail across the bay in Portree. It was great fun, but it was effin freezing! One time I was showing off and going too fast when I capsized my canoe. The water was like ice. The air blew out of my shocked lungs as I floated in the brine. Shivering. We had life jackets on and I was a half-decent swimmer, so I was not worried. Mr Roberts and another teacher came over to me and the both of them drained my canoe of sea water and helped me back in. Frozen, I carried on with my paddling.

Skyeku 11

Raked hay sun set

Coils glory in the gloaming

Winter cows fed full.

Another time they drove us out on the Staffin road towards some rocks we had to climb, and it was great fun but the rain was pelting down and a mist had settled. It was exciting to be hanging off the rocks, quivering in the cold. I was a skinny Clint Eastwood starring in my Skye 'Eiger Sanction'.

Through all of this outdoor action I had developed a crush on Alison, who happened to be one of the headmaster's daughters! I didn't really think too much about that. I was only thinking that she was nice. Before I go any further, I will report that the feelings were not reciprocated. But when you're young, you don't know any better.

The Christmas dance of 1977 for our year was held in the school cafeteria. I wanted to go and my Aunt Margaret allowed me. After school finished at four, I went home with Neil MacFarlane, who had this nice big house. His folks were super nice, and they fed me. We went outside after dinner for a while as Neil had a skateboard and I wanted a shot of it. Under the yellow streetlights on the rough Skye road, I tried and failed to master boarding.

We then headed off to the dance. He told me it would be mostly Scottish Country dancing, and he informed me about what happens during the 'Grand Old Duke of York' dance. This I did not know, but there was a chance of getting a kiss during this tune! My mind planned to be near Alison when that song was played. Was it Ian Macdonald's Dance Band that night? I think so or someone similar. I danced with a few people, doing the 'Gay Gordons' badly. Not much better at 'Strip the Willow' or any of the others, the names I have forgotten. I spied Alison and moved closer to her, but not too close. Eventually the 'Grand Old Duke of York' came on and I thought I would make my move! She was nowhere to be seen. I looked, but she had vanished. I walked to the outside doors and opened. There in the distance running home was Alison. Perhaps she knew I was waiting for that particular dance?

Not being academic at school, I was never in any of her classes so I would only see her in the corridors now and then. My immature brain was thinking, how can I get close to her to express my feelings? The only thing I could think of was a letter.

Yep, I wrote a love letter to the headmaster's daughter delivered to their address. I even included a SAE so she could reply to me! Great idea, eh? I waited, and I waited but no reply, so I sent another. What did I write in these love missives? Probably something incredibly cringeworthy and embarrassing. No doubt ending with asking her to 'go out'. Again, I waited and waited. One day my SAE returned to Linicro. All it said, and I'm paraphrasing, 'I'm not interested. Don't write to me again. If you do, I will have to tell my father!' A dagger to my heart! I wasn't worried so much about her telling the headmaster. I was only thinking about being 'knocked back'. Sad! After a month or two I had developed other crushes, but this time I decided not to do too much about them. I did some stuff, but the end result was always the same. Having no luck in school love was to be my destiny.

Over the years I would see Alison, but we were never in the same class. Probably a good thing too, as it would have been embarrassing for the both of us. Poor lassie!

Many years later I met her older sister Jackie, who was a Pharmacist in Edinburgh's Royal Infirmary. I was a Staff Nurse in the Renal Isolation Unit. I asked after Alison, who I think was working in Glasgow. I asked her to pass on my hellos. I should have also asked her to say, 'Sorry if I caused you any embarrassment all them long years ago'.

My success rate over my Portree years with members of the opposite sex was not what you could call high, unlike my pals who always seemed to find a bird easily! The reason for my low scoring is unclear. I will report however that it got exponentially higher from 1982 until 2007. Then I met my darling wife Janya and decided my single man years were over. It was time to settle down and get married. Best decision I have ever made!

Crush

Who remembers the first high school crush?
I do, and what a rush.

Second year in the games hall, I saw this vision of beauty.
From the table tennis table, I could not stop looking, but she did
*   not even know me.*

Courage built, I made a move to speak to this new-found face.
A friendly smile and a wee chit chat sent my head and heart all
*   over the place.*

The love was unrequited as our paths didn't cross much in school.
And though this didn't discourage my admiration, young love
*   can be oh so cruel.*

In a light bulb moment, I thought I would send her a SAE love
*   note.*
My heart sank when I got the reply. It was not what I had
*   hoped.*

No matter, I thought, there is always the Christmas dance to try
*   one love last time.*
But it wasn't to be her and me, and soon she disappeared from
*   my mind.*

Years as they roll on, and many more crush cases would come
*   and go.*
And I consider myself lucky, to have had the chances, to put my
*   heart on show.*

Message in a Bottle

This is the God's honest … honest! It was probably around the end of 1977, my cousin Bobby and I bored. We were down at the shore near to the slipway at Kilbride. This would have been a Sunday afternoon and nothing special would be happening at the seaside except that on this particularly lazy Sunday afternoon I found the proverbial 'message in a bottle'! The bottle just caught my eye. It was only when I bent down to pick it up that I noticed it was sealed and had a rolled-up piece of paper inside. My mind went into overdrive thinking it had come from some poor stranded Robinson Crusoe type, on a far, far away, tropically kissed island. The reality was closer to home! The message was from a girl in Daliburgh and it said if anyone finds this please call me and let me know how far it has travelled. Unfortunately, her name is lost in time, but I decided that as it was Sunday, we would normally go to the phone box outside Linicro PO to call our folks in Glasgow. I decided I would also call the girl who sent the bottled message!

Come the evening, I was feeling a wee bit nervous to call her. I had briefly fantasised about her being this beautiful girl who

MV Hebrides

would immediately fall in love with me and get on the Heb immediately straight to my arms!

Skyeku 12

Cool dark milk bucket

Ruddy cheeks squeeze softly

Eyes wide hot drink drunk.

So I called, and she answered. I told her I had found her message. She was surprised but sounded a little disappointed that her bottle had not floated further than Skye. She explained that she had thrown the bottle into the Minch at Lochboisdale earlier that year and had forgotten about it. Eager to stretch out the minutes, I asked her questions about herself and what age she was, which was me doing my best at 'chat up'. It was nice to speak to a female as I only had Bobby to speak with and he could be boring. No doubt he was also bored listening to me. She was a couple of years older than me (so no chance that she would be interested in my pale white self). Her big hobby was country dancing of a Scottish nature. It did not take long for my meagre coins for calling to run out and I said goodbye before the pips. That was my exciting Sunday, but not exactly the end of the story.

About a year later there was a dance at Uig Hall and the band had special guests, one of which was a Scottish country dancer. I recognized the name and wondered if this was same the girl from the message in the bottle? She did her dance, which was very good after which I tried my best to talk to her. Stalker like, I waited at the entrance of the hall until she eventually came out. She was very nice looking too. By this time some Dutch courage emboldened me (swigged in the nearby toilet) and asked her if she was the girl who had written the message in a bottle? It was she! She remembered me and was surprised to see me. I tried to keep her chatting a wee bit longer, but it looked as if there was a parent or guardian in a waiting car. I'm sure she would not have fancied a skinny wee keelie like me, anyway. She said her goodbyes and disappeared up the dirt road into the Uig night! Bye-bye my message in a bottle girl, I might have said if I had thought of it at the time!

Shepherd's House and Smiddy

The Smiddy

Black and grey boulder built.
By the tobar's life water rushing you sit.
Roof rusted brown and broken.
Holes frame clouds letting in Skye rain.
A deep-set solitary window, one eye open, looks over croft grass,
*   never blinking.*
Across the road, the shepherd's cottage mocks, with its
*   weathertight building.*
From the gravel and tar your door creepy and dark.
Green grass, overgrown nettles shout, keep out.
Brave the mud-soaked path, bend down and enter.
Mind your head, the lintel whispers.
Many don't.

Smell the past as welly booted feet sink into the moist floor.
Birds of a feather have long left their white mark.
Marvel at the impossible.
Rowing boat, not horse's hoof.
The furnace stack intact.

Soot blackened and strong, unlike the weak of the building's low roof.
Anvil iron, aged black hole dark, rests on a spongy, worm food wooden log.
Both pensioners now long retired.
How many hammer blows have rained down?
Iron to iron, ear piercing noise, and wet dropped from brow sweat.
The grim walls hooked and chained.
Torture chamber chic.

Random nails with horseshoe scarves.
Some powder brittle, others steel strong.
Wooden work benches crumble under tools coloured rust red and coal black.
Untouched in decades by hard skinned hands.
Linicro's last light, cat like, creeps in.

The atmosphere vapour heavy.
Broken bottles scattered, mostly by us, crunch under boot as we exit.
The air outside welcome's our lungs.
Fresh and clear, our escape made.

As darkness descends, we look back.
The black building, small and empty, creaks and groans.
Our young feet, faster now, carry our bodies home.
The wee hoose light, a magnet of safety.
The promise of strong leafed tea and cupcakes, our adventure's reward.

Rankin's the Baker

Saturday was the day I would be armed with a shopping list and two bags for my weekly trip to 'the baker's' in Uig. My bike took me there in sun, rain, hail and snow! The climb up the Totescore road was my first barrier, made easier if you had a blowing wind at your back. Should the Skye wind be at your front and should it contain the wet stuff, then the journey could be miserably soggy!

Once you plateaued at the top of Totescore's, cycling past my second favourite fank, the journey was pleasurable, and you were on easy street (or easy single-track road with passing places)! There is no finer summer sun view than cresting at the top of Uig and seeing the village in all its Skye beautifulness. The pier arm and hand reaching out into the bay which might be glassy calm or white horse rough. As you scanned your further surroundings, your eyes would be greeted with a wonderful sight of the cliffs, Earlish and the Camus Baig.

Rankin's the Baker,
then

It was all downhill (in the positive sense) from there. Occasional traffic had to be negotiated as well as the (in) famous hairpin bend! I loved to bike past the Idrigal road and into the village, looking at all the local activities of daily living (Linicro could be lonely with few signs of life). Down and across the stone bridge spanning the Rha and past the Mutch farmhouse, onto the dual carriageway of Uig. Past what would become my local haunt for alcohol imbibing the then (in) famous Ferry Inn and along to the objective, which was the (old) baker's shop. I would park up near the side which housed all the baking action, where your nose enjoyed the aroma of fresh-baked bread and other sundries. Mmmmmmm!

If it was busy no matter, you could enjoy being in unfamiliar company, as locals stocked up on supplies. If I was lucky and had some money (not a common occurrence) then I could plan my sweetie purchases. If I was doubly lucky, there might be a member of the opposite sex to eye up! I would pass over my Aunt Margaret's handwritten 'message' list to the baker's daughter Margreta, who would then busy herself selecting the canned goods and fresh baked products destined for my poly bags! I loved the bread from there, although I remember Margaret complaining if she suspected James the baker's son made the loaves whom she considered second best to his father! Nothing tasted better to me than a couple of sawn off hunks of brown/ black crusted handmade bread. Spread with Stork margarine and topped with thick slices of rounded Orkney cheese! Yum Yum for my tum tum! I particularly favoured the round 'milk' loaf and can still remember that chewy goodness till this day.

Bags in hand, I would exit the building and, should the weather permit, I might also have a piece of something sweet to eat before heading home. Life was good sitting at the roadside watching the world go by to the rushing water sound emanating from the nearby River Conan. The journey back to Linicro could be challenging to say the least. Two bags full of Margaret's messages could weigh an effin ton!

One had to get the message weight ratio just right so that when you hooked the poly bags over the bike handles and onto the bars, one either side, they had to be of equal weight in order for

Rankin's Supermarket, now

me to cycle in a safe fashion! The short run over the dual carriageway ended at the pier turn off, there was a slight decline going back towards Rha's bridge then it was uphill all the way till the top of Uig was breeched. It was bad enough cycling with two full bags on level ground, as they both would be swinging pendulum like, not in sync, making you constantly off balance. The hill climb only exacerbated the problem, and you also had to contend with your knees bashing both bags as you attempted to scale the hill road heights. I hated that part of the journey and could not wait till the endurance test was over!

I'm naturally lazy and look to cut corners when I can, and more than once I pushed my bike and the messages up the bealach path rather than take the road! I actually believed it was time saving! Imagine, if you would, a skinny Glaswegian teen pushing a lady's bike filled with shopping up that steep hill path. I did it more than once! From the top of Uig to the top of Totescore, past the Macinnes road was easy enough and then it was all downhill to the wee hoose. Yaas! Finally, I would deliver the goods to my Aunt and then get stuck into more sweet stuff surreptitiously to prevent suspicion that I had used message money to make a sweetie purchase. Yum!

The Baker's

Long ago in Uig we would visit the baker's shop.
We wee keelies from Glasgow, looked forward to making that
   stop.

Sometimes we went in the back of a car, other times we went on
   the bus.
Most times it was Shanks's Pony mode of transport, the walking
   choice for us.

Long before I Linicro lived, the baker's shop was a tasty sweet
   treat.
And we got so excited at the thought of all the sweetmeats.

The walk up to the top of Totescore, not so tough for our young
   lungs
To be greeted with that view from Waternish to Harris, brought
   chit chat to our tongues.

Scudaburgh road we passed, which also led to my Totescore
   mates.
I would go down to see them later, if we didn't return home too
   late.

On and on we walked till we reached the top of Uig, our old
   friend.
Like croft clowns we tumbled down the bealach, to avoid
   walking round the hairpin bend.

Past Idrigal road we inched ever closer, as our tasty goal was in
   sight.
Across the stone bridge over the rushing Rha, we peered over the
   bridge's edge in delight.

On the home stretch now, we could almost smell the cakes
   permeating through the air.
In a jiffy we neared the entrance, our smiling faces said we were
   there.

That smell as you entered was nasal heaven and our stomach was
   in need of sweet food.
A plethora of choices, from chocolates to doughnuts, each one
   you knew tasted so good.

*Service with a smile was the case, but we only were interested in
  cake.*
*Then outside we would head, wanting to be fed, by the River
  Conon's bridge we would take a break.*

*Satiated and happy we had to make our way home, the bealach a
  mini Mount Everest.*
*Our wee legs reached Linicro and after walking so long we were
  all in need of a rest.*

*Later on in the evening the baker's treats kept coming, with round
  sliced milk loaf and cheese.*
*And we chewed and chewed the delectable food. That bread
  was the baker's bee's knees.*

Bible Study

The wee hoose in Linicro was not what you would call well
sound proofed!

Every voice could be heard easily in each of the four small
rooms. My first bedroom was above the living room and every
Sunday either morning or at night I would hear my Aunt
Margaret read to my great Granny from the big brown leathery
looking bible with the brass lock. It sat on a square four-legged
stool and it weighed an absolute ton. Not that I ever had any
actual interest to read it, but I must admit lying in bed and
hearing Margaret recite some passages was kind of cool and
relaxing. I think the bible was in English, but Margaret spoke in
Gaelic! I also liked the fact that Margaret and my Granny got
some comfort out of the readings too.

Ode to the Corncrake

Oh, Corncrake where art thou?
I hear you but I've yet to see you.
Are you big or small? Your sound is big.
Your summer song. So familiar.
Are you not tired singing all night long?
Behind the Smiddy. I know you lurk.
Bedded down in my Auntie's hay.
As I lie awake on my spring sprung wee hoose bed.
Wallpaper peeling. Your song lullabies me to sleep.
Your call my alarm. Sleep rubbed from my eyes.
Totescore bound you're with me. Hidden yet heard.
Double note rasp attracts my ear and your mate.
At Uig's top midsummer.
Your call across the bay.
From Glen Conon to Earlish.
Idrigill echoes. I hear you.
Your summer long song. My comfort.
In winter you are missed.
Your song the sound of pen drawn across comb.
Decades gone since your voice I heard. You still there?
Oh, Corncrake where art thou?
I've yet to see you and long to hear you.
Oh, Corncrake where art thou?

Hot Hay Days

What one activity would you say sums up the 1970s Skye crofting life? To me it's the manual production/preparation of winter dinners for crofters' cattle. Making hay in the Skye summer was a beautiful thing for us kids. It was not all fun – you had to put some work into making the endeavour a success. I would say that 1977/78 saw the end of a hay making era for most of Linicro as it was the last time that hay would be made into coils, the wetter summers soon demanded that hay be put on tri-pod 'sticks', which helped the cut grass dry quicker and be a wee bit more impervious to the falling water.

My Aunt Margaret's hay field was opposite the two Linicro houses, behind the byre. Arrangements had to be made with Norman Macinnes so he and his trusty red David Brown would come to cut her hay with the mower (firmly attached to its rear). I would be his help (or hindrance), I would ride on the back of the tractor only to disembark when the mower blades clogged with thick moist grass and needed to be unclogged. It could be a precarious, potential finger losing business! Luckily to this day I still keep my 10 digits! I loved that job and I loved Norman like a big brother. There was no doubt about it. He was my all-time crofting hero (still is).

We cut the top half of the field first, and we gave the downed vegetation time to dry on the ground. Anecdotally these couple of summers seemed to be a lot drier than the ones to come. At least this is what my memory tells me. The first job would be to turn the mown hay. This would be done after Margaret inspected the field and the weather permitted. In the byre's loft, sitting amongst the roof's cross beams, lay hay making accoutrements in the shape of long and short forks and wooden rakes. The forks were what was needed for the turning. Under Margaret's instructions, I would do my best to shake and turn the green stuff for maximum drying effect. My cousin Bobby was very adept in the hay making art and would often help me out. After the passing of some more sunny drying days, it was time to coil the crofting cow food. Again, we would reach for our weapons of choice, which would be a selection of forks and rakes.

Most days I was on raking duty, and as I gathered the tinder-dry hay my least favourite part of this job was the removal of skin shredding, desiccated thistle skeletons. Ouch! Coiling hay may have looked easy to the untrained eye and the uninitiated child of the croft. The reality was that it was a skill that could only be learned by years of doing! Making the body of the coil was easier, but the 'topping off' was not, and I never gained that specialist skill throughout my Linicro life. Margaret and Bobby were the experts. I have a memory of brown rope unwound from a ball, being used to secure these organic masterpieces.

The days were long and Skye summer hot. Throughout the afternoon we would break for food and liquid refreshment. I would occasionally go to the nearby 'tobar', where hill fresh cold uisge would be gathered for our drinking pleasure. Once or twice I would be allowed to complete a coil, but the next day anyone could tell which coils were 'Raymond's'.

Overnight the hay would settle and if the coil was not made properly, it would flatten and would not keep out the water of summer showers. My coils were always flat and had to be redone by Bobby or Margaret to withstand any watery weather! By the time the coils would be ready for haystack building, school was in session, and I would miss out on the creation of these grass monsters. Usually two or three placed in front of the byre's loft door, opposite the wee hoose. There they would stand, ready to be taken, bit by bit into the loft, eventually ending up in the stomach of the four-legged milk-producing machines. A delivery of baled hay bricks would also supplement Margaret's hay to ensure the cows did not go winter hungry.

Totescore Hay Tractor, now.

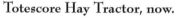

Long gone are those postcard perfect Linicro summer days which lasted long hours with very little night. The smell of freshly cut greenery is still with me, and that familiar aroma of dried hay. Every time I pass the hospital gardeners working with their lawn mowers I might get a whiff of the newly cut lawn creeping up through my nostrils, and in an instant I'm back in that 70s Linicro croft. My hand on a wooden fork, waving to the visitors in the passing tour buses whose smiles and return waves made you feel glad to be alive and on the Isle of Skye.

Whilst we worked on Margaret's small hayfield, not far away on the croft at 5 Totescore the Macinnes-owned red baler that would attach to their David Brown would be in use and producing many bales of cow food. I'm sure it was a New Holland as the red body had branded yellow writing on it. When Skye's summer sun allowed, their hay would have been cut, shaken and then swathed to prepare for the baler. The mechanical making of hay for me was far more enjoyable than the rake and blister causing hay fork. How easy life was when the creation of blocks of dried grass caused great excitement and an opportunity for the creation of mischief.

Unfortunately (for me) my Aunt restricted my access to mischief; I could only go over to Totescore at 7pm returning at 10pm. Only three hours per night to cause havoc? Not good! I vividly recall many evenings after dinner wishing that the hands of that chiming clock on the shelf of the wee hoose dresser would actually move. That hour between six and seven took days, weeks to complete! Come the seven chimes and with Margaret's permission (not always granted), I shot out the half door of the corrugated wee hoose and was past Morton's house in a flash!

Until I got my wheels (old woman's bike that I spray painted silver), I always used Shank's pony to the Macinnes home. I would reach the top of Totescore, before that bend that revealed the fank, and then cut off-road onto the well-trodden (by me) path and continue downhill at speed till my destination was reached.

The Macinnes's had several fields growing hay and when it was time for hay making work whoever was in the house and whose surname was Macinnes would be out dealing with the dry crispy grass. I loved to be there for the baling. Norman or Duncan would be in the driver's seat, Archie and I would walk behind carrying on and catching the bales. What a magical machine. What a privilege to have helped (mostly hindered) in providing winter dinners for their cattle.

Once the grass was cubed, weather permitting, we would leave them in the field until the day the David Brown would have the trailer hitched and we would load up the bales onto it. These would be taken to their byre and stacked in the loft until winter's dark short days. There was one warm summer evening with Mr blue sky above us and an almost, but not quite, cooling breeze rushing up from a still Minch. Archie and I along with Duncan and Norman had come across a wasps' nest exposed by the cut hay. Unsure what to do, we nervously skirted around it until (brave or stupid) Norman used a hay fork to rid the field of this pest. Big mistake! Out of the wasp factory came a swarm of angry flying stingers who, cartoon like, formed a small dark cloud above Norman's head as he made a run for it down the croft. Arms flailing above his shoulders, he found no escape from the mini wasp cloud. We offered no help, just belly laughed at his stinging plight! Norman managed to lose the irate insects, suffering only a painful sting or two to his big calloused crofter's hands!

Even now, as if this just occurred yesterday, I see him running. The memory imprinted and crystal like in its clarity will be mine to have a chuckle at forever.

Byre

I remember the byre when it was big and full of adventure.
I remember being excited to bring Murdy the milking cow from
    the croft to her stall and watch my Auntie milk her.

I remember laughing as I scooped up cow pats and shovelled
    them outside to the dung heap.

I remember being shoved by my cousin feet first into that dung,
my green wellies sinking, and squelching deep.

I remember the dark cool of the stalls on a hot Skye summer's day.
I remember the scary Tilly lamp lighted darkness, when winter's
blanket covered our stay.

I remember the smell of treacle hay being fed to the cattle.
I remember the hen's sleeping tight in the horse pen as we locked
the old wooden door.
I remember the old sink and cold water tap filling buckets of
uisge, getting caught in a downpour.

I remember the time when we lit a line of methylated spirits, and
it blue flamed outside.
I remember panic that if we got caught my Aunt would be swift
with her chide.

I remember lowering the wooden steps that lead to the hay bailed
loft.
I remember the creaking as I climbed, hoping that my skinny
frame would not slip off.

I remember the stifled heat and the smell of hay dust and
corrugated iron.
I remember the story of the weary hitchhiker who spent the
night in our hay cavern.

I remember searching for kittens buried way deep in the back.
I remember the feeling of finally finding them covered in dry
grass from our haystack.

I remember the patter of rain as it bounced off the old byre's roof.
I remember daydreaming on the hay and how we played,
knowing that we were waterproofed.

I remember the rusted hook that locked the loft door as we left the
cats all alone.
All these things I remember as an adult now, working and
wishing that I was at home.

(So Here It Is) First Christmas

The Christmas of 1977 was the first one that I spent away from my family in Glasgow. It was a rather underwhelming affair, to say the least. At age 13, the excitement of Christmas and the promise of new toys was a thing of the past. In fact, if it was not for the Christmas cards atop the big hoose fireplace, you would be hard pushed to tell this day from any other. The school was on holiday and although I'd spent my first few months waiting for the school bell to ring so I could get back to Linicro, lately I was so happy to go to school, as that's where the action was!

There was to be no white Christmas. It was just dark and cold! I was to wake up to no surprise gifts, save for a couple of pair of socks from my Aunt Margaret. My folks had asked me what I wanted and good for them, they sent exactly what I requested. By mail, not Santa! What I had asked for and what I got the week before Christmas was an Adidas holdall (for schoolbooks etc.), a House of Fraser calculator and a watch. The watch was cool; it was a diver's style watch, but it looked massive on my skinny wrist. I eventually swapped it with a Seiko watch with a metal expanding strap. The swapper was my Uncle Peter. He was happy with the diver's watch. I was happy with the Seiko.

Lawnmower Man

One thing we had plenty of in Linicro was green, green grass. This was, however, not of the lawn variety. The big hoose back in the 70s had two small patches of lawn in front of both ground-floor windows, the rest of the garden space was taken up with the growing of a myriad of summer fruits and vegetables. To the side of the house, near the burn, there was another lawn type patch of green stuff used for clothes drying au naturel. This lack of lawn meant that heavy duty mowing equipment was not needed and my Aunt Margaret made do with an electric Black and Decker 'Lawnderette' mower and an old hand pushed cylinder cutter of grass! The 'Lawnderette' was hardly a manly cutting tool, but even so I was not allowed to use it. They relegated me to pushing the old, red manual cylinder mower over the blades of Linicro grass. How old this manual grass cutting machine was is unknown and I believe it was found by Bobby somewhere in the undergrowth unloved and unused for years. He cleaned it up and sharpened the blades the best he could and with some wheel oil applied, the hand-pushed beast was lawn mowing ready! To say using this ancient implement was my favourite pastime would be a colossal lie! I hated it with a passion, but as the Black and Decker was a no go, I had little grass cutting choice. Boring! Our next-door neighbour, going towards Totescore, was an elderly lady known as Miss Morton. She lived in Inverness and used the house as a holiday home.

Big Norman Macinnes was to look after her outside area, and the lady had some nice lawn space. More importantly, hidden in the wooden shed beside her back door was a petrol-engined Flymo! Wow! This baby was top of the line and probably the biggest on the market. Best of all, Norman was not fussy about who used it! As long as Miss Morton didn't find out!

This epic machine was not a toy and needed to be handled with maturity and care, so naturally I wanted a shot! A rather short safety lesson was given by Mr Macinnes, which entailed only two instructions?

1. Don't go over any rocks!

2. Don't go over your feet!

Simple!

He would drag the mower to the large lawn area at the side of Morton's house and leave me to get on with it. Yaas! With a brisk pull on the starter cord, the motor roared into life and the big blade/fan began its chopping duties!

Everyone knows the premise of the Flymo is that it's like a mini hovercraft that rides on a cushion of air. Once it's up and running, theoretically it's easy to swing back and forward, cutting your lawn's green hair! The reality was that this monster machine was very heavy and should not have been operated by a weakling weegie like me!

It was difficult to use unless you had Popeye arms. I had Olive Oyl limbs! Still, I would do my best to swing it back and forth with the end result being an unevenly cut lawn which almost always had to be tidied up by Norman or Bobby! Did I go over any rocks? I did, and any pebbles caught underneath its whirring blade and downdraft got shot out sideways like a speeding bullet. Had anyone been in the line of fire they might have found themselves with a large pebble sized body hole! Did I ever go over my feet? Nearly, and on more than one occasion! Luckily, my tootsies remained attached to the rest of my body! It was fun though, and 100 times more manly than the 'Lawnderette'!

In more recent years my Aunt Annie and my late Uncle Peter have made a beautiful landscaping job round the big and wee hoose, it's almost unrecognisable! Would they let me loose with a Flymo these days? Doubt it! I would be lucky if they let me operate the 'Lawnderette'!

Common Grazing

My heart has been pulled by its lonely strings and my head needs to go somewhere amazing.
Old eyes misted like a moor dawn, bones cracking in kindling tune, let me walk across Linicro's common grazing.

Long-time gone since I walked under the shadow of the rocks, where an echoed song bounced down to the shore.
Summer's golden eagle high above, its silhouette eclipses the sun, its wings welcome the Minch breeze as it soars.

A shout out to the hill would bring a thousand bobbing tails, running through the heather at speed.

Let me lie inside the walled fank and breathe, just breathe, the
Linicro air is all my heart needs.

In the pouring rain, windswept and interesting, I will slip and
slide on the white waved streams.
My frozen feet, sock soggy rain permeates my marrow, a breeze
skelped cheeks are my daydream.

A summer night that never darkens, that sings silently as I sit
stone bummed on the Creagan Ban.
Sunday loneliness I'm walking with myself, I'm talking as I traipse
over bog and boulder.
Can I go where the salty sea sees me in the green grazing, before
these muscles of mines get much older.

Great-great Uncle Murdo the Man in the Photograph

My great-great uncle Murdo lived on the Linicro croft at one time. My only memory of him is from an old colour photo taken of him down behind the byre sitting with his back resting on a hay coil smoking his pipe. My Aunt Annie took this perfect photo on a Kodak Box Brownie. He was a very hardy soul.

According to my cousin Flora, Murdo was a seasoned veteran who fought at the Somme and saw action in Egypt and the Sudan. He was in the Cameron Highlanders, never rose above the rank of a private because of differences of opinion with his army superiors! He was known as the 'piper' and not because he played them (another story which I have not heard). His abode across the burn from the big hoose was known as the 'Rookery'. It was basic but very warm and cosy with a wood-burning stove, bunk-bed, table and chair. Flora also tells me he had a pet bantam hen named Isabel who shared meals with him.

Great Great Uncle Murdo, Linicro 1960s

I was told that he had an old one-man rowing boat somewhere at Kilbride. This is where the slipway is the locals used to set off fishing from and also to park their boats. Bored one day, my cousin Bobby and I went to the shore and it was on my mind to look for this fabled wee wooden boat. Once we reached Kilbride, there was no obvious sign of an old, small rowing vessel. On further inspection of the longer grass we discovered it upturned and completely ensconced in undergrowth. We spent some time clearing the weeds and foliage. Eventually we righted the boat and pulled it towards the jetty. Indeed, it was a one-man boat. It was petite but solidly made, it also weighed an effin ton! I had the idea of trying to launch it from the slip, and we dragged it closer to the water's edge. Luckily Bobby was strong, and the tide was in, so we thought rather than launching from the slip, we will just push it over the edge into the salty sea. It was not quite a Govan launch, but it slowly slipped into the brine. What happened next? It sank. Like a stone! The problem for us was that it was now blocking the slip!

Linicro View

We had to wait for the tide to recede and then do our salvage best to remove it. The old wood became sponge like and doubled the weight as we struggled for dry land! Job eventually done, phew! That old boat probably still lies where we left it, undoubtedly hidden from prying eyes by years of plant growth. If anyone ventures down to Kilbride, have a look in the under-growth, you may find it's a skeleton by now!

Sunday Shore

Sunday silence hung heavy, like a freshly spun washing hanging from the kitchen pulley.
Outside, the autumnal weather had turned from green to brown, desiccated and crackling.
Jacket weather was coming, but today the sun shone as I walked down the Totescore road.

Gravel soon gave way to grass as this Sunday trip terminated at
the seashore.
The walk to the water is further than it looks, every step edging
slowly closer.
Harris hills are clear and I can almost touch their heather coats,
but not quite.

Hurdled fences and spongy ground disappeared, and Kilbride
came into sight.
A welcome from white waves caressing smooth pebbles salted.
Ankles need to be strong, as the rocky shore takes no city
prisoners.

My reward a seat near landed boats, a well-earned rest for my
skinny legs.
Ghosts of fishermen past, carrying on unseen, preparing creels
and lines.
My mind wandered across the sea as nosey seagulls flapped above
my head.
To find some rock pools I meandered, unhurried and schoolboy
free.
A saline breeze cleared my nose, and the tide waved cheerio on its
wave way out.
I found a rock pool worth investigation; I hunted for crab and
stranded shrimp.
Cold water froze my fingers. My prey disappeared under a
boulder, two eyes peeping.
Impatiently, I gave up the search and headed across to the
point.

Alone yet not lonely, I grappled with age old stone, climbed and
climbed again.
Jaggy edges, unkind and cruel, tried their best to block my way.
Behind me, some woolly white sheep watched with disinterest,
and I stared into the depths.
Crystal clear, aqua green water revealed nothing swimming
down below.

The wind whipped up and snuck under my shirt, a sign from God
it was time to move.
My feet kicked some limpets from their spot, and they sunk down
into pure white sand.

*For hours my time I passed, wandering and sitting, surveying the
 sea.*
If only the water was warm, I dreamt of a salty mouthed swim.

*No ferry today to wave at, no other sign of life except distant
 beasts with four legs.*
*The Linicro hills, way behind my back, called me ever so quietly
 to their feet.*
Time and tide wait for no boy and I left the water to its devices.

*Homeward bound, the sea air had stirred my stomach, each step
 closer to a cheese scone.*
I reached the road tired; my hunger drove me on at pace.
*My life on a Linicro Sunday afternoon, spent exploring this
 wonderful place.*

The Totescore Bodach

The patriarch of the Macinnes clan in Totescore was John
Macinnes. Anyone who has read any of my stories on Facebook
knows how important his family were to me, and the amount of
love I have for them cannot be measured. He would have been a
good age in the 1970s, but he was hardy. He had hip replace-
ments done, and he walked with two sticks, but that didn't slow
him down. He always wore those thick woollen trousers high
above his waist, held up by braces; a shirt, with white vest
underneath trying to control a bush of grey chest hair and a
matching woollen jacket – always with a flat cap on his head.
He could be a wee bit scary and if he told you to do something,
then you did it. Quick!

Like me, he got married later in life to a younger woman and he
had a big family. Four girls and four boys! He and his wife
treated me like I was one of the family and I always felt at home
in 5 Totescore. I spent a fair amount of evenings there over the

John Macinnes

years, and every Friday and Saturday I would be there from 7 to 10. Old he might have been. In pain, no doubt. Reduced mobility definitely, but the Bodach was a hard worker. He was also a hard taskmaster! Every evening he would be involved with getting the cows in for milking and he would shout orders that we all had to obey! After we did the byre work, we would all head back to the house to watch some TV!

I loved their living room; it was always warm due to it having a big cooking range in the middle of one wall. This blast furnace was a welcome sight during those cold, wet winter nights! Above it on the ceiling was the obligatory pulley. Always full of drying clothes and what seemed like an inordinate amount of 'lumberjack' type shirts, no doubt big Norman's. A lino floor on top of which stood a big dining table on the other wall opposite the range, wooden chairs either side. Always covered by a patterned tablecloth made from wax cloth.

Up in the far corner, on a creaky shelf, sat their black-and-white TV. It was a fairly old model in silver plastic, and it could only receive one channel which was BBC1. In the corner opposite was the Bodach's chair which was one of those uncomfortable wooden arm affairs and it had many cushions piled high making it easier for him to get up. Beside that was a three-seater sofa with the living room's only window at its back. There was also the brother of the Bodach's chair, minus the extra cushions, under the TV. On the window frame sat a pair of binoculars, no doubt used by the old man to check that we were carrying out any of his work orders exactly!

To me he was a man of few words, but beneath that weather-worn grey stubble face there was a kindness and dare I say it? A gentleness, and he always had a glint of mischief in his eyes. Archie, Duncan and I would sit on the sofa, usually with me in the middle and the old man would be in his corner chair puffing on his Embassy reds and we would all be glued to the TV screen watching Starsky and Hutch. He loved that show. We boys would misbehave on the sofa and quick as lightning, he would grab one of his sticks waving it like a light sabre and threatening to strike us if we did not be quiet! He never carried out his threat, and I knew that the old guy's bark was always worse than his bite!

Whatever croft work was going on in the summer months, he would be there directing operations and making sure that us boys were not causing chaos! During the hay days he would work and on fank days too he would ensure that everything was done to his exact specifications. I can still see his face now and him removing his cap and wiping the sweat from his brow!

The last time I would have seen old John was before I left the island in 1982, and when I heard he had passed, I was very sad. His memory lives on with his children, grandchildren and great grandchildren.

In my heart there will always be a soft spot for him and his wife Chirsty Anne whose kindness and generosity had a major impact on my life which carries on to this day and for that I'm eternally grateful.

Milking

The summer sun arched towards the Harris hills, smiling at its
rippled Minch reflection.
Nesting birds settled down, a rolling breeze made its way,
cooling in our direction.

Tick tock the dresser clock announced it was milking time. My
sister and I wore smiles that were too big for our face.
Our excitement palpable and our legs ran us all over the place.

My Aunt donned her green wellington boots and grabbed her
white hooked stick.
We three walked at pace on the path beside the wee hoose, our
speed made us diaphoretic.
The metal red gate sandwiched between two grey strainer
sentries.
I raced my sis to see who would be first to grab the sliding bolt to
gain entry.

With branches for walking sticks, we ran up the croft. My Aunt
called out the cow's name.
Murdy, the milker, made her way to us, hips swinging and
swaying like a pantomime Dame.

Before the gate, she moved in the direction of the water brimmed
old aluminium bath.
And she sucked the cool fluid in gallon gulps. The noise made
my sis and I laugh.

At her own pace and with no instructions, she made her way
across the Linicro road.
Through the wee wooden gate she squeezed her big frame, on
the way to her byre abode.

The sun sat watching on top of the hills as we followed my old
Aunt. Her cow strode nonchalantly into the coolness of the
darkened room.
A circle of rope round her neck, she chewed her cud, knowing
that the milking would begin soon.

Our eyes like saucers we watched in silent awe, as my Aunt sat on
her wee three-legged seat, we giggled and laughed as the teats
squeezed hard, produced the white warm nectar.

Sieved through muslin pure and ready to drink.
The pail full, the job done, as behind the Harris hills, the sun
*   began to sink.*

Angela and I tossed an imaginary coin to see who would scoop up
*   the fresh cow poop.*
I lost, she giggled, the old shovel I niggled and threw the smelly
*   stuff on the heap.*

Murdy, rope removed, deeply inhaled and tip toed outside the
*   slender wooden byre door.*
Tracing her steps all the way back to her green grassed field, as
*   she has done so many times before.*

In the wee hoose excited we wanted a taste of the warm, frothy,
*   grassy flavoured liquid.*
My Aunt gave us a glass, and we both sang cheers, satisfied with
*   the job that we did.*

∾

The Totescore Caileach

Chirsty Anne Macinnes, the Caileach of 5 Totescore was a
beautiful person who treated me like one of her own. This also
meant that I could be on the losing end of a telling off if the
three of us were carrying on (which we did a lot). To my
memory she always wore blue or maybe purple pinnies. Always!
Ok, not always, but nearly, other than when she had to attend
church or some social occasion.

The big table in their living room covered with wax cloth could
hold a feast for 100. The Macinnes boys were big eaters! I loved
sitting at that table eating boiled potatoes with their skin on
and whatever accompanied it. Duncan, Archie and I would still
be naughty ensuring either the Caileach or Bodach's wrath, and
one of them shouting 'bi samhach' and 'Ithe ur biadh' (ok I
failed my Gaelic O-level)!

Chirsty Anne
and John
Macinnes

Every night at ten, before I would leave to go home, she would disappear into the pantry which was behind a door in the living room near to the kitchen. She would then reappear with something chocolate in her hands and give us one each. She always handed it to me first, then to Duncan and Archie. Every single time I was there! All those years she never once did not give us something from that secret room. I loved spending time in Totescore. When I would return to Skye as an adult I would make a special effort to see her after the Bodach passed. She still wore the pinnies and would approach me with a big smile, her hand held out to shake my hand. Her grip was strong and true and you could tell that these hands had spent a lifetime working a croft and raising a family! The firm handshake was also a ploy so you could not escape the impending big smacker on the lips!

This wee story she told me many, many times over the years. Probably around the early 1970s they had a black bull who would sit like a dog in the field. One day my sister Angela and I with not one ounce of fear went to the sitting bull and petted him! He paid no attention to us and continued his cud chewing, but the Caileach was watching through binoculars, unable to shout at us to run away as she thought we were in mortal danger! We petted that bull more than once, even when we were told to stay clear of him. She related that story every visit and she would laugh each time she told it!

Right from the start of my memories of Skye at a very early age, I remember her and the Bodach John. I'm sure over the years, we three boys drove her mad. She was tough, every night with the old man going to the byre for milking. Working in the hay and when it was fank time she was there working hard enough to put us young fellows to shame!

The last time I saw her would have been briefly at my Aunt Margaret's funeral in 1997. When I was home in Glasgow in 2009 my cousin Bobby informed me that the old girl had passed. I had to find Archie's phone number and give him a wee call. I had not spoken to him in years (the funeral was the last time I was on Skye), I only wanted to pass on my late condolences and to express to him how important she was to me growing up in Linicro. Both she and her husband were wonderful people and always will hold a very special place in my heart.

Peat Road

The peat road is waiting for my form and shape. Lonely, no more. 'Long-time no see', it says without a word being spoken.

Heather heart beating. A path cleared from the past, stained with blood and diesel.
Hard rock's hello. I hear the call acutely; with jacket torso I answer.

Mud for blood pumping. The croft's zenith I love dearly. Fence scaled I land unsteady. Ankles buckled and bent.

Linicro's common grazing, green, brown, specked yellow. Munching mouths feed.
A breathing bag of bones heads higher. Rabbit holes for company.

Beasts of burden no more seen trotting, now only rubber and metal.
Feet first, eyes front. Underneath the eagle, past her house, I go unnoticed.

*Soaring sun streaked wings. Higher ground, forehead sweat, my
    breath by beauty it's taken.*
Minch blue, or is it green?
*Fank far below, its stone housed neighbours long gone. Square
    green grins.*

In-between the hill, past woolly punters, ignoring my every move.
Air pollen fresh and breezy. I make it to the top of the rocks.

Faint heart, there is no room for you here. Eagle's gold warning.
*I back away, and on the green green I stroll. Inhaling the view
    from field to shore, my eyes feast.*
Skudiburg my dessert.

*I reach out to the Creagan Ban, my throne, moss hard pillows my
    comfort.*
*From there, I survey all that's not mine. Riches in every blade of
    grass and boulder.*

The final furlough sees the end where my journey began.
Soul cleanse repeated.

(I) Love Cats

Nearly every crofter with a byre invariably owned a cat (or two),
whose official job title was 'mouser'. In Linicro, my Aunt
Margaret owned two of these mouse-menacing beasties. Snowy
was a beautiful blue-eyed, white purring machine. Overtly
friendly and who never raised a clawed paw in anger. Bonnie
was a standoffish, tortoise-shell cat with cold eyes and an
unfriendly nature. The polar opposite of Snowy. The calloused
hands attached to my Aunt Margaret's arms could only lift or
pet her! During the summer evenings both would risk life and
limb to cross the road from the byre, climb the wee hoose's
steep wooden stairs, and peer hungrily over the inner half door.
Demanding sustenance from my Aunt. Their hunger talk would

Skyeku 13

Fank eyes gaze upwards

Blue sky silhouette golden

Caressed by mother's breath.

drive my Aunt's favourite dog, Corrie (a gruesome blackish terrier), bananas! He really disliked the cats and would jump up on his hind legs pounding the door howling like a madman (or is it a mad dog?).

The usual dinner fare for the felines was a bowl of milk mixed with Uig baker's bread or some tasty meat treats which they gobbled up quick style, licking their lips and smiling to each other. For us kids, the fun would be when either of them gave birth to cute kittens. The cat maternity hospital was the byre's loft, secreted in hard to find spaces in-between bales of hay. We would sneak stealthily over the fence and unlatch the loft door. The creaking wooden loft floorboards gave us away easily, but undeterred we closed the door and sat silently on the hay. Waiting for the sound of a kitten's meow to alert us to their position.

The summer sun shone through the opaque corrugated plastic skylight. The temperature increasing as the day went on. The atmosphere hot and musty, with hay dust invading your nose and the faint aroma of treacle emanating from the metal barrel behind the loft door. How we loved to play there, especially when one half of the loft contained loose hay which became our scratchy bed. The other half sat neatly stacked hay bales which we had to remove one by one to find the little furry bundles of fun! These hay bricks were heavy! Once found, hours of joy would be had by playing with the little cats until we got called back to the hoose by Margaret.

As they grew in stature and bravery, they would accompany their mother across the road to the wee hoose. Cute wee things sat on the steps peering over the door with heads a bobbing. Their squeaking driving Corrie over the edge!

To this day we have cats in Thailand and in Saudi. Interestingly, in his later years my Aunt's cat-loathing terrier became good friends with the ageing Snowy and Margaret told me they would often go walking together on the hill. Besties it seems!

Fanks for the Memories

One of my all-time favourite places in the world is Linicro fank. What a perfect place, in a perfect setting for sheep and non-sheep related activities (and by that I mean playing)! Who gathered the stones that were used to wall the large square of green in the shadow of the Linicro hill? Who placed them carefully forming the walls? How old is it anyway? Who decided the size of the place? Whoever it was, thank you!

As a summer holiday child, I would love to attend the fank with my big sister Angela and my Great Aunt Margaret. On fank days the excitement was palpable, and we readied ourselves for fun and clippers. Margaret would pack a lunch of sandwiches or scones with cheese or jam and if we were lucky a chocolate biscuit or two. The weather had to be Skye sunny good and my memory tells me they were all beautiful sheep shearing days. The three of us would head up the hill behind the big hoose and reach the gate at the top of Margaret's croft. We would

Linicro Fank Sheep Dipper with Peat Road in the Background

never open the metal gate, always climbed over it. Then, it was an up and down stroll across the Linicro common grazing beneath the high rocks till we reached the fank wall. Again, we climbed. The wall's boulders, probably gathered from the hill beside us, could be shaky on top, so climbing carefully was the order of the day. Once negotiated we would head over to the fank's business corner. Here you would find sheep pens, big and small, for hairy beasts in need of a haircut! Some pens at the back had a grass lining, but the ones closest to the dipper and the shearing area had cobblestones. This flooring would quickly be sheep pee and poop filled which then would be trampled by hundreds of hoofs making the cobble stones slick and easy for you to slip if you were not careful. In the summer heat, the front pen was producing a hot smell of fleece and faeces. It did not bother my young nose too much!

I was always fascinated and a little frightened by the dipper, full of grey chemical smelling water which had been left over from the previous sheep dipping time! As we only stayed in Linicro for the school summer holidays, we never got to see the dipping action, only the clipping action!

What characters Linicro had then, and they all gathered for the annual shearing of the township owned sheep. Norman Macinnes was always there as he also assisted with the gathering of the animals from the hill and escorting them to the pre-shearing pens! The shepherd was a gnarly old Bodach called Seamus Cameron. To me he looked as old as the Linicro hills with ruddy weather-worn skin, a crooked nose and tombstone teeth. In all the years I knew him, he appeared to be perpetually in a grim mood. Truth is, he was a bit scary and none too friendly to us young ones. Morag MacLeod's dear old Dad Norman Gillies was in attendance and many other Kilmuir locals. Callum the Postie would show up and the gentleman that was Carol McIntosh's father. Not forgetting Norman (Lovely) MacDonald from nearby Seaview B&B! Sometimes we would see Alistair Hunter too! Others, no doubt, that I have forgotten about.

The shearing area was small for such a large fank, but the group were ready and able with hand clippers sharpened for the days of work ahead. There was another lady who would help my Aunt Margaret roll the fleeces once we extricated them from our four-legged friends. I don't recall her name but can still see her red-cheeked and pinnie wearing, clear in my mind's eye. The woollen stuff was laid over a makeshift table of wooden planks on top of a few red rusted oil drums. Beside this makeshift workbench stood the tall, iron frame that held the sacks to be filled with fleece. My sister would often help the ladies, but my job was more important. I held the dosing gun and was in charge of the red paint pot with a wooden stick to mark the baldy sheep. The gang of sheep shearers had their own way of doing things. Some were fast, some not so! Some would tie the feet of the sheep with brown rope. Some would use their body weight to suppress any unruly animals and keep them from bolting.

Norman Macinnes was my hero. He could do anything, and he always did it well. He sheared maybe two to three sheep in the time it took others to shear one. He was a lot younger than the Bodachs of course. What a guy and what a technique he had, in the days before electric replaced hand clippers. His were made of a dark brown looking metal that had silver blade edges because of the fine sharpening he did with his sharpening stone.

Gaelic was the language of the fank and we did not mind the guys making fun of us weegies! With dose gun at the ready I would insert the angled tip into the mouth and squeeze that weird yellow stuff down their gullet and judging by the look on their Blackface and Cheviot faces, it did not taste very good. I would then reach for the painting stick and mark two stripes on the sheep's side (left or right, I can't remember). The dosing and marking job was uniquely satisfying and helped me build up a ravenous appetite which made me look forward to lunching. When the break came we all sat beside each other on the grass to eat and more often than not Norman Macinnes, whose dear Mum packed a huge lunch, would share his goodies with me. All washed down with a strong sweet thermos tea served in a plastic cup. Yum! I can still taste that tea now and the aroma of paint, sheep dip and dosing medicine did not put me off eating one bit!

As my sister and I were the smallest (and most gullible), they would place us in the large, long, brown fleece sacks. It was boiling and stinky inside, and those brown sacks have a particular odour that clings to your clothes and your skin. Standing on the fleeces looking up, you could only see a small patch of blue sky. Then more rolled fleeces would be thrown in and we would have to trample them down as best we could. Your reward was making it to the top and leaning over the big sack gasping for hill fresh air. It was not the cleanest job in the world as there was a lot of loose poop, but not once did we get bitten by a tick!

As our childish attention waned we would often go for an adventure in the wide green fank expanse. There is one area, near the far corner where a massive boulder sits and we would climb it and sit atop wishing we had seen its detachment from the hill and witnessed its rolling down to the spot we now sat at. The rocks and hills behind the big hoose have always had nesting golden eagles and if you were lucky, when lying on the grass, gazing skyward your eyes might see these winged beauties soar high above on the Linicro thermals, no doubt spying their next snack. As long as it was not my sister or me!

This was the time when the hills seemed to have millions of rabbits and hares and if you stood on the common grazing and gave a loud howl not only would you hear your squeaky voices echo but you would see loads of rabbits take-off up the hill white tails bobbing! To us city slickers, this was the magic of the island!

The first day completed we'd say our goodbyes to the men who did all the hard work and we would stroll back to the wee hoose tired and happy, encased in sheep hair and smelling like a dunghill! After our evening meal and telling our Great Granny about the day's activities we would head for the double bed we shared and fall fast asleep dreaming of rabbits running and baldy white sheep bah bah bahing!

Fank

*Sheets of air lightened rain head out towards the Ascribs on their
way to making Waternish wet.*
*Whilst my feet, Dunlop protected, carry me across Linicro's
common grazing, muscle memory never forgets.*

*The terrain, boulder grey and green is hard yet soft 360 eyes take
in hill, heather and sea.*
The stone squared, grass filled fank, my destination approached.
*Each expertly placed natural brick, smiling, begging me to
climb, and I heed their plea.*

Gone are the dark clouds above making way for blue.
The sun's heat, not hot, pecks soil like a Granny's kiss.
*As I make my road to the pens and dipper, my visit long
overdue.*

*A late spring breeze hints of the summer arriving and I jump the
sheep dip moat, long jumper like, my wellies break my
landing.*
It's afternoon now, and the rain remains absent.
*To the fank's centre I head, the space empty, with no woolly
beasts apparent.*

The large boulder sits where it's sat for an age.
*Jacket off now, I scale the rock and stand on Mother Nature's
stage.*

I recognize sheep talk, drifting down from the moor.
High in the sky, above soars the eagle of gold.
God's boulder, his gift for my bones not yet old.

Alone yet not on my own, I'm surrounded by friends.
*From high throne I bellow hello and bouncing tails trace their
rabbit's hole homes below.*

Grass green and dry, I lie on my back, to the heavens I gaze.
Is God staring back?

My eyelids close and I allow myself to dream.
*The acrid and comforting sheep dip aroma finds its way to my
nose, carried on a sunbeam.*

The sun has itself repositioned low, to the west it is sinking, the
  day, and I your narrator must be on his way.

It's au revoir, not goodbye to my fank friend as spits of rain tickle
  my forehead.
The journey home to the big hoose's Sunday is undertaken.
The sky dull with hidden sun, the breeze at my back is a
  downpour in the making.

The crofts top sees me hurdle the gate, and I bound down the field
  Olympian in speed but not grace.
I breech the ultimate fence and make for the back-kitchen path,
  satisfaction stamped on my face.

Hen Hoose Hideaway

One of the few chores that I did not make a song and dance
about doing was 'mucking oot the hen hoose'! Not everyone's
idea of a cushy gig, I know. However, there was a smidgen of
method in my Highland madness. Over the Linicro years there
had been an eclectic collection of large and small chicken
condos spread around the croft whose lodgers had been given
names like Ken and Robin. Bantam bothies sat between the two
houses of 1 Linicro. As we said goodbye to the 70s, most of
Margaret's clucking, pecking, mini organic egg vending
machines lived in the old horse stable inside her byre.

The ground floor of the animal house was primarily designed
to house the cows but there was a 'tack' room separated by
wooden planks and a chicken wire door. In days long gone, the
family would keep one heavy horse for doing the real hard
work, like pulling laden carts and ploughing unforgiving fields.
The advent of the tractor brought an end to these big beasts'
backbreaking work. Margaret had used this room for the
majority of her hens for years. It comprised a large cobbled

space with several man-made wooden ledges. Stretching from stone wall to inner wooden wall were the birds of a feather flocked together at day lights ends, sleeping till dawn's chorus.

By now one might say to themselves 'what was so good about cleaning chicken poop'? Mostly I was alone and I could take my battery-powered, solid state cassette deck with me to play the fitting 'Animals' by the Floyd! Margaret would never bother me or complain about the music or the extraordinary amount of time it took me for this relatively minor job. With my music blasting through the player's mono speaker, I would chase out any straggling feathered friends so my work could continue unimpeded.

The miasma of smells did not trouble me in the darkened hen hoose. Light snuck in from the wooden door, clattering about in the wind. Chicken poop flakes permeated the air, attracting hay dust and other friends whose final destination was my two nostrils. Not an unpleasant aroma, but I never see it being used as the basis of a cologne! My tool of choice was an ancient woodworm-decorated shovel. I attacked the poop head on, scooping up a full load, then staggered towards the door and threw the stuff onto the cattle dung heap. I would then blow the gathered poop from my nose, enter and scoop, enter and scoop until I had moved the poop from the interior to the exterior. I made this job last twice as long so I would not be seconded onto any other outside jobs. Smart, eh?

Once the organic matter was cleared I would unfurl the green rubber garden hose and wash the floor down with copious amounts of freezing Linicro water!

Finally, I would then take a hard-bristled brush and brush the viscose remains outside the door onto the dung heap. One last wash down of the floor revealed the craftsmanship of the cobblestones beneath my wellied feet. The chore done, I would then reach for the tap outside the byre door and wash off the excrement clinging to my lily-white hands and face. I could then relax inside the coolness of the byre listening to the Floyd and try to work out what the hell they were singing about?

Hunting Eggs

*Can you find eggs under the broody hens, hiding somewhere on
the croft?*
*This request to find these nests brought smiles of joy, and with
gusto we set off.*

*The promise of a cream toffee or two, the reward for finding egg
treasure.*
*To the hill we marched with a stick in our hands. Hope made
the search a pleasure.*

*Daydreams of finding an egg queen with hundreds of fresh eggs in
her nest.*
*The sun at our backs and luck on our sides, we prayed we
would hunt the best.*

*To the burn by the wee hoose, overgrown, thick with brambles
and stingy nettles.*
*Our stick swung like a sabre, promised to reveal a hidden hen in
fine laying fettle.*

*Others directed their gaze to the side of the barn in the boulders of
the old ruin.*
*Whilst I spied a feathered friend, secreted in a fern den, sitting
on its eggshell bullion.*

*With a song I rejoiced as I collected the oval riches, being careful
not to let them crack.*
*And I presented them as if they were crown jewels from a
grinning egg maniac.*

*The chook hunt resumes in the afternoon, our heads full of egg
yolk and toffee.*
*My Aunt happy as Larry with a bowl full of eggs, as she puffs on
her No 6 and sips her coffee.*

Biker Boy

My Aunt Margaret had two bikes that were parked in the byre's loft. Both lady's two-wheeled travellers. One was a fairly old one, coloured black, probably from around the early 60s. The other was a newer 1970s bike made by Raleigh. She would use her bike for going to church, visiting folk and shopping at the bakers in Uig. I was never allowed to ride the new bike, but occasionally got a shot of the old black one. Bobby was allowed to use the new bike and both of us would go to Uig for the weekly shop. With help from him, Margaret gifted the old bike to me! It was not my Raleigh Jeep, but it was better than walking. Something had to be done to this old lady's bike. It needed to be made manlier! Luckily Bobby had a job, so he financed the bike's makeover. First thing we did was spray paint it silver and although it was not what you would call a custom job, it looked better. Next thing I did was get green and yellow bicycle tape, which I wrapped round all the chrome of the handlebar. These bars were the old-fashioned design with the thick rubber, once-white handles that faced into the body of the cyclist. I can't think of another way to describe them, but I'm sure you know what I mean. Then I taped little green and yellow 'flags' on every spoke of both wheels. I thought it looked rather cool. We 3-in-1'd all the moving parts and my new old bike was ready for a test drive!

It was a Saturday, and we were given a shopping list from Margaret, so it was off to Uig's baker. That cycle up past the quarry to the top of Totescore is not easy, but once past the Fank it was all level till you came to the top of Uig. At this point I have to inform you that my bike had only one brake, which was for the back wheel. We bombed it down towards the hairpin bend. Unfortunately for me I was going too fast and catastrophically misjudged my biking skills. I zoomed into the bend but could not get out of it, and as I pressed furiously on my brake, the momentum took me straight into the stone wall

Skyeku 14

Face first in water cold

Sucking thirst away water gulps

The rest flows seaward.

at the side of the road! Strangely and luckily I was not hurt, but my front wheel was totally buckled! Bobby could do nothing but laugh, as I stared at my poor bike's wheel and what I had done to it on its maiden voyage. Bobby said don't worry about the wheel as he jumped on it with all his weight. Although it was not perfectly straight and had a serious wobble, it was good enough for us to carry on our shopping trip!

For the next couple of years that bike took me everywhere and was particularly useful on lonely Linicro Sunday afternoons. I also used it to bike to the Macinnes house and I would leave it lying in the grass at the top of Totescore and walk down the path to my pals. On winter nights I had to bike back to Linicro in the dark as I had no lights. Luckily I knew the road well and probably could have cycled down with both eyes closed and not get into an accident! One gloomy Sunday night I was cycling down to the phone box at Linicro Post Office. I had just passed the old blacksmiths at speed when I ran over something on the road. I did not stop to look but on the way back I stopped and there breathing its last on the ground was a big rabbit! Did I hit first or was the damage done by a car? There was very little trauma to it, so who knows? Anyway, I picked it up and took to my Aunt who on inspection decided it was good enough for rabbit stew! Yum, it lasted us two days!

Apart from my wheel-buckling incident, I was lucky not to have had any serious crashes on my trusty steed. I put that bike through a lot over those couple of years, including jumping off homemade ramps! The only accident I remember still makes me feel bad to this day. I was cycling down the Totescore road past old Stonegate when I saw my mate Archie walking along the road to the cattle pens. I decided to give him a fright, so I pedalled like a madman and as I got closer to him he moved unexpectedly, making me grip down furiously on my back brake. There is plenty of gravel on that road, so I and the bike went into a skid. The back wheel swung round and hit him hard and he fell on top of me and the bike! The momentum carried both of us scraping across that wee road, with poor Archie coming off the worst. He had serious gravel rash and was in a lot of pain! I came off luckier, but I felt really terrible for hurting him. Sorry Archie boy!

I wonder what became of that silver machine of mine? No doubt it's still lying in Linicro, probably hidden by decades of overgrowth.

Bike

Sad and alone you sat in the loft, replaced like so many, with a
    newer model.
Winter's rain, and summer's heat has left you craving a
    connection.

Your chain, your black frame needing love and Joan Armatrading
    affection.
I remember you when I was young. No grubby hands allowed to
    touch.

Your sixties paint job byre fresh, your seat white clean and bum
    pure.
Long Sundays past now since you wheeled it to the church in
    Kilmuir.

Usurped in the seventies by a Raleigh, all feminine and city clean.
Your winter sobbing unheard, till the seventy-seven summer
    when I was thirteen.

Set free and handed over to me, a lady's bike you might be.
With a silver spray jacket, green and yellow tape cuffs, a new life
    was yours to take.
Some 3 in 1 and a new cotter pin. Thick black Indian rubber
    block brakes.

Spokes cleaned, taped to look cool. Handlebars tipped and ready
    to go.
Mud guards gone, seat cleaned, we zoomed up and down
    Linicro.

*Wind, rain, hail and sun sometimes, you transported me to
   Totescore and back again.*
*My Aunt's message list delivered to the Uig Baker, by way of the
   hairpin bend.*

*Fresh bread and Orkney cheese rounds, bagged and ready, hung
   from your handlebars.*
*And I huffed, and I puffed with no help from you. The big hoose
   seemed so far.*

*Soon it would be lucky for me, and we bombed back down the
   road.*
*Windswept and interesting what a pair we made, till we
   reached my big hoose abode.*

*Two years or more of faithful service given, we had a good Skye
   run.*
*Through roads rough, and mud tough, over hill dyke and croft
   we spun.*

*Until my legs stretched by nature long, grew tired of push
   pedalling.*
And your wheels buckled, with tyres flat, no more for bicycling.

*Long abandoned my friend I left you. To rust and rot under a
   Linicro tree.*
*Never will I forget your silver silhouette and the fun that you
   gave to me.*

Roddy the Van

What a beautiful sight to see in Linicro. Roddy Mackenzie's
shop on wheels! We sweet-toothed teenagers loved to get inside
that tight customer space and get shopping for goodies. City
folk just don't know the joy of seeing a shop on wheels, its
magic. It was the blue van that I remember, but I know he had a

Roddy the Van

red van as I saw a photo on Facebook. I can still recall the smell inside that vehicle. It contained a myriad of aromas to tempt your taste buds.

One summer evening Peter Ridley and I were hitching from Portree back to the North End. It was a beautiful evening and relatively warm and we had got a lift to the Kingsburgh road and we had been walking for a few minutes when that big beautiful blue van stopped and Roddy offered us a lift. There we were standing inside smelling all those smells and having a friendly laugh with Roddy. He let us off at Earlish and waved goodbye to us as we continued our hitch.

Roddy was a decent bloke too. He helped Bobby and me out of a jam late one night. We had been at a dance in Portree and were driving back to Linicro in his VW Beetle. We ran out of petrol as we hit Kensaleyre! It must have been after one in the morning. What the hell were we going to do? Roddy stays in Kensaleyre and his house is easy to spot because of his van. We decided we would knock on his door and ask him for some car juice. We tiptoed round the back and timidly knocked on the door of the sleeping house. We did not want to knock too loud in case we put the fear of God into Roddy and his family. A light came on and we heard some feet padding to the back door. 'Who is it?' Roddy asked from behind his wooden and glass door. Bobby explained who he was and our situation in a low, calm voice. As soon as Roddy recognized it was Bobby, he sheepishly opened his door, a big kitchen knife in his hand! We apologised profusely about the late hour, but we were desperate. He sorted us out with enough petrol to get back to Linicro. Gentleman!

I know there were other shop/vans that would appear on the Skye roads. I remember a butcher van and I have vague memories of another grocery van and I want to say it was Lipton's? None of them stand out in my memory as much as Roddy the Van's Van.

Home
(Where My Heart Once Was)

After one year in Linicro and attending PHS, the school summer holidays of 1978 came around like a long-lost friend. Only this time everything was in reverse. This time my summer holiday was to be spent with my family in the city I had happily left behind a year earlier. I will admit that the only reason I had to go was that my parents insisted. I can also admit that occasionally I missed my Glasgow family, but only occasionally. Come the day, my small grey case was packed, and they ferried me to Uig to catch the Glasgow Bus. No more Wallace Arnold luxury, these Highland Scottish buses were not comfy and not designed to take us poor passengers on a near 8-hour sojourn! If you were lucky, you got an uncomfortable seat on your own. That day I was not lucky!

As a 14-year-old the hours passed like days and my stomach rebelled against each and every bump on the Highland roads. A brief respite in Fort William assured my stomach that it would not have to expel its contents (at least not yet). Through the hills and moors the day passed with tortoise speed. Another stop at Tyndrum made me think the journey would soon be over, but the reality was still a few hours away. Finally, on to the Great Western Road, the signs of suburbia led me and my fellow travellers into the city centre and our eventual destination of Buchanan St bus station. For those with long memories, the station was not like it is now. Then it was a windswept and ugly place with plastic shopping bags swirling in the air, a cocktail of bus fumes and cigarette smoke. A welcome home it wasn't!

From the station I had to hump my case to the nearest 45 bus stop. This once familiar journey appeared alien to my young eyes. Finally arriving in Springburn, I walked the rest of the way to 52a 7 Galloway St. So began my two-week vacation!

I had left Glasgow the year before with a strong weegie accent but over the 12 months I had softened it, and my words were spoken more properly. Some might say posh! It was great to see my family and their newish dog, aptly named Skye. It did not take long for my former friends to find out I was home and soon they rang our bell asking for me 'tae come oot tae play'.

This was a strange time for me, and not an enjoyable one at that. A year away from Springburn might well have been a century. I felt like a stranger in a strange land. I no longer talked with the same accent as my Galloway Street pals, and I no longer felt I had anything in common with them either. Then, as now, I tried to dip into a strong Glasgow brogue but only ended up sounding like someone from Edinburgh mimicking a Glasgow accent!

A few years later I was at home and I passed a young neighbour's kid who asked me who I was. I told her I was Gary Moore's big brother, and she replied 'naw yer no', I asked 'why do you think that'? Her reply was 'cuz, you're English'!

The expectation of my parents was that I should spend every waking hour outside with my old Galloway Street pals, but the truth was I hated being there, and longed for night to fall and for the days to pass with speed so I could return to my beloved

Linicro. My parents had no clue about how I felt as, true to being Scottish, I did not express my feelings.

The late 70s ushered in the decline of the old Springburn, with the demolition of its heart, to make way for a long-planned bypass. My street had recently been dubbed 'Glue St' (sniffing), by the Daily Record, and the once hidden world of hard drugs was now not so hidden! The day for travelling back to the Isle of Skye finally arrived and neither the long uncomfortable journey nor the thought of being sick on the bus could dampen my joy! I bade farewell to my old home and thanked God that I was lucky enough to spend my teenage years on my Island love.

I have to say that subsequent holidays back home were far more enjoyable, and ultimately, I would look forward to going to the City for Christmas. Spending two or three weeks with my family and being a roadie for my Dad's band was a blast!

Glasgow Bus

In the wet, windy and grey I stand waiting. Late again?
At the roadside, my body tired already. The warmth of the hotel mocks me.
Finally, my eyes, glazed. Gaze across the bay. The bus departs the pier and we will soon be on our way.
One final lashing as I'm whipped by Sheader rain.
Diesel belches as the bus coughs its way round Uig. A smoker's cough on wheels.
The smell of oil and fresh baked bread. Rankin's the bakers sneezes as the bus rumbles past.
I hear it before I see it and with my hand, half wave, half goodbye. The vehicle comes to a creaking halt.
The wind tunnel whoosh of Highland hydraulics welcome me aboard without a smile.
'To Glasgow', I announce with a pocket fumble and I scan the length for a seat.
The pungent pong of semi-soggy bodies greets my nose and the last of the rain trickles down my back. Steam will rise.
Eyes again, gaze. Glazed by the musty odour and the smell of Brut.
One seat is free, yippee! Two seats free? Lucky me. I squeeze my life into the overhead with ease.

The seat is not soft as I slide window bound. With a grinding of
  gears, we chug to the top. Will we make it to Earlish?
The driver, red faced and bored, wrestles with the steering wheel
  as we plateau. Portree, here we come.
The air inside is the opposite of fresh. My arm's hand fiddles with
  the blank-eyed air supplier above my steaming head. A faint
  wisp from one. No air from the other. I de-cloak.
Portree passes without incident, as our journey continues. Soon
  the sea smell creeps through the coach's cracks and crevices.
  Kyleakin beckons.
We troop, as if lemmings, down the greasy slipway. Tired and
  emotional, the ferry welcomes us aboard. Hard seats and cold
  bums are on the menu.
Bus boarding again, I find my seat. This time I'm not alone. A
  world-weary smile is exchanged for its twin. Fort William is
  broken up with traveller stops and lunch is quick and
  disappointing.
Heavy stomached I lean against the window, passing green and
  hill and river. Winter's joy. Glen Coe as lonely as a widow.
  Overcast like our bus brains.
Bridge of Orchy breeched, the rubber now kisses dry tarmac. Sleep
  is but a distant memory as lunch threatens a visit. And on and
  on we go. Window for pillow.
Tyndrum tea is welcome. My nethers rush with blood. How much
  longer driver please? 'Sit down and shut it', he'd like to shout,
  but he doesn't. Trussed up by the Trossachs via Crianlarich
  tears. Twisted minds on twisted roads admire the Lomond Loch.
Claustrophobic and excited as Alexandria hints at a city. Feeling
  great on the Great Western road. We head for Mother Glasgow's
  bosom. Streetlights, nicotine yellow. Our city guard of honour.
  Salutes us all the way to Buchanan Street. A hero's return it isn't.
Crawling into the station, the bus death rattles. Belongings over
  my shoulder, I walk off my numb behind.
'Tis the season and all that, the shops sing their Yuletide hits. The
  night sky is crispy, clear and cold. Glasgow's smile's better,
  don't you know?
My journey's end is near, and I wait at the appropriate stop.
  Another bus to board and fare to pay as the 45 to Colston
  draws me near. Finally, Springburn and its Galloway Street
  pal. Let the Christmas cheer begin.

Ghost

All I can say about this is what I believe I saw and heard when sleeping in my big hoose bedroom. It was the winter of my third year of school. Bobby and I shared the same room for a while upstairs. Bobby slept on the double bed at the far wall and I was in the single bed along the wall that leads to the bedroom window. I don't know what woke me up, but something did and my eyes opened with my body facing the tongue-and-groove woodwork of the wall. I turned myself round to face the other way. Immediately I saw it standing right beside my head. A figure in white. It looked to me like a female. I did not stare at this ghoulish apparition for long as I was totally crapping myself (not literally). I swiftly turned to face the wall again and hid my head under the covers. I listened but could hear no footsteps and I waited for what seemed like an age before I was courageous enough to turn back round to see if the lady in white was still there. She wasn't. Thank God! I eventually fell into a dreamless sleep. Years later, when Bobby and I shared a flat in Bruntsfield, Edinburgh. He told me of a time when we shared that room and he woke up and looked over to me and he saw a ghostly figure standing over me, apparently watching me sleep. Spooky! Real or not, I got a fright!

I saw no apparitions again in the big hoose, but there were some strange sounds in the winter nights. The nightly routine was always that I would go to bed before my Aunt Margaret and later I would hear her and her favourite dog, Corrie, climb the stairs to her bedroom opposite mine. On more than a couple of occasions I heard what I thought to be her footsteps climbing those creaky wooden stairs. Only to later hear Margaret talk to her dog as they both walked up to go to bed! Creepy. Also, and whoever I have told this to always say it was my overactive imagination. When I would lie in bed, I was positive I could feel the floor vibrating, almost shaking. This happened a lot. Later I was told that my great-great Uncle John (or Johnnie), slept in the room below me after the war, and he had contracted malaria during his service. Was it him shaking in his ghostly bed with malaria? I never heard or saw anything else. Just the floor shaking at night!

Nothing spooky ever happened in the wee hoose!

Big Hoose Ghost

There's a ghost in the big hoose of that I'm sure.
Creeping up and down our wooden staircase in the Linicro wee
* hours.*

Waiting patiently till I'm on the edge of sleep
Lurking outside my door, making the floorboards creak.
And when I'm far away in the land of nod.
That's when it floats beside my bed.

I saw it once through my eyes, tired, and half closed.
Translucent and white, it gave me a fright and sent me under
* the bedclothes.*

If you're awake after the midnight hour, dark and winter dreary.
You can feel the floor vibrate enough to stop sleep and make you
* feel ever so weary.*

Many times I heard my Aunt prepare to go to sleep after ten,
* and when I thought she was asleep in bed, I heard her*
* footsteps on the stairs again.*

When the electric meter runs out of its fifty pence food.
Inside the middle bedroom is where it stood.
Of this I'm sure and I know my Aunt thinks I'm immature, but
* that ghost is waiting, every night, bladder full at 3 AM, a*
* scary white toilet face I'm anticipating.*

Will tonight be the night for another fright, when I get ready for
* my bed?*
There's a ghost in the big hoose, of that I'm sure, and my
* bedroom is haunted.*

Old Man Hojan

In a croft house opposite the wee hoose, a way down the fields, there was a Bodach known as Hojan (not sure of the spelling). He had lived there for as long as I had been alive and he was a tough old soul who lived the life of a crofting bachelor. I don't think he had been married. You did not see him much up close and personal, but we could hear him every day shouting orders to his dogs! I remember him cycling to church on a Sunday on one of those old 1950s black bikes, smartly dressed in a dark suit, white shirt and tie. One leg had the metal ring round it to protect the cloth from getting caught on the chain. I believe Norman was his name, but I heard no one use that when either talking to or about him. He was a rough and tough individual who was probably younger than he looked. Grey hair, short back and sandpaper. Deep-set eyes showed a sense of fun behind them and a bit of a pointy nose. His face was well weather worn and his cheeks and lips sucked in by a toothless mouth. As kids we would go outside and wait for him to appear on his bike and wave as he casually cycled by! He always had a smile on his face. One time Norman Macinnes was doing some work for him and I was helping. He invited us in as the evening fell for a wee strupag. On entering I noticed how dark it was in his living room, then I realised that it was because he had no electricity! The light came from the window and a Tilley lamp! The room was crofter Spartan in decor and held a range where he boiled the water for his tea. I don't remember seeing any comfortable chairs, and I sat on what looked like an old church pew beside an old wooden table. The tea he served was as thick as tar and very sweet. He offered some old-looking biscuits from a tin. We sat there for a while listening to him, and it was obvious that he was a man used to his own company!

There was one time he came to visit me and Bobby in the big hoose when Margaret was in hospital in Inverness. He came to inquire about her health and we brought him in for a wee dram. Margaret kept a bottle for such visits. He had a kind face and liked to talk mischief about the ladies! We did not drink, but over the course of his relatively brief visit we filled his glass to the brim a number of times. He never refused! I remember him being very merry as he left with a wave and a smile! He may have had a wee hangover the next day!

Digging

The month and my Aunt tells me it's time to bring the old garden fork out.
Behind the byre, down on the croft, the green leaf tattie plants have long begun to sprout.

Winter's food for the big hoose table, underfoot they hide in the moist Linicro soil.
If we don't get down with our big boots on, the tubers will start to spoil.

The tattie patch promises buried treasure for those willing to break their back.
Standing under a grey sky umbrella, watching my Aunt's tattie digging technique, listening to her knees loudly crack.

It's time for me to thrust the rusting fork deep into the dark, croft dirt.
With a groan and a strain it begins to spit rain, as I reveal what's underground.

Like a madman I'm shaking, the plant's roots are quaking, and I'm happy with my first haul.
And as I move down my row, with my Aunt in tow, I'm having a gardener's ball.

Our rusting buckets are overflowing with mud, white and purple tasty treats.
Both arms aching, the sun breaks a smile, and I wish our job was complete.

Still, I'm happy when a handful I've dug, muddy and in my dirty hand.
My auld Aunt's still working with no sign of fatigue as she reaps rewards from her land.

I'm knackered and panting as the work comes to a close. We spread our booty out to dry.

*If the sun disappears and the clouds leak tears, I swear I will
    start to cry.*

*The next day we're in luck as the weather is fine and for a while
    we survey what we've done.*
*To the byre, we carry our winter chips in metal buckets that
    weigh a ton.*

*The end now is in sight, and we surrender the fight. The tatties lie
    on the loft floor.*
*With a satisfaction sense, we head home for a rest. My Aunt
    Margaret locks the wooden byre door.*

The Only Living Boy in Linicro (Fank)

70s Sunday afternoons in Linicro required a vivid imagination
and it was lucky that I was happy with my own company.
Deprived of my fellow mischief makers, the Macinnes boys,
meant I had to amuse myself until Ian Ogilvie entertained me
as the (new) Saint at 7pm on ITV. On crisp winter days my legs
would take me up the hill onto Linicro's common grazing as I
moved towards the stonewalled Linicro fank. Before I could
climb the aforementioned wall, I would have to negotiate the
boggy strip of common land that acted as natural moat,
repelling man and beast from breaching the fank's front and
sides. Most times I would emerge victorious and dry footed in
the battle of the bogs! One had to carefully choose the part of
the fank wall to climb. If I made the wrong choice, I might find
that I toppled myself and some loose stones. Ouch!

Winter Sundays rarely were sun days. More often than not a
light grey overcoat of sky hung high above my head, threatening water at any given moment. Those occasional crispy cold

days were ideal for my fank visits. There is something about the Linicro fank that would draw my personage, and now my mind, to its green and winter brown grassy

Skyeku 15

Skye sky cries tears

Hill brown and purple burn flows strong

Welcome home Minch mouths.

enclosure. If you are ever in the township, I recommend a visit. My Sunday visits would see me walk the perimeter and then head to a massive stone that had rolled down from the rocky hill many moons ago. It's big! Here I would sit atop, surveying the land 360 like. The silence was loud. The hills in front of me, my only company. To break the silence, the wind would whistle across the common grazing and through the gaps in the fank's wall. It whispered also, and no matter how hard I would listen, I could not make out the words.

I was the fank King with only a rabbit or two for subjects. In no hurry to return home (unless the weather changed). I would wander my kingdom for hours. It might appear that it was a lonely affair, but it rarely was. In the shadow of the hills, the Linicro light would change through the afternoon from a silver grey, pierced now and then, with a sabre of bright sun Skye light. I could have been the last of us, as I could see no other living soul from within these stone walls. I would often hang around the 'dipper' which was never empty and almost overflowing with a bone chilling, sludgy grey soup, giving off a chemical bug killing aroma. I would jump from side to side like Evel Knievel minus his bike (and leather suit). I would usually finish my visit with a walk to the Greaulin side of the fank.

Peering over the wall across to the long-deserted village; its only occupants now were the cows of Linicro Township, grazing in-between the cottage ruins. What a stunning place for houses. Now I wonder why they deserted that beautiful area at the foot of the friendly Linicro hill? My stomach transmitted the return to home signal to my brain, demanding to be fed. Traversing the wall and hopefully making it dry footed past the bogs. I would walk over the faded purple of the winter heather to our top croft.

I would then charge down the faded green field like a Braveheart extra. Jump over the gate and make my way to the big hoose's back door. Hoping that there were foodstuffs on the wax-cloth -covered kitchen table and that there would be no complaints from my Aunt Margaret about where I'd been all afternoon.

Totescore Fank Sunday

Walking in winter fashion no bike today, Sunday is as Sunday does.
Church traffic has subsided, prayers said, waiting for answers.

The only sound is my boot, on ground gravel crunchiness.
Clear weather reveals the Ascribs. Closer than usual, perhaps lonely?

My walk takes me to Totescore's top, and a wee wander round the fank.
My only company are two crows, catching up with each other's news.

Grey concrete pens, inactive for months, welcome me with indifference.
The dipper, full and smelly, waits for anybody wanting to get clean.

I sit down on the concrete pen edge, throwing pebbles at an unseen enemy.
Mother Nature calls and I heed, so I jump behind a pen wall.
Only my head is visible to passing sheep, who fail to notice steam rising.

Hop, skip and jump, I'm running in the grass pen, like an athlete I clear the fence.
Local council land now, as I tramp and stamp through dried mud, nothing of interest here.

Then it's back on to the road, with Waternish bored, following behind.
A few Sunday hours passed as the sun starts its dip, and it's back to the big hoose for me.

Shotgun Showdown

How brave (and stupid and immature), I was when I was younger. Not terrified of anything in those early Linicro days. Now I'm not so brave most probably because my brain has developed a wee bit. There was one winter weekend afternoon when Norman and the boys were over at the Morton house, so naturally I joined them. I would be around 14 years old. Norman Macinnes had with him an ancient-looking double-barrelled shotgun that he said would be used to frighten the crows around the Morton house. Immediately I wanted a shot of that long metal crow killer. I don't remember what the poor crows had done to deserve to be shot, but when you're young and an idiot you don't think of these things. On the Morton driveway just before the gate, to the right are a lot of trees which we thought might have crows in them, so we planned an attack.

The shotgun only had one barrel that was operational, so Norman put in a pellet cartridge and snapped it shut. He gave the weapon to me with the instruction being don't point at anyone. Stupid I was, but I was not a complete idiot. I made sure everyone was behind me! I aimed at the treetops with Norman whispering in my ear 'watch out for the kick' and I fired! The recoil was strong, but I managed it ok and as I said I had no fear!

Some birds flew out and behind us across the road to the hill opposite. I wanted another shot and so another cartridge was loaded and I moved across to the ditch beside the field. A bunch of crows were sitting on the electricity poles that ran through Linicro. These had white ceramic things round them, and close to these glossy things was a crow. Without thinking, I took aim and fired, missed the crow, but clipped the ceramic stuff that flew off into the field! It was not a direct hit, thank God, and it did no actual damage to the Township's power supply!

I think it was Bobby who took a turn next, and he aimed at the trees, firing off a blast. Nothing! All flying life had gone. We took a wee break when I noticed some sort of bird walking on the grass beneath Morton's trees, and I asked for one more shot. I aimed, I fired, and I missed but shot up a big mound of earth that was fun to see. The crows were lucky that day. That was the one and only time we went crow hunting!

Bridge

Time at times has no meaning, past is present. Present past.
Wandering my consciousness travels and settles on a rest place
    at last.

Across common green grazing, Polaroid colours, and the view
    amazing.
Hill climbed, plateau reached, within eye distance my wooden
    goal.
Sleeping wood spans water meandering. I gaze through time's
    keyhole.

Eyes closed, deep inhale, I'm there I swear, all skelfed and tar
    stained.
Legs a dangling, I smell the peat permeating from the brown rush
    below.
Hot head, hot hands and I exhale, feeling God's love as delicate
    as a feather pillow.

All around, I'm surrounded by Earth Angels. Purple, green and
    mud brown.
Life flows below, it's his bridge, cold and inviting. Banks wishing
    my come down.

I resist water temptations and I gaze at the sun, clouds, cotton
    woolled, high overhead.
Nature and me at one, Golden Eagles breathe on my neck, and
    it's love I know unsaid.

How long have I been here, my mind wonders? Office chaired;
    computer screened.
I'm always here, Father Time answers, as he cuddles and comforts
    me.

Maths then Arithmetic

I freely admit that the subjects of maths and arithmetic were not what one could call my favourites. The truth is my brain just is not built for such academic activities. At PHS my poor maths teacher was Miss Collins Taylor, who had the unenviable job of trying to teach me long division, etc. I still can't do long division. Thank god for the phone calculator. Not only was I not good at maths, I could not be bothered to learn it either, so I ended up being a bit of nuisance to our long-suffering teacher. Her class was across the blaise in one of the huts and on more than a few occasions I drove her to distraction and was punished by doing hundreds if not thousands of lines! My classmate Peggy MacLeod reminded me recently that there was one afternoon when (I think it was) Steven Isles brought a stray dog into the class and locked it in the store cupboard behind Miss CT's desk. The inevitable happened and the poor dog relieved himself of a number two! I think she breathed a sigh of relief that in fourth year I was chucked out of her class and put into Mr Mackinnon's arithmetic class, which was in the wooden huts near the technical block.

Anyone who knew that class knew that it was for the people who like me were hopeless at maths and arithmetic. I thought that going there would be a bit of nightmare and it would be a wee bit embarrassing, but it ended up being one of the best classes I had in 4th year.

Mr McKinnon was from Broadford and was a stout elderly gentleman who had in a previous life done some boxing. He could look intimidating, but he was a bit of a teddy bear. His classroom had the old-style desks which were double seats. My seat mate was Neil MacFarlane, who luckily for me liked to get up to a bit of mischief too. Some of our classmates who we would torment were Simon and Kenny. There were others and a few females too. I do not remember having learnt anything from that class, but I do recall laughing a lot! One of Neil's crackers was sitting on the seat beside Kenny or Simon (and some others) and whilst they readied themselves for class, he would slide across the bench fast and bump them off the seat onto the floor! How many times he did that I don't know, but he did it more than a few times and the victims were always unsuspecting as though it had never happened to them before!

The most common trick that we would do was putting drawing pins on various people's seats. It was the only reason we hurried to the class so we could lay our trap and see who fell for it. Again, I have to say that Kenny and Simon suffered the most! We would watch them saunter in, never checking their seats. They would sit down, then jump up in an instant. Drawing pin stuck to bum! We would kill ourselves laughing. Let me say now. Hand on heart, a big apology to Kenny and Simon! We tried it a few times with Mr McKinnon, but he was too smart for us. There were a couple of times we were sure he would sit and then just before bum touched wood he would pick up our pins. On more than one occasion he would get me to stand up and he'd come close to me and quick as lightning he would punch my stomach, but very gently! He could easily have winded me if he wanted, but his goal was to scare and make me flinch, not to hurt. He was a good guy and I'm sorry to say he did not teach me much, but then again with arithmetic I'm pretty unteachable!

Feathering the Nose

Winter Sundays could be ever so long and boring in Linicro. Especially when the weather did not permit you to go outside for an afternoon adventure. No TV was allowed until after seven, so I had to find ways to amuse myself. If I found my Granny sleeping on her chair by the fire, I would look for a long feather pulled from the birdcage or cushion. I would then creep behind her back and gently tickle her nose. Half asleep, she would wave her hands about as if shooing a fly. Once she went back to sleep, I would take the feather and tickle her ear. This time she would mumble something and her dentures would slip. I waited again and tickled her nose. Now she awoke and shouted, but looking around she could see no one. I hid silently. I was very bored so I could wait until I thought she went back to sleep. I raised that feather and tickled her nose again. This time she did nothing, but her hand drifted slowly towards her stick. I tickled her ear and, as fast as a speeding bullet, she grabbed the stick and swung it behind her head. She nearly caught me a good few times! Eventually I would get up and she would wave her stick and threaten to skelp me! She would laugh about it later, though.

Linicro Winter

I remember the freezing cold as I slept in my big hoose bed.
I remember the condensation on my sleeping bag duvet, my
nose the colour of reindeer red.

I remember hopping about on the cold lino as I slipped into my
frigid school clothes.
I remember the frozen face water in the igloo-like bathroom as
an outside gale blows.

I remember shivering in front of one electric bar, fake coal
radiating no heat.
I remember icicles in my cornflakes, the under table stamping to
heat my poor wee cold feet.

I remember the rain for days and nights that seemed would never
end.
I remember being stuck in the house with only two smelly dogs
for friends.

I remember days so grey and overcast, the sun but a distant
memory.
I remember walking on Wentworth streets, through hail and
wind blustery.

I remember the boredom of always being wet, my shoes all
covered in mud.

*I remember looking to the hill, white water in full flow, the burn
   by the wee hoose in flood.*

*I remember a fire burning with peat as I sat with my legs stretched
   on the mantel.*
*I remember being comfy and watching Bruce's Big Night, the
   weather outside truly awful.*

*I remember long hot baths whilst my Aunt was at church and
   listening to the top 20 on the radio.*
*I remember a mug of tea, a plate with bread and cheese, me
   singing along to Ritchie Blackmore's Rainbow.*

*I remember the dread at the thought of bed as I slinked my way
   up to my room.*
*I remember my red-hot rubber water bottle being of some solace
   in the winter gloom.*

*I remember ice between the sheets and an inferno at my feet as I
   tried to count those sheep.*
*I remember dreams of Lillie Langtry and Francesca Annis, and
   I'm smiling in my Linicro sleep.*

Monkstadt Shore

For the brave adventurer there is a spot on the shore way down
behind Monkstadt that has some very cool rocks to dive off into
the freezing Minch. There is also a cracking wee cove that I
could imagine smugglers of old using as a landing place for
their smuggled contraband. Bobby and I discovered it one
Sunday summer day during a mini heat-wave in 1977. The
weather was scorching and it being a Sunday we had nothing
better to do than to make our way to the shore. The Minch was
glass, calm and inviting. As the crow flies we ended up away
behind old man Hojan's house and walked over the rocky
shoreline near the Monkstadt fields. This is where we

discovered this rocky outcrop and I felt like we had discovered an unknown land!

Sweltering we sat on the rocks looking out to sea when Bobby stood up and peered over, eyes looking at the crystal clear almost green of the water and the pure white sand below. It was probably two metres deep and as it was such a calm day, there was not much movement in the water. I stood beside him and pushed him off the rocks. I still remember the splash as he hit the water feet first and headed to the sand below. Within a second or two he surfaced and that deceptively cold water pushed the air out of his lungs with a loud gasp! I was killing myself laughing but knew that my turn to hit the salt was coming soon. He swam to the rocks and climbed up, and rather than wait for the inevitable, I removed my top and shoes. Took a deep breath and dived off the rocks. I hit the water hard, and like my cousin before me, quickly surfaced with no breath left in my body. The cold water had stolen it all. I quickly grabbed on to the rocks and climbed up, shivering. The hard part done, I jumped off again, landing feet first into the water that was no warmer. Bobby joined me with a dive bomb, but both of us swam very little as it was totally effin freezing. We eventually climbed back up onto the sun-warmed rocks and let ourselves air dry. That was one of only a few times that I swam in the sea surrounding the island. I can still feel the coldness of that water.

Linicro Rain

When is it going to stop raining? I'm tired of being stuck in the house.
My Granny is snoring this weather so boring it's driving me to drinking the Grouse.

When is it going to stop raining? My Auntie won't let me watch TV.
And even if she did, the set is so old that the three channels play abnormally.
BBC 1 there's a picture but no sound. BBC 2 there is no sound but a picture and forget about ITV.

When is it going to stop raining? Outside the big hoose windows,
    it's pelting cats and dogs.
There's sheets of rain rolling down from the hill and the Minch
    has been swallowed by fog.

When is it going to stop raining? I've read and reread the week-
    old Sunday Post.
Oor Wullie and The Broons are bringing me down on strong
    sweet tea I've overdosed.

When is it going to stop raining? I did all my lines and homework.
The dogs are barking for the walkies they're wanting and the
    budgie is driving me berserk.

When is it going to stop raining? Daylight has turned into night-
    time.
If I don't get out and run about, I'm considering committing a
    crime.

When is it going to stop raining? I ask God as I lie in my bed.
I wait and I wait with cold sheets at my feet for an answer that
    remains unsaid.

When is it going to stop raining? The pittering patter of gallons of
    water hitting the roof rock me to sleep.
In my dreams I'm complaining because in them it's still raining
    and I'm stuck inside counting sheep.

When is it going to stop raining? In the morning, I wake with a
    start.
I jump out of bed, shaking off my sleepy head with this
    downpour I'm falling apart.

When is it going to stop raining?
It's stopped.
It's started.
It's started to stop. For a dry day I would give anything.

Skidding on the kitchen floor, I open the back door to reveal a
    blue sky in the process of birthing.
When is it going to stop raining?

Totescore Fank Fun

Totescore fank holds many fond memories for me. These two incidents may have happened on the same day. The Macinnes family were having their annual shearing fank on one of those days that was hot tempered with a cool breeze blowing its way up the hill from the Minch. A cloudless blue sky overhead made for a postcard moment.

My job was to wrestle the unshorn sheep from the concrete-walled pen to the hand off to either Duncan or Norman. My work partner was Archie, who easily possessed twice my strength in both his Totescore brawny arms. Anyone who has done this fank job knows how hard it is and that sheep are surprisingly strong.

You begin inside the hot smelly pen, choosing your prey carefully, then wrangling them out by almost sitting on the sheep. Once they are between your legs, you lift them by the horns, high enough so they are standing only with their two hind legs. You then struggle to manoeuvre them out of the pen gate. Hopefully, this can be done with no rogue sheep escaping behind you before the pen gate can be closed. You then guide them over to the shearer.

There I was inside the crowded pen looking for what I hoped would be an easily straddled four-legged woolly beast. My quarry chosen, I bent to grab its horns when suddenly another sheep jumped up at the exact time I was reaching down. A sheep's head butt straight to my right temple. Ouch! Stars and tweety birds in front of me, I was half out of it for about a minute, but I did not want to show weakness, and luckily nobody saw what happened. At this point, I should tell you that the troosers I wore that day had a small hole in the left cheek area at the rear. Again I went to grab a sheep when another ewe inserted her horn into that trooser hole! I went one way to grab my chosen victim and the blackface with its horn in my troosers went the other! Totally tore the arse out of my breeks! There I was handing over a sheep to Norman with my white butt cheeks in full view! The horn also

Totescore Fank, now

ripped partially through my y fronts! They remained semi intact, however, so that was ok!

Luckily Janet Macinnes was on hand with the large needle and string that they used to sew the fleece bags shut. Unluckily for me was that anyone who knows Totescore fank knows that it's close to the road and fank activity always attracts tourist with their Kodaks. So there I was, stretched over Janet's knees as she darned my ripped clothes. This produced much tourist laughter and camera clicks.

Funny that it was it was not the funniest moment of the day. Later, one tourist asked Archie, 'What's going on here?'

To which he replied, 'We are having a fank.'

Unsure of what he heard, he asked, shocked, 'You're having a what'?

Skyeku 16

Coal lumps frosted white

The old wooden hammer smash

Wee hoose smoke rises.

We laughed about that comment for many years. It still brings a smile to my face when I think about it today! Later on I had some serious bruising from the earlier sheep butting episode!

Tech Talk

I know the arguments made by today's parents (including me) that kids don't play outside enough and are glued to their electronic devices. I love my tech just like any kid (probably more) and I believe if today's tech had been available in the 1970s Linicro, I would have embraced it as I would a long-lost uncle. I know that it would not supplant my love for the outdoors, and I would have incorporated tech into my island adventures. Thankfully, there were no camera phones around when I was growing up, particularly when I would make a total idiot of myself at local dances.

Case in point being the two burns that cross the second Totescore road, in particular the first burn that runs past Stone Gate ruins, and specifically the concrete pipes that carry nature's lubricator through the road on its way to the Minch. I spent many happy Highland hours inside that 'tunnel' playing and sheltering from Skye's elements. If I had a cell phone, then I guarantee I would have been posting Facebook pictures of me peeing into the water and generally having some wholesome water fun!

This tunnel had a twin which you could find further down the road. This underground concrete structure was harder to get to, and the burn was way wider. The pipe/tunnel diameter was larger too. I would be there hiding from the sun or sheltering, legs akimbo, from the rain and no doubt updating my Totescore status on a regular Facebook basis! My symbiotic tech relationship could easily have worked in my Highland home. My adventures could have been Facebooked live or on YouTube for posterity! I could easily have been Tik Tok (ing) my way around Linicro and up the hill to the highest heights sharing my bird's eye view with my FB friends and family. Having internet access would not have dulled my outdoor enjoyment, in fact it would have doubled the fun.

All things in moderation apply to alcohol and tech. Imagine the photos I could have been posting should I have had a personal device back then? Some of them would be beautiful, most would be OK, and a few would be blackmail embarrassing (OK maybe more than a few)!

Get the kids out in the hills with their action cameras strapped to their noggins so that memories can be made and enjoyed with the amazingly affordable tech of today. And if it's really bucketing down, then get them editing inside and uploading to their YouTube channel for friends and family, far and near, to see and enjoy. Let them play their Xbox or PlayStation now and again without shouting too loudly at their finger exercising fun!

On the Hill

Norman Macinnes was a very hard-working guy. He seemed to work for everybody, and I rarely saw him in a foul mood. I'm not saying me and his younger brothers didn't drive him mad. We did, and occasionally he would appear angry, but it didn't last long. Often he would work for the Linicro Township, gathering the sheep for fanks, either dipping or shearing. He stopped at the wee hoose late one morning and asked me if I wanted to go to the hill with him as he was searching for Linicro sheep. I jumped at the chance to be with my big pal. It was a typical grey day but dry as we walked up Margaret's top field towards the common grazing. From there we would walk the peat road and head into the hill in search of four-legged woolly friends.

Far behind the rocks of Linicro there is a deceptively high hill area. You would think you had reached the top only to be greeted by further hilly heather and grass. As a young teen, it was a hard slog. I was familiar enough with this area but had never been this far behind the rocks. If it had been a clearer day, we could have seen the bealach road. We stopped for a rest. Norman, courtesy of his mother, had a knapsack with a thermos of tea and scones with cheese. He unscrewed the thermos lid which doubled as his cup and underneath he unscrewed the smaller plastic cup for me. So, there we were, sitting in the heather on the hill, drinking his mother's sweet tea, when Norman pointed out something (or someone in the far distance). I looked, and I could see a dark figure at the top of the hill. I asked Norman who it was. He said it was nobody. It was a cairn. I had never heard this word before, and I asked him what it meant. Norman told me someone built it to remember somebody who died on the hill after getting lost in terrible weather (he was pulling my leg, I think). I thought it looked very creepy, but I wanted to get a closer look at it. He said no as it was out of our way and he thought the sheep had moved to the other hill above Greaulin. I stared and stared at the cairn in the distance, and I could swear it was an old man wearing a hat and smoking a pipe. I was a wee bit scared. The more I looked at it, the more it seemed to move. A fine mist had descended above it and made it look even creepier! We moved on, sheep searching, and it relieved me to be out of the sight of that old man cairn. I dreamt about the creepy cairn that night. Not quite a nightmare, but slightly scary!

The following summer I decided that my Sunday adventure would be to find the cairn on the hill. I was older and not frightened, after all it was daylight blue. It took a while, but I made it and there in the distance was this grey form. I moved towards it, thinking I would see the hat and the pipe. I saw none of those as I reached it. All I found was a pile of rocks, stacked up to about my height. Not very frightening. They were probably used as a marker for people's sheep gathering throughout the years. I placed a stone on top to add to the 'hat' height and made my way back down the heather.

Camping Stove Nightmare

In the wee hoose my Aunt did most of the cooking on a two-ringed Calor Gas camping stove. This was situated near the worktable up against the wall. There was a hole in the wall for the hose and the gas canister which sat in my Aunt and Granny's bedroom. We also had a Baby Belling cooker that was in the corner near the window, but that did not seem to get used much. The current stove had seen better days and my Aunt had ordered a new one which had arrived. Bobby was tasked with fitting it and I was to help him. It was not a big job. Unhook the old one from the hose and reconnect the new one. It did not take too long. Once the job was done Bobby tried out both rings. With a struck match in one hand and the turning knob in the other, he leaned down to light it. As soon as the flame lit it burst upwards making a helluva racket. Bobby jumped back and I just about peed my pants! I got a real fright and thought the whole contraption was about to explode. I hid behind him, quaking in my wellies. He turned the gas off by going round into the bedroom and twisting the knob on top of the canister. Thank God it went off, and the noise stopped. I moved well away from it and Bobby inspected the stove and for the first time read the instructions in the box. It turns out that he had not fitted the regulator. He fixed it quickly and relit the flame, which burned as normal.

That night in my wee hoose bed I must have had a nightmare about it as I was shouting in my sleep saying, 'Turn it off'! I also got up and half sleep-walked down the stairs where Margaret, Bobby and Norman Macinnes were sitting chatting. They looked at me and wondered what the heck I was doing. I sleep-talked with them for a minute or two and then climbed back up the stairs to my bed and a no further nightmare sleep!

Ever since then I have always been nervous around gas stoves and cookers. I prefer an electric appliance for heating and for cooking!

Islands in My Dream

The islands of Gaeilovore are part of the view that greeted me every new day in Linicro. My one desire was to one day get up close and personal with them. The summer of 1977 promised that I might achieve this goal. The Martin family were from down south and had been regular visitors to Skye, staying in my Aunt Margaret's big hoose. The father was a diver, and this summer they brought a fast rubber-type boat with what looked like a rather large outboard at the non-pointy end of the black floaty thing! They asked me to join them on a ride starting from Camus Mor and ending somewhere near the islands. Wow! I was very excited as we drove to the slipway and even more excited as I put on my life jacket and, with other members of the Martin family, I climbed aboard!

I sat on the rim of the dinghy as the Martin father opened up the throttle and the front of the boat lifted and we bounced across the waves. Yikes! I was never so scared in all my young life! The sea was not even that rough. I held on to the side of that boat like an overgrown limpet! This was not going as planned. I could not show my fear as one of the Martin family was a pretty girl my age who was a lot more used to this mode of transport than I ever was! If only they would slow down, I thought, but they only went faster with everyone laughing except me! Those islands looked a lot closer from the shore, but the faster we went the further away they seemed. Were they moving? We would never reach them. We made it about halfway before we turned back and headed for shore. My landlubbing body was glad to get back on to the slipway and get as far away as possible from the rubber death bouncer! That was the first and last time I would attempt to get near those islands and I promised myself that the next time I went on the Minch I would either be on the MV Hebrides or on a gentle rowing boat not far from land!

The Rha

It might not have been the Nile or the Amazon, but Uig's River Rha was a Sunday explorer's dream! The brave adventurer could start their journey from beneath the bridge in Uig. Or if you were truly fit, you could start at the end by following the river from Uig's rocky shore where the Rha's fresh water meets the salt of Uig Bay. Beware you don't slip and end up bum in H2O. It happened to me more than twice!

On a summer Skye day underneath nature's canopy, you could make believe you were a million miles away in some foreign jungle minus the humidity ... and animals that could kill you. The land underfoot could be treacherous, so only the fierce need apply, but if you do, then the scenes you will discover will make you believe in magic. For me, the adventure would start by cycling along the road to the Quirang. Then it was off-road and on foot down to the river's hidden secrets. What a place of beauty and awe! There are many mini waterfalls to find that end in pools of dark peaty water. Fresh and cold await the hardy soul who fancies a swim. One had to be careful though as it could be treacherous and some of those dark pools of water were deep and iceberg cold. I knew my limitations and fancied myself a splendid swimmer, so was happy to make my way up through the meandering river that sliced through the hill above Uig. It could be tough going and you could be forgiven for thinking you were the only living boy in Uig!

The summer smells mixed with the water spray could clear all blocked noses and hours could be spent just enjoying your own private view of heaven on earth. Lagoon-like pools harboured fish, and who knows what lay beneath in the dark depths? Most of my adventures were on a Sunday and on my own but occasionally I would be accompanied by Bobby and later on I would take my girlfriend Karen on a love expedition.

Most people usually start their river view from the path in Uig and it is exquisite there, especially on a sunny summer day. The colours are radiantly green lit by light spikes piercing the leafy trees above. For me though, it was better to walk down from the Bealach road where you could find yourself some lovely wee spots to sit and daydream! Even in winter when the sky was grey and angry the water of the Rha took on a different hue and could mesmerize you into thinking it would be nice to take a winter dip! I could spend hours there on the holy day and each time that I would go I would find something new and cool to look at. Most of the time I was happy just to sit on the bank and watch the water run away from me as it raced to the sea. Occasionally I got caught in some winter showers and would try to find a natural shelter. The water's edge frothy and brown would not assist in this, and many times I just sat it out and waited for the heavens to close their watery eyes. If I got too muddy, it was OK. I could tell Margaret that I fell off my bike and anyway Sunday night was bath night!

Potato (Memory) Chips

When a city slicker leaves his family home in the smoke and ends up in the crofting community of Linicro, there is a fair amount of acclimatising to your new Highland life to be done. One of the biggest cultural differences for a young city teen is the fact that they boil the tatties with their skin on and you have to eat the skin (it's the best part of the potato says every adult ever)!

Also, the tubers or as I like to call them Solanum Tuberosum (I just Googled it) are not served on each individual's plate, rather they are unceremoniously plopped on to a Pyrex pie dish in the middle of the wee hoose's dining table. From there one can jab at the carbs with a fork and drop them onto your plate. For the longest time I would fiddle with the recently boiling food balls, trying my bestest (is that even a word?), not to burn my fingers as I clumsily removed the skin from each tattie! No amount of encouragement from my Aunt or Granny would make me try to taste the skin. I left them to be added to our hen's food. Rarely did a chipped potato grace our Linicro table. Perhaps once or twice in a year. As time marched on my inherent laziness kicked in and I ate potatoes and the skin which, as it turned out, was pretty tasty, especially with a wee bit of melted butter. There were times when your gnasher's crunched on some Skye soil, but as it had been boiled it was clean (wasn't it?).

My Aunt Margaret had two (maybe three) potato patches on her Linicro croft. The ones in the gardens of the big hoose were for tiny new potatoes and the ones on the lower croft, below the byre, were for feeding us three (four when cousin Bobby was at home), during the winter time. I freely admit to not being interested in anything garden related and would do my utmost not to be involved in any chores whatsoever, but digging the tatties was something different.

There was something earthy and naturally organic about having a garden fork in one hand and a plastic bucket in the other as we would march down to dig for potato treasure! I'm not saying that it was easy, or that I did most of the digging (that was usually Bobby or Margaret), but there was a feeling of satisfaction when your metal instrument pierced the soil around the plant. The pushing down with a welly booted foot, the tipping of the dirt to reveal the root made you feel at one with Mother Nature. Even though your back might be breaking, bending down and shaking the dirt from the plant to reveal a host of potato prizes. It was almost like a competition to see who could dig the plant with the most tatties attached. Who could find the biggest potato in the field, and whose bucket would be filled first? Sometimes I was lucky and would produce an enormous bunch of lovelies from the dirt, other times I would discover some squelchy rotten stuff that oozed like a wound, the smell of dead chips in each nostril!

These potatoes, once collected and dried, found their temporary home in the byre's loft, only to be picked at over the winter, ensuring our stomachs were full each night. My wife, who is Thai, more used to boiling rice, will search Saudi supermarkets to find fresh new potatoes for me. These she boils (in their skin) dabs on some butter and grinds black pepper to feed my Scottish stomach at least once a month if not more! Yum!

Primrose Yellow

Another task that was assigned to my young self by my Aunt Margaret, was the annual painting of the big hoose windows, drain-pipes and guttering! The Trinity of total boringness for a teenager in the Linicro summer months (when the sun would shine).

For many years DIY was something that held as much interest to me as watching drain-pipe paint dry, but now the thought of it is very attractive (I even like going to the Saudi version of B&Q). The teenage me was given a bristle-losing brush and a can of primrose yellow paint by my Great Aunt and told to get on with it and stop complaining! Old big hoose photographs show the previous colour, which looks like a sky blue or is light green? I have a colour deficiency, not diagnosed until adult life, so perhaps it was not even primrose yellow paint?

No, I remember it said it on the tin! Anyway, there was never any pre-paint preparation like washing off the previous year's collected Highland dirt from the cast iron water collecting receptacles. Nor was there any prepping or sanding of the window frames' wood. I just splashed that yellow stuff on raw, and generous I was too! The guttering and the pipes were easy enough apart from the precariousness of my ladder perching. I had no one to ensure my safety by gripping the base of the wooden and metal steps. Man, I coated that paint on very thickly and none too smoothly! It gave a very rustic appearance to the old cast iron (or so I thought).

The windows though were a different matter altogether. One had to be very careful not to leave the yellow stuff on the windowpane and to ensure that it was evenly applied in a semi-professional manner. Not easy, as I was not particularly delicate with my touch. It did not help that these wooden windows were probably the original ones installed during the birth of the big hoose.

The Skye weather had taken its toll on the wood and rot had taken hold in a fair few places. I would generously apply putty. Then, once it had hardened, I would paint over it. To be honest, some if not all of window frames were probably more putty than wood! For the streaks of yellow that I inadvertently applied to the glass, I used a turpentine rag to clean as best I could and hoped not to be overcome by paint and turps fumes! The entire job could take days in my unskilled hands and if the weather changed, days could turn into weeks!!

With my wee mono cassette deck blasting Pink Floyd's 'Animals', I would sing-along with Messrs Waters and Gilmour till the paint pot ran dry! Finally, I would be done and could stand on the lawn admiring my handy work; glad knowing that I would not have to repeat this mind-numbing task for another year. Then I would do my best to hide from Margaret, lest she would have another boring chore for me to do!

Sitting in my office today in the desert sands of Saudi Arabia, I would welcome, with arms wide open, a chance to be in the fresh Linicro air, paint brush in hand, with (hopefully) the sun on my shoulders! To feel the wind cooled by the Minch. To gaze over to the outer isles from my high ladder vantage point would be a desert dream come true, and I promise I will be very careful this time and not get any paint on the big hoose's glass panes! Honest!

Praise Be

These days as an adult I do my best to show my appreciation to people and to congratulate them on a job well done. Big and small. Whether it's my staff, my co-workers, or my family. In particular, with my kids. No matter what they have done, I make sure that I always praise their efforts. I think it's incredibly important for their self-confidence. At my work I have seen the effect of saying 'good job' or 'excellent work' and the results of a myriad of surveys on staff satisfaction undertaken by my employer frequently show that praise is more important than money (this surprised me). A quick internet search will reveal this to be true across the globe.

I'm living proof of the negative effect that lack of recognition can have on young folk. My Aunt Margaret was hard to please. Let me rephrase that by saying I could never please my Aunt Margaret. No matter what I did. Or how hard I worked. I have no memory of her ever showing me any appreciation for any job I did around the croft. In those first few years of living in Linicro, I tried. I really did. One weekend we had been delivered a load of firewood which had to be sawn into fireplace-sized pieces. This day I was determined to get some praise for doing a good job and working hard. All day I placed each long piece on a trestle and cut them into smaller pieces with a rusty blade saw. It was hard. My hands and shoulder were killing me by the end, but I wanted her to be proud of the enormous pile of wood I cut. Not one word from her mouth. There was another time I had to dig up the garden just inside the big hoose gate to prepare for her planting. The earth was dry and hard. My spade was as blunt as a blunt butter knife. Weeds were as tough as barbed wire. It was back-breaking, forehead-sweat-producing work. All day I toiled. Not one word again. I didn't crave much, just a wee show of appreciation. It was possible she would always tell me how good a worker Bobby was. She would also tell me how hard my pals Duncan and Archie worked on their croft. The closest I got was one hot summer hay day. I raked, and I raked. The palms of my hands had blisters from the rake's handle. We worked all day into the warm evening when she said 'we have done enough hard work for today, time to rest'. That was it. Ultimately, I don't blame my Aunt. She didn't know any better. You could say it's a typical Scottish thing. It's easier for us to praise strangers than it is to say thank you to those closest to us. I understand that but when you're young, you just need a wee thank you now and then. How hard is it to say well done to a teenager? It never happened, and the consequences of it were that I gave up trying to please her. The less encouragement I got, the less I wanted to do. I know you might think that's just a cop out, but that's how I felt.

Skyeku 17
Love it must be love
Lifelong strong and life enduring
Linicro love it is.

I truly believe it had an influence on my self-confidence as I grew into adulthood. And in some sad way probably still affects me to this day, even when I receive words of praise and thank you. I find it hard to accept and truth be told hard to believe that something I have done is worthy of such stuff. What it has taught me though is that I won't be like that with my three kids. I'm not like that, even with my wife. I do my utmost to say positive things. With me, I hope that negative circle is broken.

My Pal David Brown

I want to talk a wee about the Macinnes's tractor. Everyone knows that I wear my love for David Brown tractors on my sleeve like a high school letter. I think it was a 996, but I can't say for definite. It was red with some yellow. It had a white-roofed cab and ever since I can remember it lived in its own wee shed at 5 Totescore. As a young kid Norman would let me steer it, and as a teenager I got to drive it (occasionally). This four-wheeled dream machine was always used to cut my Aunt Margaret's hay, and it powered all the Totescore machines like the baler and the swath turner. It's hard to convey the excitement I felt when I knew Norman was coming to cut the hay and I would be there with him. It really was very special.

The tractor though was nearly the death of me as we were driving past the Hunter house going to Kilmuir. Norman was driving and Duncan and I were standing at the back. We had the trailer hitched. Although not travelling that fast Norman opened the throttle and we were going flat out. We hit a pothole

Bobby and Me,
Linicro 1978

on the road and I lost my footing. In slow motion, it seemed, I fell. Luckily, I did not end up on the road being run over by the trailer. Duncan grabbed me by my jumper and pulled me back up to safety!

The David Brown lived in a very compact shelter on the road down to the family house. I always wanted to park it, which required reversing it in, but they never allowed me. Probably a wise decision, as I no doubt would have hit one of the walls.

I liked other tractors too. The old bluey grey Fergusons I love and I liked the Gillies's red Massey Ferguson. Later on, Norman bought a bigger Fordson Major, which I didn't like much. I often wonder what became of the David Brown? Is it rusting in some field? Has it been scrapped? If I ever win the lottery I'm buying a David Brown 996 and sending it to my house in the Thailand countryside. Definitely!

Tractor Pal

How long ago was the day we first met?
Me, easily lifted by Skye strong arms into your faithful trailer pal.
I held on to the weathered wood sides as you bumped us up your
    family's road.
Red, white and dirty yellow.

Diesel fumed perfume.
Small in stature, I took your steering wheel.
Strong Skye legs controlled your metal clutch and brakes, not mine.
My excitement when I knew you would come to cut the hay.
Waiting impatiently for the roar of your voice as you rounded
    Miss Morton's.
Your pilot big, burly and with an unshaven smile.
At last, outside our half door, you sat.
I shoed my Glasgow feet.
Gazelle like I jumped on to the metal mower.
Vice grips.
Underneath the heat of your plastic white hat, I blethered to big
    Norman.
A saint in plaid, he listened always.
To the hay boy. To the hay.
I had a job to do, and I followed you.
Your razor teeth gnashing green.
If you got too greedy, my tiny hands unstuffed your mouth.
Oil and cut grass infused the Linicro air.
Three pals laugh.
Dead thistles take revenge as they exhale their last breath.
Afternoon hot and sweaty.
A faint breeze from the Minch hints of salt.
Metal gears grinding their croft song.
Sweet sounding to my ears.
As teatime beckons we finish the last patch of the standing grass.
I brush your green teeth clean, and we head for tatties boiled in
    their skin.
For me, our parting is such sad, sweet sorrow.
You wave goodbye now on your way home to bed.
Too tired to talk I fall asleep half dressed, dreams of Totescore
    baling in red.
Where at last my body, big enough to control you by myself.
Throttled loud in second gear, petrified to push you faster.
Where are you now I wonder?
Are you alive or are you dead?
Is your colour still red or has nature taken its toll?
For years there has been no other tractor for me, no matter how
    shiny and big.
In my soul you live forever, and in my heart you will always be.

An Buth Bheag

I would have been a third-year pupil in 1978 and every lunchtime my penniless self and Ali Aitken would head into town to hang around and try our best to chat up (usually 4th or 5th year) girls! When our patter inevitably failed, we would wander in zombie fashion up and down Wentworth Street, killing time before afternoon lessons.

The Buth Bheag was a cute olde worlde shoppe that we would grace with our cashless presence. I remember the lady behind the sweetie counter (but not her name) being tall, immaculately dressed with black bobbed hair. She had the patience of a saint to put up with the influx of PHS sweetie gobblers, and we tried to test that patience with every visit.

She was always very pleasant to Ali and me, and she quickly realised that our regular visits would never make her rich! I can honestly say (to my shame) I don't remember ever buying anything there, certainly not during our school lunch break. The shop contained a world of candies and the shelves were laden with jarred sugar treats. We would often use the 'try before you buy' ploy that failed on nearly every 'try'! There were, however, a few successful attempts when she would open a jar of her choice and give us a sample taster. I think she was bored and glad of some company and our reward was a dental-caries-causing morsel.

As time advanced and fourth year came around our 'brass neck' softened so our visits became more infrequent! I will not forget the black and white checked clothes wearing lady and her sweet acts of sweetie kindness shown to two pains-in-the-butt teenagers! Thank you kindly.

MacRumours

If there had been a government music collection census taken on Skye in 1978, I think Fleetwood Mac's Rumours would have been found to live in most Skye folks' homes. Since its release in early 77, this musical treasure trove quickly made its way across the Atlantic, jumped over the Outer Isles, hitched a lift across the Minch on the Heb and slowly crept up the shore secreting itself into every household across the misty isle. All accept one. Yep, you guessed it. 1 Linicro was Rumour-less and the only music that played was Pink Floyd and Boston courtesy of DJ Bobby, and the Sunday Gaelic Service courtesy of DJ Aunt Margaret and her mono speaker'd Philips transistor radio.

My ears would be a stranger to this magnum opus until well into 1978 when I was given a home-made copy by every Portree High guy-of-a-certain-age dream girl (friend) Janette Ross. Wow! Lucky me! Major crush was in effect, so when the music tracks of Messrs Mac et al. played on my tiny tinny solid-state cassette deck all the songs of love and loss pulled at my still maturing heart strings. As time does, its passing brought other crushes and songs like 'Never Going Back Again', 'Oh Daddy', 'Second-hand News' and my personal fave 'Songbird' could be utilized in affection showing without ever having to say anything affectionate. Such is being an emotionally stunted Scottish guy.

The beauty of music is that you can wrap yourself up in a 3-minute fantasy along with the girl of your dreams whilst getting the cow into the byre for milking. Rumours remains a firm favourite of mine, especially knowing the backstory to the album's creation. When a group of talented musicians, arguing and falling out with each other amid cocaine madness still produced songs that sound like God's love in human form.

Love lost. Love found. Love lost again was the soundtrack to my adventures in the maelstrom of emotions known as my (future) love life!

If you have not listened to it in a while get it out, blow off the dust and blast it on your music reproducing device of choice! Get daydreaming again, if only for the length of your favourite track!

Personal Hygiene

Those of us of a certain age might still (in the back of their mind) consider Sunday night 'bath night'. I know I do! When I told my wife that we only had a bath once a week as kids she was shocked. Thai kids have to shower twice a day (granted, their weather is a wee bit different from ours)! You might remember that during the tourist season I lived in a hoose (wee), which had no running water! During winter at least I had the luxury of a full body bath courtesy of the big hoose and the 50p electric meter.

With the changes happening in my youthful body (puberty) personal hygiene became a real obsession. I had never noticed perspiration before, but a few months into attending PHS I became aware about the potential for wet underarms (mine) and that it may give off an unpleasant odour. What was happening to me? This had never been a problem before. My cousin Bobby advised deodorant to help combat this wet enemy. I can still remember that first anti-perspiration purchase. One bottle of Sure deodorant from the Uig bakery/shop, which was green, and the label said it was forest fresh. This became a crucial part of my morning ablution schedule in the wee hoose.

With a plastic basin of water and some lifebuoy soap I would attack my face, neck, behind the ears and now my hairless underarms! Once complete I would bare-chestedly take the basin outside and throw the contaminated water in the ditch near the hoose. Then something else changed? Once my childish hair could look clean for a week, but now this was not the case. After a day or so, I noticed that it appeared oily. This look I equated with greasy teens and to use a Glasgow term I became 'pure paranoid' about my oily hair! It was now apparent my teenage body was rebelling against me as I cultivated my first pimple. Unfortunately for me this teenage rite of passage was growing at the end of my nose and it was not small.

I ended up looking like a large red boil that had a skinny white body growing out of it. This was a nightmare time because I wanted to appear handsome for the zero number of girls who would eye me up at school!

To add insult to injury, my cousin Bobby informed me I was also cultivating a patch of blackheads on my nose. What the hell? This was growing up? Spots, sweat and greasy hair? I needed a plan of action!

Washing my hair more than once a week was tricky as I was very sensitive to cold water and my frugal Aunt would not let me boil a full kettle for hair hygiene purposes. She would often say wait till Sunday! Then I was told of this mystical product called dry shampoo. I quickly purchased it from the Portree chemist and this promised to vanish the oily look without the aid of water!

All it was, was a fine talcum like powder in a blue plastic squeeze bottle that you applied to the worst affected oily hair area. I soon used up that small dry shampoo bottle but using my critical thinking skills I found that Avon 'Lily of the Valley', old ladies' talcum did the same job. It just smelled stronger! This powder was more coarse, so you applied it sparingly and then massaged it gently into the grease-filled hair. You had to make sure you did not apply too much as it would make you look prematurely grey-haired and smell like yer granny!

For fighting the onslaught of the blackhead army, my defence was medicated face wipes. Again, purchased from Portree chemist! Man, this personal hygiene business was painful on the pocket! These wipes were used sparingly to make one wipe last a whole school week!

As third year at Portree High progressed, I was lucky in that I did not develop the teenage curse of acne and I was only occasionally visited by the zit monster. The hair was an ongoing challenge as I rifled through any and every bottle of talcum I could find at 1 Linicro. Keeping my hair short and an anti-dandruff/anti-oily hair shampoo helped keep the greasy terror at bay. Round about the end of third year a new product name had entered my personal hygiene lexicon. This was Denim for men! The TV advert clearly stated that 'the more you put on, the more that is likely to come off'. Meaning your clothes, and by the hand of a lady (they lied)! Denim deodorant was quickly added to my arsenal of grooming products where it remained for many years until I replaced it by smell-free anti-perspiration spray and CK One.

It was a challenge maintaining one's grooming habits in the early Linicro years and often, necessity was the mother of invention, but ultimately it was to no avail as I had little success with members of the opposite sex and was always financially unstable because of the ongoing cost of my hygiene armaments.

Bath

Sunday night was bath night, in my big hoose home.
And if I was lucky, my aunt fed the meter before she left me
    alone.

If I was not the immersion heater would only produce a half bath.
My Aunt all Sunday smart on her bike to church was probably
    having a laugh.

Lucky for me occasionally, I had a spare fifty pence piece.
With the water tank full of lovely hot water, just add soap to
    remove the grease.

With the white vitreous China all full of hot soapy bubbles.
I would grab the radio, turn on the top twenty, and soak away
    my Linicro troubles.

Vosene applied to my head and shoulders, I scrubbed the week's
    grime away.
With the bar heater radiating the bathroom, the lather keeping
    the dandruff at bay.

What a life it was to be stretched out in the tub, with nobody there
    to complain.
On the corner by the taps, the radio full blast, my week's worries
    soaped down the drain.

By seven o'clock I was all clean and shiny, eating my scone and
    Orkney cheese.
The black and white portable was plugged in and ready to
    watch The Saint on STV.

The rest of the week I had to make do with the sink, filled with
    freezing cold water.
Washed my hair and my face, not forgetting my nethers, a poor
    part-time bather.

I then had to wait for Sunday again to enjoy my Skye spa treat.
But for now I was clean, from my top to my tail, and made do
    with my smelly feet.

That's Entertainment

It was not all daily adventures in the 1970s Linicro. Lots of
times it could be mind-numbingly boring with very little to do.
Especially in the dark of a winter's long night. Our in-house
entertainment was limited to the frugal use of a 14-inch black
and white portable TV. When we were in the big hoose I was
allowed to watch it for a few hours at night. To get a semi-
decent picture, you had to prop up the TV on a small stool on
top of the living room table near the window. Then you had to
twist the circle-shaped aerial in the general direction of
Stornoway. For this you were rewarded with two snowy
channels in the shape of BBC 1 and STV. Top of the Pops was
the most anticipated show of the week. Thursday nights around
7.30 the TV had to be on and tuned to BBC1.

When the opportunity arose for outside entertainment, we
would jump at it. There was not much mind you, but
occasionally we got a surprise. 'The Hell Drivers' was an
American car stunt show that eventually made its way to Skye.
It was held at Broadford airstrip and Norman Macinnes had got

us all tickets! Duncan, Archie and I were overly excited to go as we hopped in Norman's blue Austin 1100. The long drive to Broadford ended at the airstrip. It was evening, and the weather was not too bad. It was dull and overcast, but it did not rain. I won't say that it was the best car stunt show in the world, but it was better than staying in the house with my Aunt Margaret. The stunt that sticks with me today was when two cars drove only on two wheels and a guy got out and stood on the outside of the door. Occasionally it looked that the car would tumble on its side, but it never did. There was also some driving at speed off ramps and smashing into parked cars. This was reasonably exciting! All in all we had a superb night and I believe we got a bag of chips in Portree as we made our way home!

One evening, courtesy of Norman again, he took us to the Cuillin Hills Hotel in Portree as they were showing the horror movie The Omen. We were super excited as I was 16 years old and this movie was rated X! I think they showed it in their function room and I must admit it was cool seeing this on a relatively big screen. It's a classic 70s horror flick, well worth watching.

Lastly, I remember going to see a wrestling match which was held in some big shed in Dunvegan. All of us boys were fans of ITV's Saturday wrestling on World of Sport. Suffice it to say we were keen to see two guys or more fighting within a canvas floored ring with a real referee! The fighters were hardly Big Daddy, Giant Haystacks, or Mick McManus! In fact, we had not heard of any of them. Still, it was better than nothing and we did our best to enjoy. The standout moment for me was when one of the wrestlers had an argument with the referee and both of them fought! It was all staged, but we laughed anyway!

Singing in Kilmuir

'You want to go to a singing class?' It was the winter of 1978, and this question was being asked by Archie Macinnes. At first I was not too keen as he said we would be singing hymns, but that they provided cake and chocolate biscuits! My sweet-toothed answer was 'Yes'! Anyway, the choice was this singing class or another night in with my old Aunt Margaret! To the singing class, then! They held it in one classroom of Kilmuir School. We got chauffeured by the ever-reliable Norman in his Austin 1300. Arriving at our destination in the Kilmuir dark, the welcome warm lights of the school's classroom were inviting. In we went, and there were a lot of familiar faces. Mostly familiar old faces!

Having loosely followed the Roman Catholic religion until I left Glasgow, I was not a hymn expert. What did I know about psalms and the singing of them? As I looked at Archie, I realised that this could be an opportunity to get up to some of our favourite thing: mischief!

A gracious lady who looked at us young ones with a knowing glint in her Kilmuir eyes led the class. She knew we were on the lookout for fun and the half-time tea and assorted home-made baked goods. Sitting down the back of the class with the younger folk, we opened our hymn book as directed and the room burst into heavenly song! Morag MacLeod's Dad Norman Gillies was giving it laldy and wow the Bodach could sing! We did our best to join in. Half-time came, and it was eats galore and some fun wandering about the school in the semi-darkness!

This class became a regular outing for us and not because we were angels, more that we were always starving and hungry for a carry on. We could make requests for particular songs and as we had recently found out that Boney M's 'Rivers of Babylon' was based on a psalm, we always asked for it but were always refused. No luck!

One thing I used to do to amuse myself was to deliberately sing flat. This I did covertly, so it was not immediately obvious who the flat culprit was. What a rebel, eh? Still, it was fun and I'm glad I had the opportunity to be around the older generation who could be strict but had a sense of fun about them too!

Uncle Peter and His Wing Mirrors

My Uncle Peter was originally from Earlish in Uig. His family name is Nicholson and his family were known locally as 'the Fiddlers' as in 'Peter Fiddler'. I assume it was because some family members played that musical instrument but my memory of him is that he could play the accordion. He and my Aunt Annie retired to Linicro in the late 1990s. Over the years he had many cars, all of which hold special memories for me now that he has passed on. My very first memories of travelling to Skye were in the back seat of this Wolseley that he owned, probably in the late 60s early 70s. I'm sure it was a light green colour but would not swear on it. I must have been small, as I believe there were four of us in the back seat. My two cousins, Flora and Bobby, with me and my sister Angela.

The journey to Skye for us backseat drivers was impossibly long, only made bearable by us having sing songs on the road all the way to the wee hoose. The only song I can remember singing is the chorus to Aquarius (this is the dawning of the age of).

I also possess a vague memory of the ferry crossing, but that is about it. However, when I see a photo of a Wolseley (I don't know which model he had back then) or glimpse one in an old movie, I think about that back seat and the tune of Aquarius plays in my head!

During my time living with my Great Aunt and Great Granny, Uncle Peter and my Aunt Annie were regular visitors to Linicro.

Uncle Peter, Margaret, Granny, Flora, Bobby and Angela, Linicro

Peter was then driving a red Hillman Avenger which was hardly a muscle car, but I had fond feelings towards that motor and still do. Many a trip to Uig/Earlish to see his family was made in the back seat of that beast and, when it was parked outside their Linicro caravan, I would spend ages sitting in the front seat practising gear changes and pretending I was a villainous getaway driver! My cousin Bobby took ownership of the Avenger and tried to spruce up the appearance a wee bit to make it look sportier. Peter's next car was my favourite, and it was the classic Ford Capri, two-tone beige type colour. I thought it was very cool, and he used to joke that once he got his wing mirrors fitted, it would be a real babe magnet!

I have only seen him and Annie sporadically over the years, but have always appreciated his sense of humour and the fact that he liked to make fun of me! One of my old pals from Galloway Street worked with my Uncle (he called him 'wee Nichie') in Glasgow and he would often say what a great laugh he was to work with. The last time I spoke to him was when my mother was visiting Skye a few years ago and I said hello to him via Face-Time. Peter was always good to me and made me laugh, and I hope that he has a flash car and his wing mirrors in the hereafter.

Boston Boston

One reason I have eventually gotten round to writing some of my teenage memories was to acknowledge people, places and music that had a positive effect on my teenage life. One of the first albums that had a musical effect on me was Boston's debut. It was such an important album for me. Released in 1976, I had a vague memory of hearing 'More Than A Feeling' a few times when I was in Glasgow but as it only reached number 22 in the charts that year and it quickly disappeared it was not in my mind long!

When I arrived on Skye for my summer holidays in 1977 this album (in cassette form) was in my cousin Bobby's collection. Desperate for some sing-along sounds that I recognized I would

Skyeku 18

Misted eyes water falls

Dreams of days gone by sustain

Skye love last forever

play 'More than a feeling' regularly. Slowly, slowly the album's other songs hooked me in and it did not take long before I loved all the songs like a brother and knew all the words. 'Hitch A ride', 'Foreplay/Longtime' and 'Rock n Roll Band' were all faves of mine (still are). I know that many people will label this album AOR (Adult Orientated Rock), and the perception of it may have been that it was outdated given that they released it in 1976, the year of Punk Rock in the UK. No doubt about it, Boston were exactly the type of band that Punk was rebelling against but a great album is a great album no matter what music fad is going on. To me, this album stood out not only because of the songs but also the production. The sound of the album is cool, and the guitar soundscape in particular is amazing. It took years to complete and if you want some 'punk', read the story about the band stealing the master tapes from the record company!

Seamus Cameron

Having previously mentioned this old guy from Staffin who was the Linicro township shepherd, it reminded me of a time Norman Macinnes took me to the Cameron croft with the promise of making some cash. I only knew the Bodach from fank-related activities and was a wee bit scared of him because he was not always in the best of moods. He rarely spoke to me and most times he was speaking to the other fankers or is it fankees (?) in Gaelic.

He lived in Staffin, and aboard the Macinnes David Brown tractor Norman and I set forth. On arrival I was not surprised to find that he lived with his sister (he had never married). She was friendly as I recall and looked as hardy as him. Prototypically pinnie-wearing with ruddy red cheeks, rough hands, one of which she extended to me to shake and nearly broke all my fingers! She went off to the house and Norman and I were left with the cantankerous old Cameron. Norman was to do some ploughing with his tractor, and I was to do some harrowing with Cameron's old Fordson Dexta. The field for me was square and relatively flat. Near one corner it had a slight incline. Graveyard-mouthed, semi-toothless Seamus asked if he could trust me with his tractor? I said yes! I think he smiled, but it was hard to tell. As I looked at him I wondered what had happened to his nose. Had somebody punched him years ago to make it so crooked?

The Dexta had seen better years. It was faded blue with a fair amount of red rust and it had a white plastic roof. It was around about the same size as the David Brown. Norman showed me how to start it and how to get it in gear (I would not go above 2nd gear). We drove to my field and Norman instructed me in the art of harrowing. Basically, I just went round and round the field making sure the harrow at the back of the Dexta harrowed all the soil. Easy. It felt good to be trusted to do an adult job. I harrowed the hell out of that field, driving slowly and carefully. It was an overcast day, thankfully rain free. I was as happy as a happy lark. After about my third round of harrowing, I noticed that there was a strange sound coming from the tractor. It eventually spluttered to a stop and would not start. Both Norman and old man Cameron came to the field to inspect the vehicle and tried to restart it. Seamus accused me of breaking his tractor! I'm not sure if he was joking or not? Norman decided that it was a 'bubble in the gasket'. I had no clue what that meant but knew that I did not do it. Looking at my work, they both decided that it was fine, and I had harrowed the field enough. I went to sit with Norman as he finished his work, and then both of us went to the house for a wee cup of tea. Strong and sweet with the obligatory scone with butter and jam. Yum!

Time was up and we got ready to make our way home. Old Seamus came out with a wry look on his weather-worn face. He handed Norman something I assume was money. And then he turned to me. He said, 'Even though you put a bubble in my gasket you did a good job'. Well, at least I think that's what he said – he was difficult to understand when he spoke English. He stretched his calloused hand over to me, which revealed a fiver. I took it with a smile and said 'Thank you.' I was rich, and all the way home I talked in Norman's ear about nothing of consequence. As usual, he just nodded.

∽

Creepy Castle Capers

It's hard not to be in awe of the eerie remains of Duntulm Castle. Situated besides one of my (all time) favourite areas, Score Bay. I could easily imagine this building taking pride of place in one of Westeros's bleaker kingdoms. Perhaps beyond the wall and the seat of the Night King himself?

I remember as a young child, along with my sister and cousins, visiting the dilapidated structure for the first time. Back then health and safety was an afterthought, and we youngsters roamed freely around the 700-year-old former clan house. We

Duntulm Castle

were not as interested in the building per se; we were more excited about the ghosts that were rumoured to roam at night when darkness fell.

We were told of the clansmen who was imprisoned in the dungeon, starved until mad with hunger, he practised some autosarcophagy by chewing on his own appendages!

As kids we could go down into the lower floor to what we were told was that very dungeon and (perhaps the same story) we heard about a prisoner who was fed only salted meat. No water passed his lips. He died a horrible dehydrated death, using the salted meat bones trying to dig his way through the thick dungeon walls. We were shown the marks on a wall, made by his dry bone! We loved the scares!

Perhaps the story that touched us the most was the nursemaid, who for some insane reason cradled a clan baby on the edge of the window that had the steepest drop to the rocks and salty sea below! She dropped said wean, and her enraged boss set her adrift on a small boat into the Minch never to be seen again. Wow! Super scary! These ghosts continue to haunt the Castle along with a few more, I'm sure. As a teen, I ventured to the creepy castle at night. The only sounds were the Atlantic wind in my ear and the Minch waves crashing on the deadly rocks below. Peter Ridley was in tow with me and I thought with his spiky hair and pointy shoes, should we meet a spirit they would be more scared of him! No ghost was harmed during our night visit!

A New World (Record)

1976 might have been the year of the Sex Pistols and when punk rock took over the airwaves. It was also the year that ELO released 'A New World Record'. This collection of cracking tunes is one of my all-time favourite albums. From late 1976 in Glasgow to 1977 in Linicro, songs from this album made their way into my eardrums. 'Living Thing' and 'Telephone Line' made it on to TOTP, not forgetting 'Rockaria' with its opera singer beginning. Although I don't remember it at the time of its release, 'Do Ya' is an effin brilliant rock song, begging for a metal cover version (I'm sure there are a few out there)! I did not get to hear the album in its entirety until my bestie from Glendale, Mr Ali Aitken, made me a cassette copy. This album is truly an 'all killer, no filler' album. I even got some tracks played on the school bus! If John the bus was in a good mood and I had not annoyed him, he would play some of my tapes. I remember hearing the opening of 'So Fine' through the bus's speaker's and thinking Wow! 'Telephone Line' is one of my all-time fave love songs and 'Shangri La' is a totally top tune! Jeff Lynne to me has a timeless voice, and that guy has written some absolutely classic songs. A New World Record to me sounds timeless and I continue to play this album now and still enjoy every single song.

Let's Get Physical
(Education)

'If you don't stop your talking, I will send you back to Barlinnie.' This phrase was said more than once from the ageing gentleman in the green and white trackie top. The gentleman in question was the 'Bopper' the location was Portree High's gymnasium. With his stern face and kind heart, it was a running joke with him and me during my first year at PHS. As soon as he met me and heard my high-pitched (pre -voice-breaking) Glasgow accent, he joked that I had been sent from Barlinnie prison.

Love it or hate it, P.E. was part of your weekly Portree High School life. Luckily, I loved it, even though I was a sub-par sporting student. My introduction to the class was from the aforementioned Bopper who, to my young eyes, looked anything but a P.E. Teacher. Along with D.F. Macdonald (and I say this with respect and love) they were an odd couple. The Laurel and Hardy (or Little and Large) of Island physical education. Did the Bopper ever look young?

Sitting smoking in their office was a sign of how things were back in the 70s. Did he ever wear anything other than that green trackie top? What a character he was with a wonderful sense of Highland humour tinged with a wee bit of pit bull aggression!

D.F. on the other hand looked more like what a P.E. Teacher is supposed to look like. His blue and white Adidas tracksuit finished by his Adidas Samba trainers. He might have been slight of size, but he was wiry, strong and fast. He was a thoroughly decent guy, who also had a pleasant sense of humour but could be tough when he needed to be.

I remember one time in the games hall I nearly got into a fight with a classmate, when D.F. in a flash was on me. I recall vividly that I was so mad, and he had my two thumbs in a vice like grip from which there was no escape until my anger had subsided.

After which he did not discipline me, just told me to calm my emotions.

From basketball in the gymnasium to unihoc in the games hall, D.F. was an ever constant during my time at PHS with the Bopper always around in the background. Usually having a cigarette!

My memory tells me we had P.E. twice a week (double periods). And on our way there we hoped we would either be playing basketball or five-a-side! I also liked to play unihoc but was a hopeless teammate! During the cold, damp and occasionally frosty winter Skye days they would force us to do cross-country, which meant running up the hill behind the school. These races were always (and I mean always) won by Donnie Nicholson! He was strong, fast, and left most of us far behind.

There was one activity, to a man, we all hated. This would be weeks before the school Christmas dance? Yep, practising country dancing underneath the harsh games hall lights. We would be joined by our year's girls P.E. class and forced to embarrassingly 'Strip the Willow' or 'Dashing White Sergeant'. This event had the potential to be crushingly embarrassing. Especially if you fancied some girls (which I did)! Also, your mistakes in the half dark of the Gathering Hall could easily be hidden, but if you fell on yer arse in the games hall, scores of laughing eyes would scan you as you picked yourself up from the floor. The positive side to this dancing was that you got to dance with girls in their P.E. wear. No amount of practising could improve my country dance moves as I awkwardly pranced about, out of time with my pale skinny frame.

So here is to our two lovely Phys Ed teachers and to the couple of lady teachers who joined them (names wiped from my memory bank).

Thank you for teaching us and putting up with our immature and annoying behaviour (mostly mine) I had fun from 2nd year to 6th year and I only sustained one sporting injury (fractured thumb in 4th year). You will both remain in my mind and heart for the fun, kindness and the occasional shouting at that I received as one of your pupils in the late 70s and early 80s.

Brand loyalty is a potent lifelong attachment that we place on material things. And though I would love to tell you I place no importance on clothing labels and the superficiality of one brand above others, etc. I would be lying through my (not as white as they used to be) teeth. I'm a slave to the brands. I buy (overpriced) Fred Perry shirts and own only one pair of store-branded trousers! In particular, I love trainers and Adidas is my brand (although I have Gola and Puma too). When I arrived in Linicro for what was only meant to be a school holiday in the summer of 1977 I had precisely two sets of footwear. A pair of black brogues (they were fashionable once) and a pair of white and blue (striped) Winfield (Woolies own brand) trainers. Trainers like these were cheap and on my Glasgow street were known as 'Adidas Nae Stripes' or 'Adidas Extra Stripes'! For my Skye holiday, the Winfields were fine as nobody in Linicro cared (rightly so), about what brand of trainers you wore. Going to PHS and attending P.E. was a completely different kettle of herring! Though nobody noticed or made fun of my footwear, I was incredibly self-conscious of my cheap sneakers. I longed for three-striped German shoes, but my empty pockets would permit financing nothing fancy. I longingly gazed at our P.E. teacher, D.F. Macdonald's Adidas Samba, knowing that at £21.99 they would never adorn my Linicro feet.

Third year came around and I able to persuade my folks to spend £7.99 on an entry level pair of Adidas shoes that were known as Kick. These definitely were a few steps higher in the foot fashion ladder than my Winfields, but my heart and eyes craved more. By 4th year I had upgraded to Adidas Bamba at around £12.99 and was happy that I could show off these black and white beauties to people who didn't care!

Fifth year was when I had summer job money (thanks to Uig Hotel) and I splashed out on Adidas Campus for street wear and the trainer holy grail that was Adidas Samba displayed proudly on my plates of meat. Yaas! Again, nobody noticed or cared! To this day my wife complains about my trainer collection and that I have more shoes than a lady does! What can I do? They have brainwashed me since I was a young Glasgow keely and there is no hope of me ever being deprogrammed!

Don't Cry for We Argentina (or, We're on the March with Ali's Army)

The summer of 78 was memorable to many, including me because Scotland had qualified for the Word Cup finals in Argentina. What a time it was. Everybody was going crazy and with Ally McLeod in charge, we actually believed we had a chance! We had a fantastic team and as we all know we should have done better but what a time it was to be a football fan and alive!

Unfortunately for me in Linicro we only had a black and white portable TV. The reception at the wee hoose was bad. For the first Group 4 game against Peru, Bobby and I watched outside the wee hoose front door as the picture was less snowy. They beat us 3-1 so we were not off to a good start! Later we positioned the TV on the sofa next to the window and twisted the aerial for a less grainy experience.

Still the optimism was high. We then had to face Iran, who we should have tanked but drew 1-1. Last as everyone knows was Holland, and we thought we had no hope, but Archie Gemmill and his wonder goal brought us to the edge of our wee hoose seats. We nearly did it, but even though we beat them 3-2 we were out of the competition! Holland went on to the final only to be beaten by Argentina. It was very depressing.

'If only' was on everybody's lips. We should have prepared better. We should have beaten Iran. Ally got most of the blame for the debacle and as a manager that's the risk you take. I don't think he was that bad, if truth be told. What's wrong about being positive and saying you have a good chance of winning the World Cup? Scotland was in a confident mood. People were excited, and it was infectious. Not since 1978 has any other campaign felt so good. We may have gone on and played better over the years, but that happiness was never repeated. Not like it was in Argentina and for that we should thank Ally. He made us believe in ourselves. He made us think our boys could take on the world and beat them. After it was all over, I saw on the TV a compilation of Scotland's Argentina experience, it might have been on the Rock and Roll Years TV show. Elton John was singing 'Sorry Seems to be the Hardest Word' whilst we see a distraught Ally McLeod on the touchline. It was moving and sad. Still, Ally and our boys gave us the opportunity to dream that we were in with a chance, oh and what a dream it was!

The Darkness

I would be lying if I told you that during my time in Linicro I was not afraid of the dark. I was a wee bit! Locals know that on a cloudy winter's night it's totally pitch outside. The only light sources being those coming from house windows and the occasional croft's outside light. Walking to and from Totescore in the winter's dark proved to be a challenge. Most of the time I had the fear under control, but as a young teen my imagination could run riot on that walk. It was especially creepy walking past the quarry on such nights. God knows what could lurk in that black hole. I always picked up speed just to get away from the unseen demons! On starless nights even the silhouette of a passing place sign could be imagined into some deranged killer ghost coming for my skinny body! Any strange noises could be misinterpreted as footsteps coming to get you. Worse still were those damn coughing sheep! They sound very human in the dark, and that sound was enough to make my young heart pound!

One particularly pitch-black Sunday night I was walking down to the phone box to call Glasgow. As I walked past the pens just before old man Bradley's I thought I saw a shadow. My heart moved to my mouth when all too soon I bumped into someone walking in the opposite direction! I nearly died, and I ran to the light of the Linicro Post Office phone box! To make the night complete after I finished my call, I had just opened the door when there was a loud metal banging sound as if someone was drumming badly. I ran down the path on to the road like a Scottish Speedy Gonzales! The sound was probably from an expanding or contracting diesel barrel near Calum the Postie/ Tailor's workshop at the back of the Post Office.

Even when I had my bike, it was still creepy at night. At least I had a faster means of escape from those imaginary lurking monsters. I always hoped that when we had a full moon, it would be a cloudless night and Linicro and Totescore were bathed in the dark vanquishing silver light of a Highland moon. Most full moons it was cloudy though!

Dark

*The light has gone from the Linicro sky above as I jump off the
   school bus.*
*God is saving his fifty pence pieces for future heat when the
   weather is atrocious.*

*The big hoose lights are already on as I step inside, my Aunt is
   making my tea.*
*My bedroom cold as I change my clothes, and there is only a 50-
   watt bulb for me.*

*Come seven, I'm ready to head for Totescore with a mini torch
   gripped in my hand.*
*As I tread the mud to the road so bleak, I head into the grim
   winter wonderland.*

*There is no hint of a star above my head as I pass by the Morton's
   home.*
*The silence of sound is all around, my sight's 20/20
   monochrome.*

*It's creepy as hell as I walk alone, and my young mind begins its
   tricks.*
*Is that a shadow I see in front of me as pass by the first Totescore
   sign?*

*The quarry ahead fills my beating heart with dread, and I wish I
was in sunshine.*
*A cough from below makes my breath disappear, I'm too scared to
exhale.*
*Was it a sheep or a man? Do I have an escape plan? As my torch
light begins to fail.*

*The quarry, deep, dark and menacing, laughs as I walk and my
feet move ever faster.*
*My ears acute, chest pumping, I pass Stonegate without a
disaster.*

*I'm at the road's top now and I scan the land, looking for a bright
light friend.*
*Down my pal's well-worn path, I need a laugh. The Macinnes
house, my sanctuary.*
*Another night of fun is what we have planned as I leave the
dark and scary.*

*Three hours pass in three minutes, and soon I have to sadly head
back.*
*The boys, my bodyguards, and I'm brave and fearless, even it's
just for a wee while.*
*All too soon I'm alone as I quickstep back home, my pale face
missing a smile.*

*Tonight, I'm in luck as the outside light shines and I safely reach
my destination.*
*And I'm back in my room getting ready for bed, the hot water
bottle my just reward.*
*Burnt feet and rubber smells, I laugh to myself, as I slip into the
land of dreams.*
*And in them I'm all right because there is no night, the dark
scattered by God's moonbeams.*

Sounds of 1978

1978 was an interesting year for me musically speaking. Slowly but surely my tastes were refining. ELO's 'Mr Blue Sky' was one of my favourite songs, but 'Rat Trap' by the Boomtown Rats was equally good. Boney M's 'River of Babylon' sticks in my mind because of the hymn singing classes in Kilmuir although they never allowed us to sing it! The Cars had 'My Best Friends Girl' and Gerry Rafferty had his 'Baker Street' both great tunes from opposite sides of the Atlantic. Grease songs still charted, and it was hard not to like a lot of the singles (just don't tell anybody). The Bee Gees had some cracking songs from Saturday Night Fever, but again you did not admit that out loud! One-hit wonders Clout with 'Substitute', Yellow Dog with 'One More Light' and The Motors with 'Airport' kept my foot tapping. This was also the year that we would first hear the weird and wonderful voice of Kate Bush with 'Wuthering Heights' leading me to have a wee crush on her! The Commodores had a hit with 'Three Times a Lady' which is up there with the all-time great love songs! They would feature heavily with me and my first love as she had a tape of their greatest hits, but that was four years away. Rose Royce had two crackers with 'Wishing on a Star' and 'Love Don't Live Here Any More'. I really loved 'What a Waste' by Ian Dury. More one-hit wonders in the shape of Jilted John with 'Jilted John' and City Boy with '5705'. My favourite glam rock era band, The Sweet had their last big hit with 'Love Is Like Oxygen'. The Clash had the sing-along 'Tommy Gun' and the Sex Pistols faded out with 'Silly Thing' and 'No One's Innocent' with Ronnie Biggs. Let's not forget the underrated 10cc and 'Dreadlock Holiday' and the Double A-Side 'Girls School' and its more famous 'Mull of Kintyre' sung by Mr McCartney. I eventually got to go to the M of K and walked along the beach singing that song as loud as I could! Finally, a few Sunday nights I spent up in the big hoose miming along to Rod's 'Do Ya Think I'm Sexy'. Many more songs caught my ear that year, and the next year was only to get better!

Army Boots/Nudie Books

Linicro weather requires that you wear sensible footwear. Wellies are almost mandatory. Trainers can be worn if the summer months are kind, but a good pair of boots are ideal for all sorts of business be it fun or crofting related. Into 1978 I was desperate for a pair of boots. I would eye up Doc's in the Great Universal Catalogue belonging to Janet Macinnes but was put off when Norman told me that the soles were not great on wet grass and this could make walking slippery. The search continued.

There is a storage area at the top of the wee hoose stairs and peeping out from beneath the junk I saw what looked like shoes. Having cleared everything away I saw that it was pair of brown boots! They must hae been there since the 1960s. My Aunt Margaret thought they might have been hers. On closer inspection they kinda looked like women's boots but beggars can't be choosers and they fitted me. Once covered in mud they looked OK and not too ladylike. The sole was the problem as these were for walking on pavement or road. Not hill and heather! Still, it was better than nothing. They lasted less than a month! The soles began flapping like an old dog's watery tongue and soon gave up the ghost no matter how much Bostik glue I applied!

Bootless again I planned to get my folks to buy me a pair when I was in Glasgow for the two weeks of the 78 summer holidays. My old man Big Gerry suggested that I go into the toon and check out the Army and Navy surplus store. This I did and I found myself a cracking pair of army boots for less than a fiver! They were a couple of sizes too big but no matter I would grow into them and in the meantime could just wear double socks!

Army booted I was pleased with myself back in Linicro. Come the day of the Kilmuir cattle show I proudly wore these too-big-for-my-feet boots. I wouldn't say that it was a beautiful day but at least it was boot-wearing weather. Wandering around the small show with the Macinnes boys we met up with local character Geordie. Short and rough with nicotine-stained teeth we could always get a laugh with him. The boys were talking to him when he spied my new boots and started laughing at me as he saw that they were a bit on the big size! I didn't mind and I told him that they were good for 'bootin baws'. Just as I said that I threw out my leg as if to kick him in the nethers. I did not allow for the fact that these hard leather boots were a lot bigger than my feet and completely misjudged my move catching him full on in the nads! He dropped to his knees and made a sign of the cross then fell face flat on the grass grasping his toilet area. I knelt down and apologised profusely. I truly never meant to hit him. The poor guy was rolling about in agony. I felt terrible but as is often the case with me I started to laugh! The sight of him dropping like a stone and making the sign of the cross was very funny. We got him to his feet and by this time the pain had eased. I apologized again with a big smile on my face. He accepted my apology and said that my boot just 'clanged his clocha' and it was the shock more than the pain! For the rest of the day I could not stop chuckling about it! I still felt bad.

Not too long after that incident we were out and about in Norman's car. We had heard that Geordie was alone in his folks' house and by way of a belated apology gift we took a half bottle of whisky with us and a couple of nudie books. Probably Penthouse. It was dark when we arrived outside his place and he invited us in with a smile. He asked us not to make a mess or his Mother would kill him. He was happy with our gifts. We all sat in front of his living room fire chewing the fat. The boys passed round the half bottle as Geordie eyed up the ladies in the magazines. I hate whisky and when it came to me, I had a joke planned. Of course I did. Sitting on the corner seat by the roaring fire I took a large mouthful got up and handed it back to Geordie as I walked back to my chair, I spat the whisky out into the fire! We all know what happens with alcohol and fire don't we? The flames whooshed out and licked his Mum's mantelpiece! Everyone laughed even Geordie! Archie started doing the same thing and we all rolled about like pyromaniacal maddies. I had the horrible taste of whisky in my mouth and asked Geordie if he would make a strupag? He agreed and I asked for milk and lots of sugar. Whilst our host was in the kitchen, I began to rip some of the pages from the porno mags and hid them under the chair cushion. The boys realized what I was doing, and they followed suit. They tore out some mammary material and hid it around the living room and under the sofa! I got my cup of tea but before I drank it, I had to again do my party piece! I was an idiot! The flames looked good with the whisky spit. We eventually made our excuse to leave and left Geordie happy with the remaining whisky and the nudie books! We were in hysterics in the car thinking at some point when his folks came back his Mum would be tidying up and find the naked women photos! If she did, we did not hear about it, but we still laughed! Sorry Geordie!

Snowboys

I'm not a big fan of snow. It's nice to look at on hills far away, but not nice to walk in when it turns to grey slush. As a kid in Glasgow we would love when it snowed and would spend hours out in the cold white stuff.

As a teen in Linicro when it snowed the hill looked beautiful, but the road was a mess of freezing, shoe-penetrating, grit-containing slush. It did not snow that much when I lived there and even when it did, being so close to the sea it didn't lie too long, unless you walked on higher ground. Sometimes the roads were that bad that 'John the bus' and his bus could not make it up Score Bay. The first time it happened, I enjoyed the day off as it was my first Linicro winter. A year later, when it happened again, I got my big jacket on and got on the road and hitched to Portree. That's how much I enjoyed going to school. Not for the academics but for the carry on! I had just passed Morton's when I got picked up by a car who took me to Rankin's in Uig. From there I walked up the road towards Uig Hotel when a truck, probably just off the ferry, stopped and picked me up. The driver was nice and friendly but didn't talk too much. That was fine by me. He took me all the way to Portree, and we listened to Terry Wogan on Radio Two. From that time on, I was a Wogan fan. 'John the bus' managed to get to Portree later after the council were out gritting the roads.

My favourite memory of the snow was after a heavy fall and my Totescore buddies, Duncan and Archie, came over and we decided to 'sledge' on the hill behind the big hoose. It was a beautiful crisp night with a full moon shining its silver light across the township. With the light bouncing off the snow, it was as if it floodlit the hill. We did not have a sledge, but we had found this enamel side panel from an old cooker. It was not big, but it could fit one and a half bums. On some short 'test' runs this shiny piece of metal proved to be a speed demon, so we took it up to near the top of the croft. One of us (and I don't think it was me) had an idea to build a snow crash barrier in front of the fence which separated us from the trees and the big hoose kitchen. We all thought this was a good idea so got working packing the ice as high as we could. This we thought would slow us down, preventing us from hitting the fence. Big mistake. At the top of the hill Duncan, being the biggest, sat on the enamel panel first and we sat on him. We let ourselves go. We did not account for how slick this makeshift sledge would be, and we bombed it down the field like a bat out of hell. It all happened so quick that my memory of it is in slow motion. The panel turned round, and we sped down backwards. As we neared the snow 'crash barrier' we lost Archie. He rolled down the hill sledgeless. We totally missed our barrier and rammed legs akimbo into the fence. Luckily, we did not sustain any nether region damage and any other pain we had, we laughed off. If there had been no fence (or trees) we no doubt would have sailed straight through the kitchen windows and into my Aunt's double sink! That night was fun with a capital F. It was also effin freezing (more Fs), but we ignored that and continued our play.

Fighting Friends

I would always say (jokingly seriously) that I was a lover rather than a fighter. I have had very few physical fights in my entire life, and I'm happy with that. At school in Portree there had been the occasional threat of a fight but nothing ever materialised into fisticuffs apart from one time. It was around third year and on a wet lunch time us boys were hanging out in Mr Nicholson's/Miss Collins-Taylor's hut, which was our form room. There were the usual suspects, Donnie Nicholson (Noddy), Angus Gordon, Alistair Aitken and me. I don't remember exactly how it started, but it was with my best pal Ali. Both of us had a crush on a certain older lady, and I was probably jealous of the attention he was receiving. What I do remember was that I was sitting on one of the two-person school desks, swinging my legs and doing my best to annoy Ali. Whatever it was I said it had the desired effect of making him so angry that he dived straight at me! The table turned and my legs went up in the air as we did a half somersault to the floor with Ali on top of me! Luckily, we did not sustain any damage in the initial attack. He was a lot stronger than me and had me pinned to the floor. I was apoplectic with rage, but his arms kept me from punching him and I even tried to head butt him in the stomach. This caused him no pain whatsoever. I was effing and blinding when Donnie and Angus jumped in to break it up. They eventually dragged us apart and I think one of us left the class. I don't know for how long afterwards, but we did not speak to each other for a good while. I believe I made the first move to apologise to him and to assure him that my crush attentions had moved on to another older lady at school. The incident was immortalised in my one and only school written song when we were in fourth year. Titled 'You're a Friend'. The words though puerile and derivative were heartfelt, and this was what I wrote, 'Remember the days of trouble? Remember the fight we had? We were young and in love, but with the same girl. Now that's all over, that's all done'. Ali put a pleasant tune to that song, and it had a nice sing-along chorus that went, 'You're a friend, you're a friend and we stay here till the end. Just us two. Me and you. Because you're my friend'. Ok, it won't win any Ivor Novello awards, but it was nice to sing at the time!

Great Granny

As far back as I can remember when our school summer holidays were coming to a close and it was time to leave Linicro for Glasgow, it provoked the same reaction from my dear old Great Grandmother Annie. Upon our departure we would say 'we will see you next year', tears would form in her sad Highland eyes, and she would respond 'I probably won't be alive next year!' This went on for years and probably was said to my mother and her sisters when they left Linicro long before!

November 1978 arrived unkind and dark. Those nights could be long and cold. The big hoose fire would burn logs, coal and peat and unfortunately for those sitting in front of it, trying to warm our damp bones, most of the heat disappeared up the lum! One such evening my old Granny went to spend a penny, walking stick in hand. I was sitting with her watching something on our 14-inch black and white portable that had more snow on the screen than was on the Linicro hills! I suddenly heard a crash

Granny, Linicro 1960s

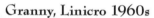

and a door bang coming from the toilet. I jumped up and rushed to the bathroom. My old Granny had fallen but appeared to be unhurt. My Aunt Margaret was behind me and between us both we got Granny into the living room and on to the sofa. The rest of that evening was a bit of a blur, and I don't recall how Margaret called for an ambulance? Did we have the phone in then, or did she go to a neighbour? The strongest memory I have of that dark night was sitting with my Granny as she slept on the sofa, holding her frail hand. As I waited, she would occasionally squeeze my hand with a sturdy grip and this made me think everything would be ok. This would be the last time I would see the old lady of Linicro. The ambulance arrived after a while and took Granny and Margaret to hospital in Broadford.

I slept alone in the big hoose that night, and the next day I was told by my sad Aunt that her mother had passed away. This was such a shock to the young me as I thought with that forceful grip, and the fact she looked unhurt seemed to be a good sign. As teenager grief is an unfamiliar animal. How do you do it? I just carried on and lived my school life as usual.

The days before the funeral were dark and miserable. Margaret was coming to terms with the loss as best she could. We Scottish folk don't wear our emotions on our sleeves and seeing Margaret in distress tugged at my heartstrings. There were no touchy-feely moments. You just had to get on with it as best you could. Annie was a well-known lady, from Linicro to Glasgow, and all points in-between. We had many visitors over the following days. The mood was sombre and reflective. The funeral was in Uig; the service being at the church beside Uig Hotel, finishing at Annie's last resting place, Uig Cemetery. The family had gathered from Glasgow and they decided I was too young to attend. The Skye sky was grey and heavy like our hearts, and I was told that the church service was a gothic type affair replete with lashing rain and a leaking church roof.

My Granny was a good age when she went on her last journey. Born in 1887, she lived through two world wars, spending the Second World War in the 2nd city of the Empire. What changes she must have seen in her 92 years of life? Both in Glasgow and in Skye. If only she had documented those experiences, I think they would have made a right riveting read! We are lucky, though. She may be long gone, but because of her singing talents and her ability to remember many old traditional Gaelic songs, they recorded her voice for the audible delectation of future generations. Her singing can be heard online or purchased as part of the Edinburgh School of Scottish Studies Gaelic collection. My memory of her singing was when her voice was less strong, but not her desire. She would sit in the wee hoose's corner in her Great Granny cardie, giving it Gaelic laldy! My sister and I would join in and try to do our Gaelic best! I still hear these songs in my head and consider myself lucky to have been related to such an important traditional mouth music torch bearer. Many years have gone under the water bridge, but her memory remains fresh in my mind. I recall the many times I would draw her ire by pulling out her wallys as she slept when the top set slipped from her sleeping jaw! She was a real character whose personality was twice as large as her 92-year-old frame! Her (selective) deafness and refusal to wear her hearing aid was a source of frustration and laughter for many of us, and I know she always heard what she wanted to and filtered out the rest.

I'm happy that she was my Great Granny and a special thanks goes to her as I know it was her that made it possible for me to stay in Linicro past my 1977 summer holidays and who said 'boys will be boys', when I nearly wrecked my chances of Linicro life by getting up to some stupid teenage mischief.

My Granny might be 40 years gone, but in my heart and mind she lives forever.

Foxes 1. Fox Hunters 0

The only times I have seen a fox are once in a playing field when I lived in Tottenham, London and many times as they raided the bins at the back of my sister's Park Road apartment in Glasgow!

It's the late 1970s at the river Rha in Uig. This was the designated meeting place for a motley bunch, including yours truly. The aim was a fox hunt. As we know fox hunting for sport is bad but fox hunting for foxes that have been causing croft mayhem is acceptable. The charges against our quarry seemed vague, but it appeared that across Glen Conon and above Uig there had been said fox activities, hence this gathering. Amongst the group were the Macinnes boys, Willie 'Potty' probably John Neil and his brother Grant from Glen Conon and others. Some had shotguns! It was exciting, and I was just a tiny wee bit scared. When you said fox, I imagined wolf! So, the plan was to fan out on each side of the river and push any (hidden) foxes up the hill into the open, where they would be met by some gentlemen with heavy arms. With trepidation I climbed the undergrowth with my fellow hunters (it was difficult, think Vietnam jungle). There was a lot of shouting going on and apparent sightings of the animals. Truth be told, we looked like a gang of Elmer Fudds going after an uncatchable rabbit as opposed to a well-oiled hunting machine. Further we climbed when a shout went out and from the other side of the river Willie's head popped up beneath the green fan ferns. His (old) shotgun raised and pointing to us on the other side! We dived to the mossy ground expecting to hear the bang, but nothing. Carefully we raised our noggins above the greenery, but Willie was gone. We seemed to be there for hours with nothing actually happening and The Sweet song 'Fox on the Run' was playing in my head! We breached the top of the hill and met up with the others, and nobody saw a four-legged thing. At least we didn't get shot! We all went home alive including the fox and for that I was happy!

Foxes 2. Fox Hunters 0

The next hunt was above the Linicro rocks, and this time we had a professional fox hunter being paid by the local community. If I may, I will tell you I never saw or heard any foxes at any time during my Skye life. I did not see any damage caused by these invisible foxes either. Only stories told about their viciousness and dangerousness! Our crack team was small, only me, Norman Macinnes and the fox hunter plus his two Jack Russells. The hunter had a fancy rifle with a telescope and a heavy-looking backpack. He was a wee guy, wiry and English, but he seemed to know his stuff.

It was one of those Skye summer evenings when darkness refused to fall and lucky for us Mother Nature's gentle breath kept away the midges. We walked across the rocky ridge and bypassed the peat road and climbed the hill again. Once we reached the plateau high above Linicro, the dogs got scent of something and we halted. One wee dog disappeared as if swallowed whole by the heather, while the other was running about like a lunatic and barking orders that we could not understand. To my surprise, the hunter put his ear to the ground and swiftly produced a small spade from his backpack and dug furiously. Strange, I thought, but intrigued I was. To my amazement the hole he dug opened up and there looking up was the recently swallowed dog, neck deep in dark peaty water inside what I assume was a foxhole.

Wow! We are going to catch something, I thought. We moved swiftly on to see if there was another exit but could not find one and after a short while our pot-holing small dog re-joined us. Shaking the brown liquid off his coat, he and the other terrier continued to sniff the grass as we moved across the green and purple ground. It now seemed that they lost the scent. We stayed outside till well past midnight, then we made our way down to the peat road and cut past the Linicro fank heading towards the cattle pens and the foxhunter's Land Rover Defender. No luck for us, but lucky foxes!

He dropped us at the wee hoose in the half-light, and we said our farewell to the foxhunter. I was knackered as I climbed the wee hoose stairs to my bed to the sound of Norman's Austin 1100 leaving for Totescore. That night I dreamt of fox/wolf hybrids chasing my skinny body across the Linicro common grazing, but thankfully I had a secret weapon? In my dreams, I could fly! I awoke the next day, excited to tell my tale of hunting to anyone who would listen!

Sick

I was very fortunate in all my time on Skye to be blessed with good health (but not good looks). However, during my Linicro years I had one bout with a virus that KO'd me for days. The reason this ill memory stays with me is that it was the only time in my life (until then), that I was too sick to get out of bed!

Around the spring of 1979 I was bored and looking for something to do when I spotted two ladies on the Linicro road out for a walk! On further investigation it was none other than my friend/neighbour Morag MacLeod, nee Gillies, and a friend of hers who I did not recognise. I walked with them and we gathered at the gate on my Aunt Margaret's lower croft besides the old Smiddy. The weather must have been good because I remember we stood there for ages and I was doing my level best to chat Morag's friend up, using all my best lines. I'm not sure if these 'killer' lines worked, but I continued to show my sparkling personality over what could have been hours.

I remember that the three of us had a good laugh (although I don't remember the friend's name).

Having been away from the big hoose for several hours I guessed (correctly), that my Aunt Margaret would wonder where I was and she surmised (correctly), that I was shirking my weekend chore responsibilities. Eventually, the two lovely ladies said their cheerios and continued their walk down the road and I headed back towards the hoose with a smile on my face, thinking I had made a favourable impression on Miss Gillies's friend (I hadn't). When I got in Margaret complained that I was a lazy, worthless so and so (she was correct, well, maybe not worthless). The following day I woke up, and I was feeling a wee bit strange and my stomach was roller coaster churning. I had also developed the thirst of a guy stuck for weeks in the waterless desert, and I was drinking copious amounts of H2O from the cold water tap in the bathroom. No sooner had I quenched my thirst when the water in my stomach rebelled and an exit was required either by projectile vomiting (in the true sense of the phrase) or from the other end of the alimentary canal. It was out at speed without very much warning! My body was so fatigued that I could hardly move, so I was exiled to my room and my bed.

No more could I drink, and I was 'puked' out! If I had needed to sit on the loo, I don't think my legs, which were Rowntree's jelly quivering, would carry me downstairs. I might even have been delirious for the first day or two. It was bad enough that a call was made to the District Nurse, Annie Ross, who scheduled a visit.

The last time that I had had some of Annie's care was years before when the big hoose's kitchen door was slammed on my wee pinkie, slicing the top off! Ouch! Red-cheeked and out of breath (from climbing the stairs) she stuck a thermometer in my gob whilst asking me how I was feeling. Whatever I said, she diagnosed that I needed a butt injection, which she duly administered and left me with a 'don't get out of bed' warning!

Delirium gave way to acute abdominal pain and insomnia! This was in the three TV channel era, but no matter, we could only receive one station and the portable TV was nowhere near my bedroom. Boredom replaced my stomach pain and my 'new' Nurse, cousin Bobby, needed to work on his bedside manner. My Aunt Margaret visited a few times and blamed the illness on me spending hours outside talking to the girls. Eh? Perhaps she needed to work on her bedside manner too, but in traditional Scottish style, sympathy/empathy was in short Linicro supply.

By the fifth day I was feeling better and could get up out of my sick bed. And by the end of the week I was back to normal with Aunt Margaret continuing to blame the lady-chatting and spending hours in their company as the source of my illness!

Don't think so!

Mr Marshall the Music Man

I wanted to mention the man who introduced many of us to Runrig's Recovery album (and much more). Housed in Portree High's Technical block and sporting a spiffy 1970s moustache. I'm talking about our favourite music teacher, Mr Marshall, of course. His music class was always fun, and he was a great ambassador for all styles of music. If my memory serves me right his record deck and speakers were clad in a light wood and it may have been a Garrard turntable. I loved the fact that he really liked to blast the music, and this habit has stayed with me throughout my adult years. My daughter Isis often complains that I play my music too loud!

Some standout tracks he used to play included the aforementioned title track 'Recovery', and I recall he loved the chord change at the end of the song, which is indeed a beautiful touch. 'Village Ghetto Land' by Stevie Wonder introduced us to this musical legend and remains one my favourite songs of his. On the folk side he played Silly Wizard's 'The Valley of Strathmore', which is a touching song of lost love, I advise everyone to listen to. Classical music was often on the menu and for me Vivaldi's 'The Four Seasons' became an essential addition to my music collection.

John had a wonderful teaching style which was relaxed and full of humour, this definitely made his class a very popular one. I attempted O' level Music but proved to be the opposite of talented in this subject. This class was a tiny group including my bestie Ali Aitken, Lorna Cormack, Margaret Gunn and John Don Macleod. All (it must be said) much smarter (musically) than me! One standout incident comes to mind, and this involves a confession? There was to be a recording for radio at the Skye Gathering Hall and our small group were to take part! I think it was a hymn we had to sing and there was a part that was only to be sung by the ladies, then we guys would join in. After many rehearsals the day of the recording came, and we made our way to the venue. Sitting beside John Don, Ali and the girls it was exciting to know that they would play us on radio (I don't remember which station).

For the song we had to sing, Mr Marshall was out front to conduct, and all I had to remember was Do Not Sing at the beginning with the ladies! The tape rolled and what did I do? Yep! I sang with the ladies! Mr Marshall's head whipped round looking for the offender and realising my mistake I turned to look at John Don as if to say, 'What are you doing'? I never admitted officially to the mistake and let it be thought John Don made it! Sorry! Later on, I listened to the broadcast on the radio and could hear my mistake permeate the airwaves. Double sorry!

O' level Music proved too baffling for my simple brain, and eventually I left after one year. There was one other thing that Mr Marshall was involved in and I wanted to mention it but my memory is dimmer about this. I think it was Christmas of 79 or 80 and he held a Gaelic Christmas Carol competition and asked for submissions. My poor brain memory tells me it was someone from Staffin who won with a beautifully composed Gaelic tune. I won't attempt to write (even phonetically) but the melody and its wonderfully simple chorus are still with me today. For your services to the development of my musical ears I would like to say a big thank you John, it was a joy to be taught in your class.

Bomb Boys

I'm sure my cousin Bobby won't mind me telling this wee story, I hope not anyway. Do Not Try This At Home (or anywhere). Bobby knew a lot of stuff, was very handy with his hands, and in those days long before Google he collected a lot of unusual information. There was one afternoon we were over at the Morton house along with Duncan, Archie and Norman Macinnes. Norman was there doing his handyman work, and we would help with the lawn mowing. We all stood outside her wooden shed where all the garden tools were stored. This was opposite her kitchen door. Bobby told us he could make a bomb with a certain weed killer powder and sugar? We all laughed and basically said he was talking nonsense. He said he could prove it. So, he hunted around, and he found an empty whisky half bottle (from where I don't know) and he proceeded to pack it full of a mixture of weed killer and sugar. We still did not believe him at all. There we were, the five of us behind the Morton house, and Bobby lay the powder-packed bottle on the ground and then covered it in sugar. I did not know sugar burned, but it did, like a fuse! We all stood behind him as he attempted to light this sugar fuse, which eventually caught fire. We still believed nothing would happen. After about a few of seconds the sugar flame lit inside the bottle and the next thing that bottle took off across the concrete like an effin rocket and smashed up against the Morton outside kitchen wall. Not quite exploding, but near enough! Wow! We loved it and us young ones wanted more, but the mature heads of Norman and Bobby said no more! In retrospect that was definitely an excellent decision because no doubt we would want to go bigger and louder! It's lucky that none of us was hurt by the flying glass!

Cold Comfort Croft

The cold and I are not friends. We can just about bear each other's company only if I'm outside dressed in the appropriate attire! We really don't see eye to eye when it comes to a cold house and in particular a cold bedroom!

Our council apartment in Glasgow was not known for its warm bedrooms and hallway. The council had neglected to fit any type of heating in the room or in the stairway cum hall. Subsequently, it was freezing during the winter months. Springburn was a stranger to continental quilts, so we had to make do with Skye Woollen Mill scratchy blankets and a counterpane decorated with Smokey the Bear (all the way from my Dad's sister in California)! When temperatures dipped, we relied on two of my Dad's winter overcoats to keep us toast-like! Waking up in the morning was a torturous affair as the Glasgow cold invaded our nethers! At night, luxury for us was having a Dalek-shaped paraffin heater 'take the chill off' our bedrooms. Paraffin fumes permeated our dreams as we sang Esso blue in our sleep!

The move to Linicro did not improve my relationship with the cold, in fact it made it much worse. My bedroom in the big hoose was immune to warmth with winter nights and mornings being an absolute waking nightmare of freezingness! I doubt the traditional tongue-and-groove cladding on the Highland walls possessed any insulating properties and my agony was to last all winter long. My bed was covered with more scratchy wool blankets, but this time I used the sleeping bag that I had brought from Glasgow as a luxurious Linicro continental quilt! This undoubtedly kept me warm whilst asleep, but in the morning the shiny sleeping bag material was moist with the condensation from my breath. Moist and cold!

My Aunt Margaret was expertly frugal with heat-producing equipment and the morning saw the electric fire in the big hoose living room with only one bar glowing orangey red. Eventually she capitulated to my ongoing request for some type of heater, and one was duly ordered from the Freeman's catalogue. Finally, the 'heater' arrived and calling it a 'heater' might have been stretching the definition of the word ever so slightly. It was a small white convector type affair with two very thin 'heating' elements curly and stretched from side to side. Underneath turned a 'fan' and underneath that was an orange bulb. The bulb gave you the (false) impression that heat was actually being produced. In order for it to heat my big hoose bedroom, I reckon it would have to be on all night, and that was an Aunt Margaret no-no! It could only be switched on in the morning. For the duration of me getting dressed in my school clothes. My school shirt and jumper had been removed together the previous night. Quicker to remove (and to apply), and they hung over a wooden chair which backed onto the convector. In the morning I would jump out of bed on to the freezing lino, turn on the heater, jump back to bed for ten minutes, just so I could remove the chill from my clothes! I think the only way for it to produce any proper heat would have been to pour petrol over it and set it alight. Now, as an adult and in control of my life (and the electric bill), I have always ensured my morning room was sub-tropical! Even now as I live in the desert I'm always arguing with my wife and kid. They like to keep the AC going all night, so it is effin freezing when I get up and I have to run into the shower quickly just to get a heat!

Bedroom

The steep wooden steps at the wee hoose front door led you up to my wee, wee hoose bedroom on the second floor.
Watch your head on the lintel, as you push open the creaking door.
With booted feet forever not silent, walking on the creaking floor.

My room, a dream for an Antiques Roadshow crew.
A spinning wheel silent, as a wooden butter churn sits and stares at you.
A wooden bookcase rests forever lonely on the crumbly gable wall.
Each shelf a home to dust encrusted books, all about to fall.

The Z bed behind the door is layered with three different mattresses, and if you forgot to close the skylight, you were the victim of the midges.
After cocoa it's up to bed, with a small candle my only source of light.
Wee hoose Wee Willie Winkie climbs and says goodnight.

Lying on the lumpy surface on top of the rusting bed I crawl, if I turn over please don't laugh, when onto the floorboards I fall.
A battery and a torch, a posh luxury, as I flick through my Dandy and Beano.
Shadows on the peeling ceiling, ghost shadows in the afterglow.

If your bladder wakes you in the night's middle, sleepy eyed and scared to go to the outside loo.
Into a potty you could piddle, and under the bed you would push, that's all you could do.
Walls and floors are thin, this place holds no secrets, so be careful what you speak.
In the morning all are laughing as they heard me singing in my Linicro deep sleep.

Wee Hoose and Big Hoose now

Sunday summer morning, lazy underneath the metal corrugated.
Outside is the sound of Sunday silence, and it's me being
serenaded.
At night my Aunt reads from the bible and it's music to my
Granny's ears.
Whilst I nod off under a spider's web and the moonlight
reappears.

Small and dusty it might have been, but it was the first room I
could call my own.
In my daydream state, I'm back again under the roof of my
Linicro wee hoose home.

Mistaken ID

Did you hear the one about the drunken fisherman asking a
teenage boy for a dance? No, it's not a joke and yes that teenage
boy was me!

Uig Hall 1978 and I was there sporting hair by (cousin) Bobby.
Otherwise known as a bowl cut! So, I'm at this dance with my
cousin and it was the usual scenario of guys outnumbering the
gals by about six to one! I believe that the music makers this
fine winter's evening was a Highland dance band and could
have been the ubiquitous Ian Macdonald. There I was standing
at one side of the dance floor looking innocent and apparently
like a lassie! This short English fisherman whose name has
slipped from my brilliant mind, but I think he lived in Kilmuir
or perhaps further north staggered drunkenly towards me and
tried to engage me in some semblance of a conversation.

At first, I assumed he we just being 'friendly' but his beard and
accent made it difficult to understand what the hell he was
saying. Being a polite kind of guy, I just smiled and nodded.
This was not enough. He persisted with his drunken words and

nervously I edged closer to my cousin out of fear! The music continued to drown out his words, but Bobby was big, so I felt safe enough. The drunk turned to his friend and said something that set him off in fits of laughter. I did my manly best to ignore but stuck close

Skyeku 19

Rear view island eyes

Long years gone Linicro lost

Hearts scrawled on window.

to Bobby just in case. The next thing I know the fisherman's friend and he approached, and his friend stood in front of me saying some words to the drunk fisherman. The friend then patted both his hands on my chest and as he did, a dim (imaginary) light bulb appeared above the drunk fisherman's head! The realisation of what he had tried to do apparent on his drunkenly embarrassed fisherman's face! He then disappeared, not to be seen for the rest of the dance! His friend explained to Bobby that he thought I was a girl and that he was asking me to dance! WTF? I can laugh about it now, but back then it was scary and creepy! As I mentioned he lived past Linicro and fished out of Uig, so he drove the same road that I walked.

His car was one of those long Peugeot estate cars, easy to see at a distance. For months afterwards I was still creeped out a bit and, if spotting his motor, I would jump to the side of the road and hide in a ditch or I would turn my back and put my hood up so no traces of my bowl cut could be viewed! Who knows, he might have stopped and asked me for another dance!

Luckily, I got rid of the bowl cut (eventually) and sported the more traditional short back and sandpaper. I saw the bearded creepy guy at a few local dances, but thankfully he did not recognize me! I still stuck close to cousin Bobby, though!

The Quarry

To me, the Totescore quarry has always been there. Although I don't recall it ever being quarried as I saw no earth-moving motors in the near vicinity. It appears to have increased in size over the years; perhaps under cover of dark an earth-eating giant secretly scooped out handfuls of yummy dirt, stuffed his face and then made off into the night undetected?

How many times did I walk past it, back and forth, as I visited Archie and Duncan? In the light of day this country chasm is a benign neighbour but in the Skye dark, walking past the vasty nothingness of the quarry's innards, was creepy, especially if one is being followed by the ever-present coughing sheep! Scary! I guess some consider this piece of wounded earth as the proverbial blot on the landscape. Ugly and unloved. No doubt tourists have a negative opinion of this Totescore spot, but not me. It is, was and always will be 'the quarry' and if it was not there, it would be missed!

A book I'm reading triggered a long-hidden memory when as a seven (maybe eight) year old I decided I wanted to find the source of the quarry's stream. I'm sure many of the Island's children undertook similar adventures.

The first obstacle for this Linicro Livingstone (me), was scaling the high(ish) mini waterfall. This entailed climbing the hill to the non-quarried side of the running water. There you will find a dip and a small plateau hidden from a roadside viewer's eye (there is a reason I know this and it involved a future girlfriend and me enjoying nature and getting up to natural things). From there, looking up, the journey took on Everestian (is that a word?) proportions but determined, I moved on. When not pouring with rain the stream meanders all the way to the Minch and as I hopped either side of it on my way up the hill, I was sure I would find its source sooner rather than later. The thing about being young and small is that the hill can fool you easily. Just over the next hillock I was sure I would achieve my goal, but no. The hill had dips that tricked my young mind and the climb continued. Though not steep it's deceivingly high and just as you're sure the summit is close, it requires more climbing. The higher I got the smaller this water tributary became, and I could feel that I was getting near my mini Nile source. The view from the top (on a clear day) is breath-taking in its entirety, and you felt that you were King of the non-existent castle. Soon there is no stream just boggy green underfoot and disappointingly there is no viewable source; no doubt it's hidden under the hill but at least it has an end. With no Stanley to greet me at the top I caught my breath and crossed over the 'ridge' and ran (occasionally falling) down the purple heathered hill until I'm caught in the net that is my Aunt's croft fence behind the big hoose. This I scale over like a hurdle, continuing my run until I'm at the red iron gate. The source of the Nile it was not but the sense of accomplishment and the sheer innocent pure joy of my afternoon adventure has stayed with me all these years.

What's in a Name?

One thing I loved about being at Portree High School and living in Linicro and Uig was the wide variety of weird and wonderful nicknames people had. Often, I wondered where they got them from. Some got labels from the areas of the island they lived. Some got their nicknames from their Christian or family names.

Some from the way they looked or the habits they had, and others got their moniker from God knows where? I never had a nickname at school but was called plenty of names, usually of the four-letter variety. So, I thought I would share a few, hoping it will stir you, my dears, to thinking about people in your past and their nicknames. I mean no disrespect to anyone and would like to thank them all for playing a part (big and small or not at all) in my Skye life!

Snippet	Knocky
Donnie Glen	Staffin
Black Angus	Tatties
Sniper	Gibbon
Bloat	Patch
Holy Joe	Gudge
John the herd	Lovely
John the bus	Teuchie
Angus the student	Willie Potty
The Loon	Bambi
The weed	Cloudy
James Tornado	Boofie
Geordie	Speedy
Oddbod	Aussie
Klanky	Fiddler
The Bopper	Canada
The Beak	Mandy
The Fruit	Noddy
Rosebud	Busty

To name but a few!

Many of these were given to folk from a very early age and still stick with them until now. The genesis of most I'm unfamiliar with but some were easy to guess. Canada was a guy called David who hailed from Canada. Neil 'Aussie' was from Uig who had spent years in the antipodes before returning home to the island. Mrs McFarlane my old English teacher was well endowed in the (to quote Frank Zappa) mammalian protuberances department! Lovely was a neighbour of ours who kept his 'Seaview' B&B lovely! Patch I went to school with and his mostly black hair was broken by a 'patch' of unusual white hair. Teuchie's nickname was derived from Teuchter which is a lowland Scots word for describing someone from the Highlands. It was odd that Highlanders would call him this, but I think the reason was that he had a strong crofter accent when speaking English and was probably more used to speaking Gaelic at home. The late Donnie 'Glen' was from Glenhinnisdal and Staffin was from Staffin! Mr Roberts our chemistry teacher was known as 'Oddbod' and if I'm not mistaken it's because some people thought he looked like the character from the movie Carry On Screaming. The three Maitland brothers were known as 'Gibbon' and who am I to say that they resembled such tree climbing cuties? Our biology teacher was known to everyone as 'Klanky' perhaps it was his robotic teaching style? I didn't give him the name, but I did refer to his wife as 'Mrs Klanky'. Angus 'the loon' was a well-known character from Uig. Let's just say he was a wee bit on the eccentric side and leave it at that! My Uncle Peter and his Earlish family were collectively known as the fiddlers. The instrument was played by some of his family members and Bobby recently told me his Dad could play a wee bit. Although their surname is Nicholson, everybody called them fiddler as in Norman fiddler, Archie fiddler and my Uncle Peter fiddler!

Willie Clippit

As far back as I can remember a black and white etching of a sailing ship hung above the fireplace in the wee hoose. The artist was signed as John Arnott. He was the oft talked about but never seen son of my Aunt Margaret's brother Willie. This 'great' Uncle of mine was rarely seen in Linicro during my time, he lived and worked in Glasgow.

Willie was a short bald guy who looked like my Aunt Margaret if she had had male pattern baldness. He had a fondness for the deoch and that is probably why we did not see him often, especially whilst his Mother was alive and kicking. No doubt he was afraid of what Annie would say if he was in Linicro attendance and under the influence!

Willie visited Linicro twice during my time there and it would be fair to say that in my teenage eyes, he had 'short man' syndrome. I really did not warm to him. He could be a pain in the rear when tipsy and was partial to complaining about me being in Linicro 'eating food' and 'using electricity'. He also portrayed the tough man image whilst drunk and was fond of swinging his arms and punching a clenched fist into his open palm. Not scary, and not tough!

The last time I saw him probably was around 1979/80 when he came for a brief visit! One afternoon I returned home from school to be greeted by him and Margaret in the big hoose kitchen. Margaret started complaining about me not helping her enough around the croft (which was true) and alluded to the fact that I was a lazy bugger (also true)! Willie, obviously with a few inside him, stood in the middle of the kitchen, legs akimbo, arms swinging as if dancing to some tune only he could hear. He took over from Margaret and he shouted about the fact that his sister worked hard to keep me in food and in school! Fist slapping and arms swinging he shouted that if I did not wise up, he, and for some reason our neighbour Donald, would go around Kilmuir banging some skulls together and generally taking care of business! I would have to change my (lazy teenage) ways fast or else have him to deal with and the aforementioned neighbour Donald MacDonald!

This rant continued for a while alongside his body popping and clenched-fist slapping until I could take no more. I shouted at him to shut the hell up and stormed out of the kitchen door with a loud closing thud! I was in tears as I went upstairs to my bedroom. Later on, he disappeared to Boyd's (The Ferry Inn). By the next day, he had returned to the big city and my skull had not been banged!

208

So why Willie Clippit? This name was given to him by my brother Gary, who had met him in the 80s whilst he was staying in Linicro. Willie would like to operate garden shears whilst whisky-full and would usually start off in the garden clipping anything that looked too long. He was industrious! Once satisfied with the big hoose garden, he then started clipping around the wee hoose and the dyke in front of the byre. In a clipping fervour he would move towards the burn clipping either side of the council land heading up towards Morton's house and beyond! I'm sure if Margaret had not called him in for his tea, he would have clipped his way to the Ferry Inn and possibly all the way back to Glasgow!

I dare to think what he would have been like had he got hold of the strimmer!

Hankering for a Hobby

Being a third-year student at Portree High, I slowly turned away from toys and childish things. My voice was fully broken although I still looked young and as yet did not possess the official school dress and I don't mean a skirt; I mean a blazer (that came in 4th year). My attention was taken up by members of the opposite sex. Which entailed trying to act more mature and manly! Truth be told, I was not what one could call highly successful with the ladies throughout my PHS years, albeit with some notable exceptions (secret)!

1978 was the year of Star Wars. Unfortunately, Linicro would hardly be the scene of a major movie premiere. All we had was a B&W Ferguson portable TV that produced more snow than entertainment.

What was a Sci-Fi guy to do? The closest I could get to the Lucas world was the first edition of UK official Star Wars magazine. Would the newsagents on Wentworth Street have it? Would it be sold out? Did I have any money? Stressful times! Made even more stressful by the fact newsagents closed around the same time our lunch bell rang, but if you ran like the Six Million Dollar Man, you could just about catch the last 10 minutes before they closed for lunch. I never understood the newsagent's shop closing at that time. Surely, they would have made a lot of money from us school kids if they stayed open?

Eventually I procured a first edition Star Wars magazine with the X Wing Fighter free gift and the second edition with the TIE Fighter gift – very cool although I hid the magazine in my bag just in case in case I was made fun of! Another kid's craze caught my Skye eye in 1978, and that was skateboarding. Wow!

The nearest we ever got to skateboarding in Glasgow was stealing my sister's 4-wheeled skate, placing a piece of wood on top as a seat and zooming down the hill road in Springburn park. Not too bad for fun, but when I first saw a real skateboard, man, I wanted one badly! My issue was the lack of any substantial funds. The next best thing was skateboarding magazines. After catching up with Luke Skywalker et al., I would gaze longingly at the boards, ball bearings and wheels in this shiny mag!

All could be mail ordered and paid by postal order. Unfortunately for me, my pot to pee in did not exist, and the likelihood of speeding down from the top of Totescore on a fancy board to my Linicro front door would remain a total fantasy. These types of fantasy would soon be replaced by fantasy girlfriends!

Later I was to become a devout reader of the music press. Specifically Sounds and the NME, when I had money of course! My school bus friend James 'Tornado' Macdonald would buy either of these from the newsagents and I would pay him when he handed it over to me on the bus. I was so grateful to him. I could never read the music paper on the bus and I didn't like anyone else asking to read it whilst we rode home. It was for my eyes only! I loved to be tucked up in my big hoose bed reading about the latest bands. I remember being totally obsessed with the 'Indie' charts, even though I did not quite understand what 'Indie' meant. 1978 was a significant year for lots of types of music, and as we moved into 1979 the New Wave of British

Heavy Metal (NWOBHM) was a big musical thing! I wished to hear these new and exciting heavy metal and Indie bands but had to make do with just reading about them! I read Sounds and Melody Maker for decades after Linicro, and now every month I download e-music magazines to read on my tablet!

Last Night Tom Ferrie Saved My Life

In the late 70s and early 1980s more than a few of us on the island would be tucked up in bed with a tranny! Around about ten o'clock Tom Ferrie hosted his show 'Night Beat' on Radio Scotland. I have Googled the show name but find no mention of such it. I'm almost 100% sure that the name of the show is correct, and I will tell you why. In 1979 The Jam released one of my favourite songs of theirs, 'Strange Town', and I mistook a lyric, 'I've got blisters on my feet' as 'I've been listening to Night Beat'. I remember, (naively) thinking, 'Wow, the Jam listens to Night Beat on Radio Scotland'. I'm an imbecile and I know it!

Anyway, Mr Ferrie's show played hits of the day, but what we all were most interested in was the dedications that could be phoned in by anyone with a phone (we were phoneless in Linicro). We (and by 'we' I mean me), fervently hoped that a dedication read on air was from someone you knew. This simple gimmick was a magnet to my ears. In Linicro I would secrete my Aunt Margaret's solid-state device into my room and pray that there was some juice left in the Ever Ready batteries. I believe we could only get the MW broadcast, with all its atmospheric interruptions ensuring a poor listening experience. DAB it was not! The sound quality in and of itself was of secondary importance as I could only play the volume at less than 1 in fear of being discovered by my Aunt who would frown upon me draining her batteries!

I, like 100s of other young Skye ears, would hope to recognize a dedicated name. It was also a medium that was commonly used for people to declare their love for their B/GF or to announce that you had a fancy for someone. In my dreams I conjured up many PHS ladies phoning in a dedication for me, but that (sadly) never happened! Still.......I could dream! The next day's classroom conversation would contain info/gossip from the previous night's show and the sense of pride hearing someone that you knew getting a mention was a thing that money could not buy!

Kilmuir Youth Club

Saturday nights in the late 70s invariably found us going down to Kilmuir Hall as there was a Youth Club held there at the weekend. I don't recall any adults running it, my memory tells me it was some older more responsible teenagers like Duncan McDonald (Tornados brother) and John Andrew Macdonald (Bambi's brother). There was not a whole helluva lot to do, but it beat staying in with my Aunt Margaret!

It was only Archie and I that would attend – by this time Duncan was more mature and probably was having to work on the croft. If we were lucky, we would get a lift by Norman or my cousin Bobby, who by this time had taken ownership of his Dad's old Hillman Avenger. Other times we had to walk. There was a mix of ages and at least we had some female company. Most of whom I would annoy in some shape or form.

They had a table tennis table and I think a badminton net and some racquets. There was also stuff like board games. These did not interest me. I only wanted to get up to mischief. Duncan McDonald was a bit of a musician and would bring his guitar with him so he could strum and hum some songs, and I liked his voice. Latterly Archie stopped coming with me then I would meet up with Peter the Duntulm Coast Guard's son for a wee bit of Saturday night action! Mostly we would play table tennis and chat up the girls. Peter was a lot more successful than me!

Most times I would have to walk home on my own without my mate Archie. I still was under a 10 o'clock curfew, which was impossible to keep as the club finished around that time. One night I was back around 10.30 and Margaret had locked the back door. We always locked the front. I thought it was a joke she was playing as I peered in through the living room window. There she was, sitting on the sofa, doing her knitting and ignoring me. My punishment for being late. Luckily the window for the other downstairs room was open, so I climbed in and went straight to my bed!

Another time I was given a lift down to the hall by Bobby, who had Archie for company. After dropping me outside the hall, they drove off. After the club finished, I got a lift by Roddy Gillies, who was passing. It was a summer night as it was still light as we drove up to Linicro. Approaching the wee hoose I looked up the road to where the Morton house is and opposite just as the road rounds a slight corner there was Bobby's car halfway up the embankment. Holy crap! We drove right to it and soon noticed that the car was empty (thank God). We found Bobby at the wee hoose who explained to us he and Archie were bombing up the road and misjudged the corner and the car flew up the embankment which was steep! Later, with the help of Norman and his David Brown, the car was pulled back on to the road. I don't think there was any damage to the Avenger. There was also no damage to Archie and Bobby!

John the Bus

Forever it appeared that John Nicholson aka 'John the bus' drove the service/school bus from Linicro and beyond to Portree! Rarely do I remember him having a vacation. Imagine the miles he accrued over the years? I don't know what year he retired, and I hope that he is still with us.

As very young kids we used to love taking the bus to Portree and marvelled at how easily he negotiated the hairpin bend in Uig. Driving a long or short bus he would spin round that bend with aplomb. We loved to go outside and wave to him and his passengers as they zipped past the wee hoose! I vividly remember my first day attending PHS in 1977. John welcomed me aboard with a friendly smile.

Around 1978 Ali Aitken from Glendale gave me a cassette copy of ELO's 'A New World Record'. If John was in a good mood and there were few paying customers, he would slip the tape into the tape deck and play it through the speakers. How many other school bus drivers would do that? Not many, I bet!

I will freely admit that I was slightly annoying and a bit of a pain in the backside as a teenager. It must have been my hormones! How many people got thrown off their school bus during their time at PHS? How many people got thrown off their school bus more than once? Guilty your honour, 'twas me!

The details of the first time are hazy, but it involved Finn McNally and me. I seem to recall it was a song we were singing about John, but that could have been later. We were being more than immature this day and we could see old John regularly checking his mirror to see who was causing the rumpus at the back of the bus.

Anyway, by the top of Totescore he had had enough, and he stopped the bus. He stood up, pulled his trousers up and marched down the aisle to where I was sitting, doing my best to look innocent. 'That's it Raymond,' he said, 'time to get off.' I protested my innocence, but my plea for clemency fell on deaf

Pete and I
behind the bus
driver

ears! It was a service bus with paying customers, so I had to be made an example of. I grabbed my bag and sheepishly left the bus. With a close of the door, John and the bus left. Luckily it was light, and it was dry!

I said nothing to my Aunt Margaret as I entered the wee hoose. I called John all the names under the sun (in my head). His ears must have been burning because the next day he got his revenge. There I was the following morning around 8.20 and as the bus approached, I moved out into the road expecting to be picked up but with a wave and a big smile John and his bus passed me by! Damn, how will I get to school on time?

Most people would have just stayed at home if they missed the bus, but not me! I loved my school and the alternative of staying at home and being put to work by Margaret was not my option of choice. I walked up the road with my thumb out and it was not long before I got a lift to the top of Earlish. From there I walked for around five minutes before another car driver answered my thumbs call and took me all the way to Portree. I was not even late for class! I was to find out later that John also threw Finn off the bus the previous day as well, not too far from his home in Duntulm.

Around 1979to 80 we ramped up the annoying behaviour to really get on poor old John's nerves. I will hold my hand up and admit to being the ringleader along with Finn McNally and Peter Ridley. We began to sing a song about a biblical figure and a rotund bus driver being kicked in the effin arse! Very puerile, but we thought we were funny! We also began a noisy foot stamping and hand clapping in the style of Queen's 'We Will Rock You'! This really got old John's temper going!

This time he braked hard and came rushing down the back of the bus, only to be met with silence. As he turned to go back to the driving seat, we continued our feet stamping and hand clapping. By this time, I was living at Uig Hotel so I did not have to worry about John reporting me to my Aunt Margaret! However, he had a better plan.

He said nothing the following day as he picked me up in front of the hotel, but as I tried to board the bus at four, he would not let me on, saying, 'Not today Raymond'! My protests of innocence had little effect and off I went with thumb out and the bus passed me on the road out of Portree. Luckily, I got a ride quickly and passed the bus with a smile on my face. The car only took me past Borve and out on the road I again awaited a kind soul to offer me a lift. I turned to look behind me and, in the distance, 'John the bus' was quickly approaching. What to do? I did not want him or the others on the bus to see me and to laugh at my plight. I jumped into a ditch at the roadside and hid there until the bus passed me by! I managed another lift shortly after the ditch incident and made it to Uig before John! As I worked that evening I could not stand and wave to John as he went past, unfortunately. And little did I know the wheels of his revenge were in motion!

It was an afternoon PE class in the games hall when Pete Ridley and I got called out and told to go to the beak's office immediately. We entered Mr Rodger's office in our shorts to find two other people from our bus. John's revenge was reporting us to the headmaster!

I remember standing there in a line with the others with the beak standing in front of us, his legs apart, and arms on hips a la superman pose! Unfortunately for me and Pete, we found it very difficult not to laugh when we were around each other and

I was struggling to keep my face straight. I failed! The head took a ruler and prodded my chest asking, 'Do you find this funny'?

'No sir,' I answered with a smile and I could hear Pete struggling to stay straight faced. We listened to the lecture about our behaviour on the school bus and that it was not what was expected! There were to be no more shenanigans, order was to be maintained. Singled out for a specific punishment Peter and I would later find out that John had another plan for us.

That afternoon at four we headed to the bus and went down the back to sit. John closed the bus door, looked in his mirror, stood up, pulled up his trousers and came down the back. He asked Pete and me to follow him. Our punishment? Both of us had to sit behind John for the rest of the year! No more back seat sitting! Every bus scholar knows there is a hierarchy of seating. The back seat is at the top the front seat the lowly bottom!

For the first couple of weeks we ignored this punishment and tried to get down the back of the bus, but John diligently ensured we sat behind him every day. It turned out to be great fun. We really had a great laugh with the paying customers and truth be told it turned out to be a very nice punishment!

Thanks, John, for keeping us safe on the road for all those years!

School Bus

With a diesel belly full and a deep breath in, my blue and white friend you puffed up the Score Bay road.
With Captain John at the school bus steering wheel, fishing up the Kilmuir kids on the way to my abode.

Way back in 1977, teeth brushed, hair washed, outside the wee hoose I waited for you.
Butterflies battling in my belly's bottom. When passed Hunters, you were a welcome view.

As you cat crept by Lovelies Seaview, my heart pumped in anticipation.

At last you stopped with a door opened grin and I boarded in excitation.

As the years marched on at the back of the bus, school blazered I could be found.
Your captain, skilled at the helm, in minutes Uig's hairpin we would round.

In summer months, like a mobile sauna, the heat at the back was hard to take.
Jackets off, shirts unbuttoned, your sunroof cracked, the breeze was a welcome break.

On freezing cold dark winter mornings, your temperature a luxury inside the bus.
At four o'clock without fail down past the boys' hostel, there you would wait for us.

Not only school kids benefited from your warmth and sat on your lumpy seats.
Local shoppers and summer tourists, you were always more than happy to meet.

Many times, over the years, you and your Captain's patience I'd put to the test.
And more than once I waited, and you passed me by, showing me who was the best.

Lucky for me you never held a grudge. After a few days, I was welcomed with a smile.
And like a good boy I would sit in silence, and I tried to behave for a while.

No sick leave you took, through wet wind and snow, most times you made it up the hill.
Through summer, winter, autumn and spring you carried us and were never ill.

Over five years, how many miles did we travel together from Linicro to Portree?
Where are you now my blue and white friend and do you still remember me?

Dance Hall Haze

My first non-school dance would probably have been at Uig Hall. Circa 1977/78. My Aunt Margaret was not keen on me going out, but when the Macinnes boys came calling, she capitulated and begrudgingly let me out on the village! She was right to try to stop me. She knew what went on outside the halls with regards to half bottles of spirits and lukewarm lager. I only got up to highly embarrassing teenage stuff and drank too much underage alcohol. I sometimes wish she had kept me in! There were some fun nights though, especially round the festive period. At least at New Year you could try to get a kiss of a girl! And yep, even that I embarrassed myself with too!

Uig Hall is not big, but it has a stage and the obligatory space for dancing. There were chairs against both walls and the occasional table. These dances were unlicensed, so it was a case of bring your own. I never brought any, but I would drink anyone's alcohol. Most guys stood near the front entrance swigging something whilst watching the (very few) women dance. I would stagger about like a madman after having a few of mouthfuls of someone's spirit bottle. Thankfully, as I got older, I became more choosey when it came to the deoch. Usually by then I would swig on vodka and orange and not the fresh stuff either. This was neat orange cordial. One swig of voddy don't swallow. One swig of orange. Mix in mouth and swally! That's how you did it back then. Occasionally I would drink beer, but not a lot.

There were a few good bands doing the rounds back then. Both local and mainlanders. I saw Runrig at Uig Hall in the 70s. The ubiquitous Skyevers and the Ian Macdonald Dance Band graced the boards. There was even a band who played a Boston cover. Unfortunately, I could only hear from the back seat of Janet Macinnes's Mini Clubman. I was lying there, head spinning. Drunk. I still managed to sing along with them though, so that's something!

The biggest problem at Uig dances was the fighting. Nearly every dance would see at least two drunkards slug it out with one and other. I recall a fight involving more than a few people near the stage whilst the band were playing. The band had to stop and plead for calm! I saw George Cowie open the fire door near the stage and physically throw the drunken battlers outside! Eventually fewer and fewer dances were held there.

The other venue for us dancing north enders was the Skye Gathering Hall in Portree. This was our venue of choice, but because of lack of transportation we could not always get there. The good thing about the dances in Portree was that they were always busier and had more females to look at! Uig had no taxis back then, you had to rely on the kindness of car-owning adults. Usually it was Norman, his sister Janet or my cousin Bobby who would drive us to Portree. I recall one time more than a few of us were squashed in the back of Janet's Blue Mini Clubmen and her then boyfriend Willie 'Potty' was drunk in the front seat as we made our way to the Gathering Hall. Willie had overindulged in the Ferry Inn and as we drove past Earlish, he felt sick. Quick as a flash, he rolled down the window and began spewing. Most of it ending up on the back-seat side windows. The whole passenger side was sick striped!

The Gathering Hall had a bar, so getting half-decent alcohol was easier for us who were underage. The bar was to the right side as you walked into the hall and was generally packed at the beginning of the dance. I sipped a lot of Piper Export in that smoke-filled sweaty room and did my best to chat up any ladies. My problem was that I looked young (I was) and I was always chasing women who were older!

Inside the hall most of the guys huddled near the entrance. Staring at the dancing females, I suppose. The hall had chairs and tables round each side. Above them on the wall were old electric bar heaters, glowing orange and red. You could have a merry laugh, especially during (Scottish) country dancing gigs. It could be dangerous too! Being swung all over by some strong-armed Skye lady. With the hall's wooden floor wet with spilled drinks, you could easily end up on your backside during a 'Strip the Willow' or a 'Dashing White Sergeant'.

The band I saw the most was probably the Skyevers, and I liked them. They played a decent set of covers and musically they were all fantastic. They would also play a set of Scottish country dance numbers. I liked it when one of the band's sisters, Caroline – would jump on the stage and do a few numbers.

I saw Runrig there at least twice there and they were a brilliant live band. Most other bands that I saw, their names are lost to history. My memory of the drunken nights has faded!

Gathering Hall was not immune to fights. You would have drunken guys from different parts of the island all trying to out macho each other. I don't think I ever attended one dance that did not have fighting. Usually the brawlers were thrown outside to cool down. I don't think anyone was seriously hurt (I hope not).

Having attended many dances at the Gathering Hall including many school functions, I can report to you I never had a girlfriend at any of them. Sad. I tried but was spectacularly unsuccessful. Not that I was too shy. I wasn't. I just could not seem to attract anyone! Poor me, you might think but don't. The Gathering Hall was the venue that facilitated my kissing of two of my Portree High School dream girls. And I don't mean a peck on the cheek either. I'm talking about a snogging kiss! I'm a gentleman so will not reveal their names, but both these kisses left me air walking and heart pounding. Both were sweet as sweet can be and the memory of them will remain with me forever and they more than made up for my total lack of success with girlfriend finding!

Two Guys from Galloway Street

This short tale I found hard to believe myself, but it was true, and it happened to me!

We have to travel in time a little to get the back story. About a year (maybe less), before I went to live on Skye, I got involved in a fracas with two guys from up old Galloway Street. I don't remember what it was about, the two guys were a wee bit younger than me and I think it might have involved me slapping one of them. He cried and told me he would get his brother to 'batter me'. True to his word, his big brother caught me just outside the opening of our apartment building. His wee brother was laughing behind him as he explained to me, with a few punches, not to touch his brother again. It was now my turn to cry, not because of the pain but in the hope that he would leave me alone. It worked.

Forward in time we go. One fourth year morning at Portree High, who do you think I saw in the playground? Yep! It was the wee brother who I had had the altercation with years earlier. His name was Chris. What are the odds of that? And the first thing he did when he saw me was to threaten me and that his big brother 'battered' me once and would do it again. I just laughed at the wee bawbag and flicked him away like an annoying fly. Inside, though, I was worried. What if his brother came to Portree? That night I felt some amount of stress as I imagined the brother standing outside the gates waiting to kick my head in and his wee gnat-like brother standing laughing behind him. Then it occurred to me that so what if the brother comes? This is not Galloway Street, this is Skye, my Skye. What was he going to do? Come to Linicro to boot ma baws? The stress just disappeared.

It turns out that Chris had moved to Broadford from Springburn with his mother. Over the next two and half years I would bump into him at school, but I had no bother from him or his brother! I had heard from my mate Jonathan that he was a decent guy and I hope that he did well for himself. Like me, I hope Portree High School changed his life!

Sounds of 79

Was it really 40 years ago that Ian Dury was hitting us with his rhythm stick? ELO were asking us not to bring them down whilst Squeeze were cool for cats.

The Linicro of 79 was a wonderful year for my musical ears. Top of the Pops was essential viewing and Sunday's Radio 1 Top 20 was essential listening. 'Heart of Glass' was sung by us all and the year ended with us not needing any education according to Pink Floyd. With winter in the big hoose and a 50p coin in my hand. The insertion of said coin into the electric meter and a twist ensured that I could lie in a hot bath between 6 and 7pm (my Aunt Margaret was at church). Her old radio, precariously balanced on the bath's corner, blasted music through my bubble bath. I enjoyed luxury until the countdown was complete and the new Nation's No 1 revealed! Special memories when music meant that much and was as important as the Linicro air that I breathed.

What an eclectic mix of music 1979 provided. Gary Numan's 'Cars', along with The Sugar Hill Gang's 'Rapper's Delight', mixed up with The Jam's 'Eton Rifles' and Janet Kay's 'Silly Games' made for a true aural cornucopia, graciously accepted by my eardrums. Some girls liked Racey's 'Some Girls', whilst I preferred BA Robinson and his 'Bang Bang'. We all loved Lena Lovich singing about her lucky number. 'Street Life' from The Crusaders gave us soul, and I spent many an hour in front of the tiny mirror in the middle of the living room dresser. Strutting and singing 'Do Ya Think I'm Sexy' to my Aunt's budgie, Lemon. With a deodorant bottle as a microphone, Freddie Mercury and I could not be stopped now or later. It was the year my ear got confused by the cacophony of sound that was Fleetwood Mac's 'Tusk' and the time I joined Oliver's Army!

Of the many wonderful songs that 79 gave us, the one that talked to me the most was Rainbow's 'Since You've Been Gone'. I effin loved/still love that song. I was later introduced to the stunner that is Rainbow Rising when I was handed a cassette copy in Oddbod's Chemistry class by Collette Creed. This musical masterpiece blew my mind and along with 'Down To Earth' it changed my musical listening habits forever in that I became very (very) partial to 'heavy rock'. Still am!

My (Short) Life as a Peat Lifter

I always blame peat for me starting to smoke. Luckily, I gave up the habit years ago, but it began with the lifting of the peat. Way over on the road to the Quirang, probably directly behind the rocks of Linicro, was the peat patch of Norman Macinnes. Close to the single-track road he had been hard at work cutting into the ground and he called on us teenagers to help with the drying and ultimate collection of this earthy winter fuel. We did not take it too seriously; I planned on much messing around. Norman took us to the spot with his car and we passed that spooky area on the lonely Staffin road. There are some ruins to one side, and they are rumoured to be haunted. There are stories told by locals that many horses and carts would halt before the ruin and the horses would refuse to move – frightened of something. I would not like to walk there in the dark! Anyway, it was a warm summer evening with no breeze as we stacked the peats for drying. No wind meant midges by the million. The minute monsters got everywhere, biting you from your top to your toes and your nethers in-between. It was terrible, and we eventually had to finish early that night with the promise of returning the next day. Hopefully in the wind's company. That evening when I got into Norman's car either Duncan or Archie suggested that we buy a pack of cigarettes and use the smoke to keep away any of those wee flying biters. I think it was 20 Regal that was bought. We arrived at the site and like the night before; the midges were rampant. We got out the ciggies, lit up and started puffing furiously. If anything, I think it made them worse! Undaunted we carried on with our puffing. At that point we did not inhale, but it was the beginning where all three of us boys (not Norman) eventually started smoking the tobacco regularly. I was resistant for a while as I did not like to inhale Regal or Embassy Red. It made me feel sick, but as you do, I found that Menthol Consulate was easier to inhale and that was my rocky road to ruin. It was a lot cheaper in them days as a packet cost around 50 pence!

Not having money curtailed my smoking activity, so I really didn't puff a lot. I never smoked on the school bus, maybe the occasional drag, and I never found myself at the back of Mr Baptie's geography hut smoking with the professionals. During lunch breaks big Jonathan McDonald and I would head into the town for a cup of coffee, a Twix and if we were lucky, a cadged ciggie from someone with more money than us. If I went to any Friday night dance at the Gathering Hall, I would smoke, but I would never smoke at school dances or Youth Club discos. I suppose in a way I was a secret smoker! Even in later life, I did not smoke too much – rarely at work and only more when one was out on the town drinking! I'm glad I stopped, though. I feel better for it. That's thanks to my darling wife and a promise I made when we got married. It took a while, but with the help of nicotine gum it was ultimately easy. I have no desire to smoke anything these days!

Portree Kindness

I like random acts of kindness, especially when they are directed at me! Here is a wee one that over forty years later is still with me in my heart and I have done my best to pay it forward as much as I can! It was a 1980s Saturday in Portree. Peter Ridley and I had spent the day swimming then going around the town annoying people and looking to chat up girls (we were unsuccessful). As the sun disappeared, we made our plan to walk out of the town towards home and start thumbing a lift! As it does on Skye, quite a lot, the dark clouds assembled and it started to pour down. We sought shelter inside the doorway of the Portree Hotel on the corner. We waited and waited, but still the water fell. We must have been carrying on and making some noise as the Manager came out to see what the kerfuffle was all about. It turns out that she was Winnie MacDonald, who just happened to be my next-door neighbour in Linicro; I did not know her well, but she knew me and asked us what we were waiting for? We told her we hoped the rain would stop so we could start trying to get a lift home. Do you know what she did? God love her. She took us inside to that small lounge and told us we could wait there. Great, at least we had a comfy seat till the rain went off! After about 5 minutes, a waitress appeared with two plates of mince and tatties. Courtesy of Winnie. Wow! What a very nice surprise and as we were always hungry, we wolfed it down! She then sent a pot of tea and we had a few cups! All free! Very nice indeed. The rain went off, and we said our thanks and goodbyes! What a beautiful wee act of kindness shown by her. Thanks Winnie.

∽

(Is that a) New Jacket?

In the late Liniciro 70s my wardrobe was bare when it came to clothes to wear to dances and as Bobby was bigger than me, the only things of his I could wear were shirts. I had asked my folks to send me stuff, but they kept saying just wait till I came there on school holiday so I could get the right size. I was getting desperate though as by 1979 I was going to more dances in Portree and more Youth Club discos so I wanted to look my best in order for me to attract a female member of the species. I particularly wanted a jacket. Like a casual smart jacket with lapels. I also needed a pair of trousers badly! Eventually my folks sent me a jacket, trousers and a cool Adidas t-shirt. The jacket was a perfect fit for me. It was almost an oatmeal type colour, and I thought it looked rather smart and cool. The trousers that got sent were a pair of fawn cords that had a flare to them. Luckily, we could still wear flares in early 1979, but they were going out of style, fast! With the aubergine three striped Adidas t-shirt and my new jacket and trousers, I thought I looked good on the smokey dance floor of the Skye Gathering Hall.

It didn't take too long before the big lapels and flared trousers became unfashionable in favour of straight legs and small jacket lapels! My cords were no longer wearable, but I could still get away with my jacket. Well, at least until the summer of 1980! The last time I wore it I remember it well because it was a Friday Dance at the Gathering Hall in which I unfortunately missed my lift back to Linicro. My only choice was to head out and see if I could thumb it back. As I was turning the corner near the school, Silas Birtwistle was hanging out of one window in the boy's hospital. He shouted me over and asked me where I was going? I told him about missing my lift and he said to just come up and crash in their room! It was not a tough decision to make! They gave me a bed and I jumped in and tried to get to sleep! An hour later someone came into the room and came to where I was sleeping and all I heard was something like FFS and they walked away. In the morning I found out it was Derek McLennan's bed that I had purloined as he was out late with his girlfriend Christine. He was not chuffed when he saw me sleeping there because we were not exactly friends as he knew I had a super crush on Christine. Later on, in Edinburgh we became very good pals and I'm still in contact with him now and again via Facebook! The next morning, we all got up and went to the Caley for some bacon rolls and coffee. Most of the guys I was with were wearing more modern jackets with smaller lapels, I decided there and then that it would be the last time I would wear my 1970s relic! I never wore it again and chucked it before I moved into my new accommodation at Uig Hotel.

The Demon Deoch

Before I continue, I would like to preface this wee piece by saying that I do not condone underage drinking. I think that alcohol can damage the developing brain (it might have damaged mine). For those reading this who are not Scottish, I should explain that drinking alcohol young is common. My dad used to give me a swig of his can of Double Diamond beer when we would go see Celtic play at Parkhead in the mid-1970s!

It took me many, many years to find an alcoholic drink that I actually liked the taste of which was when I was around 19 and living in Annan in Dumfrieshire. It was here that they introduced me to Tartan Special, and I enjoyed drinking it for the taste as well as the effect!

In the late 1970s and early 1980s underage drinking was relatively common and apart from any school or Youth Club dance/disco I partook of the underage deoch! You know that saying that goes something like 'those who cannot learn from their mistakes are doomed to repeat them'? Well, I never learned, and I repeated the same mistakes well into my late 30s and early 40s!

I have done very embarrassing things whilst under the influence when I was young and old. Mostly related to my behaviour with the ladies and I would here like to apologise to each and every one that bore witness to my drunken embarrassments (there were lots and lots and lots)!

Thank God I had the sense to not drink alcohol at school dances! It would have been an embarrassing disaster for me! Having said that, I might have had more luck finding a girlfriend!

It's guaranteed nearly every guy on Skye my age had similar experiences when first introduced to the demon drink. I did most of my early drinking outside dance halls in the back of cars or, as in the case of Uig Hall, the front entrance! We would swig some disgusting spirit or other and take a sip of beer or two! Like most young teens I found the taste of all alcohol was pretty revolting but as we were not drinking for the taste, it was hardly a deterrent! Tennent's lager and McEwan's Export was the most common beer to chug. Both disgusting in my humble opinion (I don't mind Export now and would kill for either in Saudi Arabia)! Piper Export was another gruesome beer that I would drink mostly at dances in the Gathering Hall.

Outside both Uig and Kilmuir Halls we would swig from a half bottle of vodka and then another swig from a bottle of diluting orange to make the taste a wee bit more acceptable to our young palate! I can still taste that sickly-sweet orange and the bile producing vodka to this day! Occasionally we would swig whisky, but that was absolutely disgusting and only done if there was no vodka!

A rite of passage for any young man is to get totally steaming drunk, not know what you are doing and to make a complete embarrassing arse of yourself. Guilty your honour! I did! Once in Glasgow and once in Uig! Both times I had the worst hangover ever and swore I would never drink again! Wish that was true. I'm lucky I did not die of alcohol poisoning or embarrassment! I apologise to any girl I slobbered over.

Around the age of 15, I decided that I wanted to find a drink that I liked the taste of (as well as the effect). With the help of my cousins Bobby and Flora I could experiment a little. These were the days before alcopops made drinking easier! I first wanted to try wine as I thought as they made it from grapes it would taste OK? Wrong! My first drink was from my cousin Flora's bottle of Blue Nun, German white wine. Little did I know that it was the McEwan's Export of the world of wine! It was disgustingly horrible! I saw adverts on TV that I thought might be worth a try? Dubonnet looked promising, but it was not my cup of tea. Next was Cointreau, which was even worse! Cinzano Bianco might have had some fancy adverts, but its taste was really rather awful. This 'experimenting' went on for a wee while and I finally found a drink that was relatively palatable? Vodka and lime cordial with ice. This became my drink of choice for a few years and dealing with the hangovers the next day was manageable.

If I was in the Ferry Inn or Bakur, I would have an obvious soft drink in front of me and when Betty from the Ferry or Mike in the Bakur were not looking I would quickly swig down the vodka and lime that was beside a person of age! The bar owners were not stupid, they knew what was going on but as I would not make a big scene about it or appear really stocious, they would turn a blind eye!

Funny thing was, the only time they ever asked me my age was one afternoon by big Mike in the Bakur bar a few days after my 18th birthday!

(I've Got the) Music in Me

Around late 79 or early 1980 Portree High School rock stars Max Headroom played a short set at a school dance in the Gathering Hall. When I heard a familiar bass line, I realised that they were about to play one of my all-time favourite songs, AC/DC's 'Live Wire'. Axe master, Derek McLennan knew how to jam a rock riff and his guitar solos were up there with the best. Very cool! From then on, I had dreams of joining them and rocking out. Many a winter's night I spent in front of the mirror in my Uig Hotel bedroom. Bottle of Denim deodorant in hand (as my microphone), and AC\DC's 'If You Want Blood' blasting from my silver Alba stereo cassette player. Alas, I did not have the courage to ask for an audition as a singer in this short-lived school four piece. I really wished I had not been so self-conscious and more confident about my singing abilities. I'm not saying that I'm a super talent, but I could have made a decent pub rocker! Luckily, later on in the mid-80s my wish to play alongside Derek was realised when we formed (for fun) the under rehearsed band named 'Funnel Juice'. What a laugh we had playing at numerous Skye venues although we never did 'Live Wire'!

From 4th year to 6th year, beginning with the music of Ali Aitken, the Elgin Hostel became a hidden musical hub for us like-minded folk. My contribution was technical support and the odd vocal here and there. It was in one of the rooms that Mr Duncan Macdonald and I would strum and sing, usually on a Friday afternoon.

Long before he became a bass boss, he was rather decent at blasting out a 12-bar rock boogie tune! Heavily influenced by his beloved Quo. For laughs we created 'Purple Chicken' its only members being Duncan and me. During one such song session we wrote the 'Purple Chicken Dance'! Luckily, for most people, this song was only heard by four ears, Duncan's and mine! We would sing the Quo's 'Rockin All Over the World' to an audience of none. Also, and I don't know if he remembers this, an original song penned by Mr Macdonald about leaving Skye. It was during a loud rendition of this song (me singing as best I could), that we were discovered by Mr Nichol, who promptly chased us out of the room and the hostel.

Fast forward a month or two to a winter's night outside Kilmuir hall. In the back of a car sat me and Duncan. Sipping neat vodka from a quarter bottle and mixing it (in mouth) with diluting orange! There was a dance taking place in the hall, I believe the evening's entertainment was being provided by locals including another Duncan Macdonald (the brother of James 'Tornado'). So there we were, illicitly drinking in the dark and getting merry. We eventually finished our Highland cocktail and staggered back to the hall. In the far corner was the night's entertainment, playing to a sparse collection of (old and young) locals.

Full of (Dutch) courage, Digg's Duncan and I got up on the small corner stage to entertain. It's a wee bit hazy but I think we started off with an acoustic rendition of 'Rockin all over the World', me ad-libbing most of the verses as I only knew the words to the chorus! It was Skye surreal. Several folks got on the floor to dance! I remember dedicating a song to the dancing mother of Chris Hogg. With the vodka and orange coursing through our veins (and brain), we let loose with the chugging riff that was our song 'Purple Chicken', as in 'Do the Purple

Chicken', (dance)! Embarrassingly funny, we gave another shot at the Quo hit before being asked to vacate the stage! Our 15 minutes of Kilmuir fame over, we laughed our way outside to smoke!

The following Monday saw me sober on the school bus, and more than a little embarrassed by our Saturday night antics! At least we gave people a laugh Later on Duncan and I would entertain the folks of Skye again as part of 'Funnel Juice'.

The Times (and School Clothes) They Are a Changing

The summer of 1979 I boarded a Highland Scottish bus and headed for Glasgow. The couple of weeks I spent with my family and our dog Skye proved to be very enjoyable. I began to really enjoy vacations at my family home and enjoyed being in Glasgow. It was a time of flux for Galloway Street and Springburn in general. The city fathers in their infinite wisdom had deemed it necessary to construct a bypass which effectively tore Springburn in two. Tenement flats and the shops below them that had housed and served the people for decades were disappearing at an alarming rate, victims of Caterpillar and JCB thugs in yellow. In fact, I was lucky that summer because future home vacations would see Springburn Road in a sad state, a mere shadow of its former self.

As for our Galloway Street, the glue sniffing fad had long passed and gave way to a chronic love affair with heroin which saw our once (semi) friendly street garner a name for itself. People would say that it was full of junkies and thieves (not true). The 1980s would continue the downward drug spiral, devastating families and stealing the life light from many youngsters. Turning teens into zombies who had only one thing in mind.

Our street was not alone. Many Glasgow streets and their inhabitants suffered (and still do), the same drug fate. Sad.

That weegie summer I had other thoughts to keep me occupied. Namely, getting rid of my 2nd and 3rd year school togs (the same clothes worn in both years), and getting a new wardrobe to go along with my recently purchased PHS blazer! My plan was to look sharp, hoping to increase my chances exponentially of attracting members of the opposite sex.

With money from my folks, I jumped on a 45 bus and headed for the 'toon'. 2-Tone bands along with Gary Numan were hitting the charts and new wave was on the decline. Soon rap would be introduced to my young ears by the Gang at Sugarhill, and New Romantics would be cutting long stories short. I needed to express myself with what I was wearing and in doing so capture the zeitgeist whilst looking cool.

What did I opt to buy with the money in my pocket? Two pairs of Levi straight legged cords, one black, the other blue. Three short sleeved black and blue Wrangler shirts, another pair of brown 'thick' cords, and a pair of tan Hush puppies! Not exactly Paris catwalk fashion, but I thought I looked hot with a capital H!

Back in Linicro, I readied my clothes for the first day of fourth year. An Anti-climax experience was had as most people took little notice of what I had hanging around my slender frame and few people noticed that I had a school blazer (as opposed to the fraying grey sweater that I wore for two solid years)! No matter, I still operated under the illusion that I was one cool (for) cat and I suppose, for Linicro I was!

Sheep Butt

It was around October 1979; I got off the school bus and walked up to the big hoose where we had recently moved for the oncoming winter. I went to my room and got changed. Margaret was not in, which was unusual, even more unusual was that there was no food cooking in the kitchen. There was some work at Linicro fank that the township was doing, and I know she went there to help. I was sitting in the kitchen at the table when I saw the familiar quiff of hair that belonged to big Norman Macinnes. He walked round and came inside the kitchen holding a pair of small green wellies. Obviously not belonging to him! I expected Margaret to be right behind him, but she was not there? 'Where's Margaret?' I asked. 'She is on her way to Portree Hospital,' was his reply'! I thought the big man was joking as he lay the wellies on the floor and took a seat beside me. 'No, seriously, where is she?' 'She is on her way to the hospital, I'm being serious,' said Norman! 'What the hell happened?' and 'What am I going to eat?' Came out of my mouth. He then proceeded to tell me a story that as he was telling it, I still did not believe, and I half expected Margaret to walk in at any moment. She didn't!

Apparently, Margaret had been in one of the sheep pens at the fank when a sheep ran at her and literally butted her out of her wee green wellies! Ouch! She could not walk and was in agony with one of her knees? They got her down to the pens near the Linicro Road and someone took her to Portree Hospital! WTF?

Pre mobile phone days it was difficult to find out information about what was happening. It turned out that her knee injury was very bad, and she would have to go to Raigmore Hospital in Inverness for surgery! So, I would be on my own in the big hoose for a while, I thought? Not really. My cousin Bobby came, and he was to be the 'responsible adult'.

That period Margaret was in hospital was definitely a good time for him and me in the big hoose! The best thing was the food! Margaret's menu and portions could be a wee bit on the stingy side, but when Bobby was in charge of the kitchen, it was an all you can eat fest! In the freezer we had various sheep parts, which he brought out and roasted. Our Rankin's shopping list had everything on it we liked. Best of all for me was that I could do anything and not have to deal with anyone complaining! I could watch TV when I wanted for as long as I wanted and could go out with Duncan and Archie at any time! It was FREEDOM! For almost two months we lived like Kilmuir kings.

We did eventually make a plan to visit her in Inverness and all I remember was the uncomfortable bus journey and eventually finding the hospital and ward, spending less than an hour with our poor wee Aunt. We were more interested in going round the Inverness shops, especially the music shop. As a treat for me Bobby bought Rainbow's 'Long Live Rock and Roll' which is an absolute classic that I still listen to. He bought himself Thin Lizzy's 'Live and Dangerous' which is probably one of the best 'live' albums ever! Along with AC/DC's 'If You Want Blood'. OK, so both might have had some studio overdubs and tweaking, but they were essentially 'live', loud, and proud.

We returned home in the dark, and Norman picked us up from Portree. I was a wee bit sad when Margaret came back but as it would turn out I would only have another six months left of Linicro life!

Work (as in Finding)

Early summer in 1979 saw the addition of two strange words to my personal lexicon. 'Summer Job'. First mooted by my Aunt Margaret. Strange words indeed! Not long after that Archie informed me he had secured a position at Uig Hotel and he suggested I should inquire about any other job vacancies. I remember the day well as I was very nervous. This strange 'job' thing put me at an alien unease. It was a Saturday afternoon. I

hopped on my trusty (rusty) bike and began the journey to Uig.
A cloud-filled Skye, sky threatened rain, and I did not have a
jacket. That pedalled journey to the top of Totescore removed
the wind out of me, and I was glad that no summer sun shone
as sweat flowed from my forehead. From there on it was an easy
ride all the way down into Uig until you passed over the River
Conon bridge. Then the incline began. I parked the bike on the
grass opposite and gazed upon the former Coaching Inn,
thinking 'what the eff am I doing here'?

Archie told me to take the road up and round, past the hotel
until I came to Sobhraig, where the hotel owner lives. As I
rounded the bend opposite the church, the building came into
view and my nerves thumped my heart like a brass band bass
drum. Sobhraig was an annex of the Hotel with very nice guest
rooms. On the far corner was the Grahams' accommodation.
Jelly-like legs carried me awkwardly to the door. I rang the bell
and waited. Before long the door opened only by half and this
lady, pale skinned and dark bags under her eyes, looked upon
my nervous face. I think I woke her from her nap! I sheepishly
told her I was a friend of Archie Macinnes and that I was
looking for a job. Mrs Graham told me I was too late for this
year and that they had all the summer staff that they needed
and that next year I should come earlier if I was still interested
in work. I thanked her and with a weight off my shoulder, I
made my way back down the road to my bike.

The relieved feeling gave way to the realisation that:

1. My best friend would not be available for summer mischief
making.

2. He would have money.

3. I would be broke!

That summer my only source of income was doing some odd
jobs for the Davidsons, an elderly couple, friendly with my
Aunt. Every couple of weeks I would make my way to their Uig
House and help the husband with any garden odd jobs, etc.
They were incredibly friendly people who did not work me very
hard and provided me with afternoon sustenance. My first visit

did not go so well, though. They owned an electric Flymo that I promptly flew over the electric cable and sliced in half! I finished the back lawn with a manual push mower as Mr Davidson set about damage repair. I earned about £10 a month from them, which at the time was a total fortune.

Occasionally, I could supplement my tenner by helping (but mostly hindering), Norman as he tended to the outside needs of our (not always in residence) neighbour Miss Morton. A generous amount of land and a killer view across the Minch to faraway Outer Hebrides and the closer Ascrib Isles and Waternish surrounded her house. She owned two petrol Flymos. My job was to wrestle with these hovering green grass killers and try not to cut my feet off! Norman was kind, patient and generous. He normally would finish what I had started and still give me a fiver for helping him. What a guy. A real excellent role model for me and someone who will always have a special spot in my beating heart. So, I had some cash in 79, but compared to me, Archie was a millionaire! Next year, I thought!

Basketball Broken Bone

Luckily for me, I only had to visit Portree Hospital as a patient once. It was around about the end of 1979. This fine PE morning we were in the old gymnasium with DF and we were playing basketball. I was not skilled at this sporting activity, but I enjoyed playing. Having just caught the ball, I attempted to dribble like a pale imitation of a Harlem Globe Trotter. I looked up and saw one heavily perspiring Skye guy making a beeline for me. Remember, basketball is a non-contact sport, but it seems he did not get the memo. Perhaps he thought it was basketfootball as his knee charged the ball and the ball charged my right thumb, cracking the bone in the process. Ouch! I screamed and shouted obscenities at the guy as DF came to have a look at my paining body part. He gently squeezed the middle of my thumb. The pain was exquisite, and it was a hospital visit for me.

I walked to the hospital's front door at a leisurely pace and asked to see someone about my throbbing thumb. I don't remember waiting too long until they called me for an X-ray and duly went to the room with the lady awaiting further instructions.

She came to me and moved the back plate of the machine. But at the height of my head? Not wanting to cause a fuss, I said nothing. Then she positioned my head to the side and onto the photo plate. WTF? This time I asked what was going on and she replied, 'I'm preparing to X-ray your sinuses. 'Eh?' I said. 'It's my thumb that's the problem,' I gently added. She checked her paperwork and apologised as she had mixed up her morning clientele.

The doctor applied one of these annoying (but fit for purpose) bendable metal splints and bandaged my hand as if preparing me for mummification. OK, so I was pain free, but I had this mutant terminator-like finger.

Also, I'm right-handed, so it was virtually impossible to write properly with the splint attached to my fractured appendage! I recall having a conversation with Mr Ross, our Deputy Head as I worried about the upcoming prelims. He asked if I could take them left-handed. My reply was that my right-handed writing on a good day was illegible (still is) and that the chances of me being able to use my left hand were approximately zero! By the time of the prelims, I was so fed up with the protruding metal digit that I removed it and decided to grin and bear it. Really, it was impossible to do any activities of daily living convincingly with that contraption on. It was not so bad; heaven didn't fall and I got through all the exams pain free and passed most (but not all)!

Ch Ch Changes

This time thing can be strange. When you are 56 years of age (me now). Years pass and there is not much in the way of change. The years seem like weeks or months. It's a different story when you are a young teen. That's when years were real years, not weeks or months! The period from 1977 to 1979 is but two years, though in terms of change (for me) it was massive. I went from a squeaky-voiced Glaswegian to an adult (almost). That year between the summer of 1979 and the summer of 1980, the changes were of seismic proportions, building until this personal life-quake hit me hard and was a veritable force for good!

The year began without my Great Granny, who had passed the previous November. This changed the dynamics in the big hoose, and slowly but surely, the change, like a night cat returning home to slumber, crept in and there would be no going back. My recall tells me the argument I had with Margaret's brother Willie (Clippit) was what precipitated the change in me, as I no longer felt the need to stay silent if someone was complaining about me or my behaviour. That really was the first time I stood up for myself, so I have to thank Willie for that at least.

The other reason the proverbial times were a changing was having a new pal in the shape of Peter Ridley who was the son of the new Duntulm Coast Guard, with whom I formed an instant getting-up-to-mischief bond! We would hang around Portree a lot more on Saturday afternoons and this was new for me and something that my Aunt was not too keen on. The feeling of emancipation was palpable, especially with a thumb in the air that magically provided transport to and from Portree! By this time my 16-year-old hormones dictated that I had to attend more school/youth club dances/discos. All of which were not sanctioned by my Aunt. It's true I was supremely unsuccessful when it came to members of the female persuasion but at the very least, I had to try! I think what kept me in line before in Linicro was the fear of being sent back to Glasgow, but as 1979 rolled into the new decade that fear evaporated.

Whereas before, if I wanted to go over to see the Totescore Macinnes boys, I would agonize for an hour before building up the 7 o'clock courage to ask Margaret's permission. Sometimes permission was denied, which left me bored and alone. Now, I would confidently announce that I was going over to Duncan and Archie's and the tone in my voice held the subliminal message (to my Aunt) that there is nothing you can do to stop me.

I have no memory of when it happened, probably around March/April 1980. My Aunt Margaret informed me I would have to leave Linicro and go back to my folks in Glasgow! This was the thing I feared the most over the past couple of years, and the thought of going back to the city had previously scared the hell out of me. Now though, I was as calm as the Minch on a wind and wave free day. If I had the choice, I did not want to leave, but so be it. It was circumstances beyond my control. I had already started formulating a plan of return home, possibly including staying on at school for 5th year, which would have meant that I would have to attend my old secondary school 'All Saints'. Even the thought of this did not bother me too much. I mean, what could I do? I had no choice. I toyed with the idea of asking to stay in the boys' hostel in Portree but did nothing about it. I also seriously thought about leaving school altogether and going to Shetland where my cousin Bobby was and where there were many oil-boom jobs for the brave and stupid. The Shetland plan was the most attractive to me and I had half decided that those faraway windswept isles were where my future lay. I kept that decision to myself.

Come May 1980 Archie Macinnes informed me that Mrs Graham from Uig Hotel wanted to see me regarding a summer job. I had failed to secure such a position the year before but luckily, she had remembered me and after a quick visit to her Sobhraig home I was offered my first proper job.

Linicro Summer

*I remember when summer meant packing my grey suitcase and
Wallace Arnold transported us.*

*I remember sitting for what seemed like weeks until I could to
get off the bus.*

*I remember the journey's end safely deposited by John outside my
Aunt Margaret's door.*

*I remember my Granny's welcome hug and kiss and falling into
my bed awake no more.*

*I remember when the sun would often hide and the rain pelting
down from heaven.*

*I remember waking up to the cockerel's song but not rising from
bed till eleven.*

*I remember when I could wear a t-shirt all day long and well into
the evening.*

*I remember the light till late and the red sky sun sinking behind
the Harris hills, amazing.*

*I remember opening the gates for Murdy the cow as she strolled to
the byre for milking.*

*I remember my Granny sipping her tea and eating her oatcake
fresh from my Auntie's baking.*

*I remember mashing eggshells with a wooden spoon in a plastic
bucket ready for feeding the hens.*

*I remember running after sheep in the summer heat, gathering
them into the fank's pens.*

*I remember raking the hay and picking out the jaggy, dry, pin
piercing thistles.*

*My Aunt coiling the grass as we laughed, having fun and
waving to the passing tourists.*

*I remember the joy of playing in Totescore till late with the
Macinnes boys having not a care in the world.*

*I remember the promise of a new adventure each day as the
school summer holiday unfurled.*

*I remember the excitement of helping my Aunt as she drew two
buckets of water from the well.*

*I remember the coffee made from milk, skin floating, and that
yummy smell.*

*I remember the Uig Baker's and the aroma of fresh bread
permeating the air.*
*I remember the trips to Portree for a treat and wishing that I
could live there.*

*I remember the sadness at summer's end when Glasgow began to
call.*
*I remember the tears and the thought of waiting another year,
each drop, I remember them all.*

Postscript

Dear Readers,

If you have made it this far, I would like to thank you for your perseverance. My three years in Linicro were jam-packed with stuff and I have done my best to remember as much as my auld brain will allow.

Should you want to know 'what happens next' I have good news? There is a book two! I managed to fight off my inherent laziness and complete a second volume resplendent with wee stories and poems.

My life took an unexpected turn in 1980 and my Skye Story did not end, it just changed location.

Lightning Source UK Ltd.
Milton Keynes UK
UKHW051607210121
377454UK00001B/2